Darryl Bartlett

WordPress

in easy steps

Third Edition

In easy steps is an imprint of In Easy Steps Limited
16 Hamilton Terrace · Holly Walk · Leamington Spa
Warwickshire · United Kingdom · CV32 4LY
www.ineasysteps.com

Third Edition

Printed and bound in the United Kingdom

ISBN 978-1-84078-984-3

Contents

1 Introduction to WordPress

This chapter introduces you to WordPress and some of the things you can build with it. You will also be guided through installation and planning.

Overview

There are quite a lot of people out there who think WordPress is just a blogging platform. This is far from the truth! WordPress can build the simplest blog all the way up to a professional, complex website – there really are no limits! WordPress is a powerful tool that now powers 43% of the web (source: W3Techs) and has a 65% market share of websites with a content management system (CMS). WordPress was originally released back in 2003, and version 6 was released in May 2022.

WordPress is becoming a great starter point for new web designers and developers, since it's great for getting your website online, and it's fairly simple to pick up. As new developers become more comfortable with the platform, they can then extend their own skills to advance their own websites.

A lot of professional web developers are turning to WordPress to build sites for clients as it's a powerful tool, it cuts development time, and it provides a great CMS so that their clients can add content themselves.

Bloggers find it a great platform to work with, as they can add content quickly and easily without having to have a lot of technical knowledge.

This book will provide you with all the basic fundamentals needed to help you on the road to building your website or blog with WordPress. It doesn't matter if you're new to the whole concept of web development or blogging, as the book will guide you through each step with screenshots and detailed text to help you progress through each chapter. If you are a professional web developer, there will be things in the book that can help boost your knowledge of WordPress and how it works. You can then bring this knowledge to your own projects.

What will I need?

For this book, you are going to need two things:

- **Web hosting**: This is space online that you use to host your website. You pay a monthly or annual fee to rent space online. For the purpose of installing WordPress, I will be using a host called HostGator.

- **A domain name**: For example, **www.hello.com**

Why Use WordPress?

Web development was once considered a gigantic task involving hardcore programming skills. Websites were developed using text editors as simple as notepads. However, with advancements in web development technologies, people with little or absolutely no programming experience also began to find their feet in this arena. This happened owing to the development of CMSs such as WordPress, Joomla, Moodle and similar web development platforms. These CMSs allow layman users to develop professional-looking websites. Choosing a CMS depends on various factors. However, we will focus on why WordPress CMS is an excellent choice for developing websites.

Based on open source technologies

WordPress is an open source CMS and can be tweaked and edited by anyone to fit their needs. WordPress is based on PHP, which is an open source server-side programming language. WordPress uses a MySQL database for data persistence and storing content such as posts, comments and images, etc. MySQL is also open source and freely available.

Easy to install and manage

Installing WordPress is an extremely simple task and only requires a few clicks of the mouse. Most of the domain-hosting companies, such as HostGator and GoDaddy, provide one-click installation services for WordPress. Usability of WordPress is not limited to installation; once installed, it is also very easy to manage via the WordPress dashboard. For instance, creating menus, pages, posts, adding images and setting titles is a matter of a few clicks, and entails no programming skills.

Styling using themes

There are thousands of WordPress themes freely available. These themes can be used to define an overall style for your website. Themes can be tweaked to achieve desired styling functionalities. There are also premium themes out there for a small cost, so no two websites will ever look the same. Themes are a great way for early developers to learn how websites are built and they take out the technical challenge, so you can work on the content and look of the website without having to worry. For the advanced designer, you are able to use the editor to tweak your themes even further, or even create your own.

...cont'd

Most themes are responsive, so they will look perfect on all mobile and tablet devices. This means you will never have to worry about your visitors having a bad user interface (UI) experience on their device.

Enhanced functionality via plugins

WordPress websites can be enhanced easily via several "plugins". WordPress themes, by default, come with basic functionalities. However, additional functionalities can be added via plugins. For instance, if you want to add a login widget to your website, you can use a login plugin. Similarly, in order to add a contact form to your website, a contact form plugin can be used, not just to add the form to your page, but also to store and send on any queries that come through your website. There are many freely available plugins that can be used to enhance the functionality of a WordPress website.

Great support via a large development community

WordPress has one of the largest software developer communities. The immense developer support allows users to solve their WordPress issues immediately. Also, owing to the large developer community, rapid updates and patches are developed, which solve issues that arise in any theme or plugin, etc. Additionally, if you ever come across any problems, then you can always post in the support forum and be sure to get a quick response to your problem:

https://wordpress.org/support/

Search engine optimization (SEO)-friendly

WordPress already comes with a number of built-in SEO features, like the ability for search engines to crawl content, and pinging search engines when new posts are created. There are also a number of really good SEO plugins like Yoast, which will guide you through the process of SEO and help your website rank better with search engines.

Conclusion

Though there are many CMSs currently available in the market, WordPress is the best place to start. It is extremely easy to learn, flexible to tweak, open source and SEO-friendly. Also, with a large developer community, you are likely to get instant help and support for any issues that arise during your website development endeavors.

What Can I Build?

As previously mentioned, WordPress is not just a blogging platform. You can build a number of different websites using WordPress. Here are just a few things you can build when you get more familiar with the platform:

- **eCommerce website**: Have you ever wanted to have your own online shop? A website that can accept payments? Well, you can do just that with WordPress. There are a number of different plugins you can use; one that is free is WooCommerce (see Chapter 6).
- **Business website**: You will be surprised just how many business websites are made using WordPress. You can build a very professional website without having to know any technical languages.
- **Online forums**: You might think that forums are extremely difficult to create, but WordPress can make it a lot easier. There are plugins to help you create your own message board, so you can build a community in no time (see pages 123-128).
- **Portfolio**: If you are an artist or a photographer, then you might want to build a site to showcase your skills. With WordPress you can do just that, as there are a number of pre-made templates to help you show off your talents.
- **Membership website**: If you are looking to build a site with various membership levels – for example, a site with free and premium content – then you can do just that. Yet again, there are some good plugins on offer to help you, and you can create numerous levels of membership (see pages 135-140).
- **Directory/listings website**: Maybe you are thinking of starting a job site or a classified ads site. Well, you can with WordPress!
- **Auction website**: Have you ever dreamed of building your own eBay? There are various plugins and themes that help with this, so you don't have to start from scratch.
- **Mobile app**: There are various tools out there like AppPresser, which can convert your WordPress website into a mobile app.

The list goes on! This is just a taste of what you can do.

WordPress Hosting

To install WordPress you are going to need some space online. I recommend a company called HostGator (**www.hostgator.com**). It is very well priced, offers 24-hour support, and is very simple to set up WordPress on. There are various hosting companies out there that provide one-click installs for WordPress these days, which is great for new developers and bloggers. You can choose to set up your site using **WordPress.com**. However, there are some restrictions, depending on the package you select (see page 15).

Hot tip

Hosting WordPress through an external host like HostGator is probably the best option, as you will have full control over your site without having to spend too much.

Setting up a HostGator account

To get started, sign up for a HostGator account at **www.hostgator.com**, and if you don't already have one, pick a domain for your site. You can do both on HostGator. This is the first step to getting your WordPress site on the road! Make a note of your username and password so that you can log in.

1. Navigate to **https://portal.hostgator.com/login** in your web browser, and enter your username and password to log in to the HostGator portal. You should be presented with something like this:

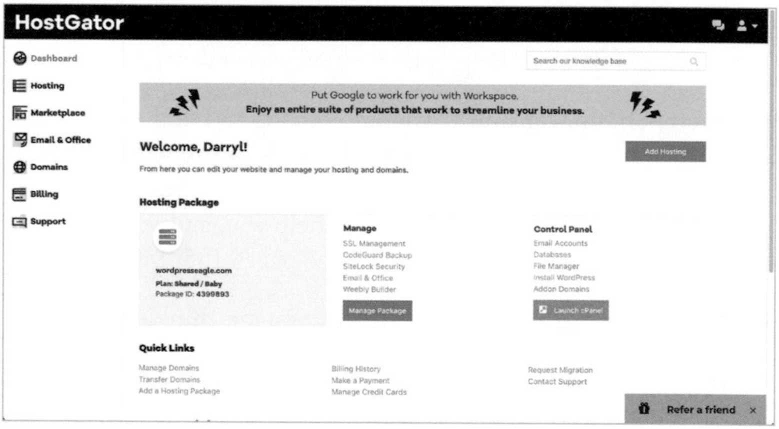
HostGator
Dashboard
Hosting
Marketplace
Email & Office
Domains
Billing
Support
Search our knowledge base
Put Google to work for you with Workspace.
Enjoy an entire suite of products that work to streamline your business.
Welcome, Darryl!
Add Hosting
From here you can edit your website and manage your hosting and domains.
Hosting Package
wordpresseagle.com
Manage
Manage Package
Control Panel
Quick Links
Refer a friend

2. Click on **Install WordPress**

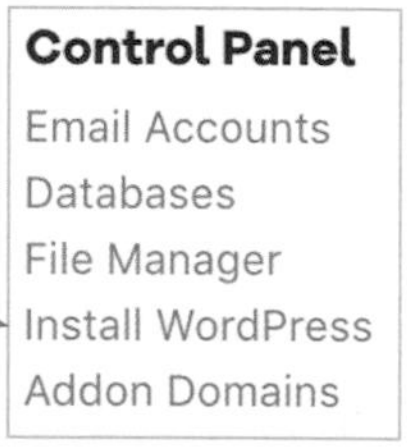
Control Panel
Email Accounts
Databases
File Manager
Install WordPress
Addon Domains

3 Click the **Install Now** button

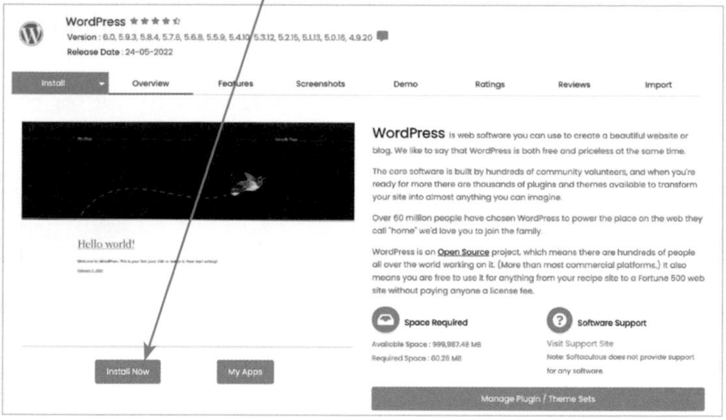

4 Select your installation URL. This is the same URL you selected when signing up with HostGator. You can leave the **In Directory** field blank

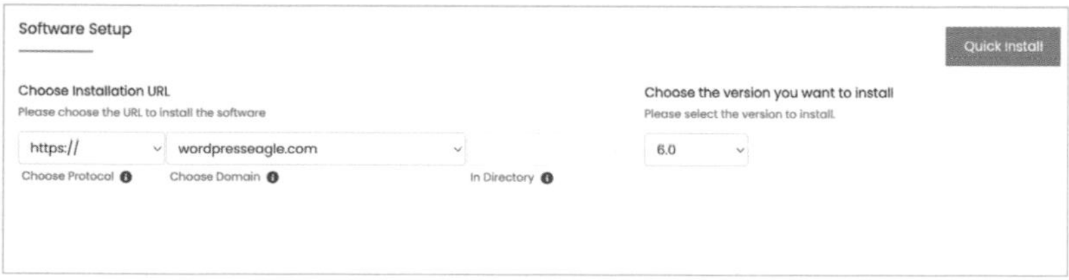

5 Fill out the form; here are the important fields:

Site Name: Enter a title for your website. For example, if you had a cake shop, you might call it "Becky's Cakes".

...cont'd

Site Description: Enter a short description of your website.
Admin Username: Enter the username you want to use to log in to the site.
Admin Password: Enter the password you want to use to log in to the site.
Admin Email: Enter the email address you wish to use for the admin user.

6. When you have filled out the fields, click the **Install** button

Install

7. Once installation is complete, you will see a message similar to the one below:

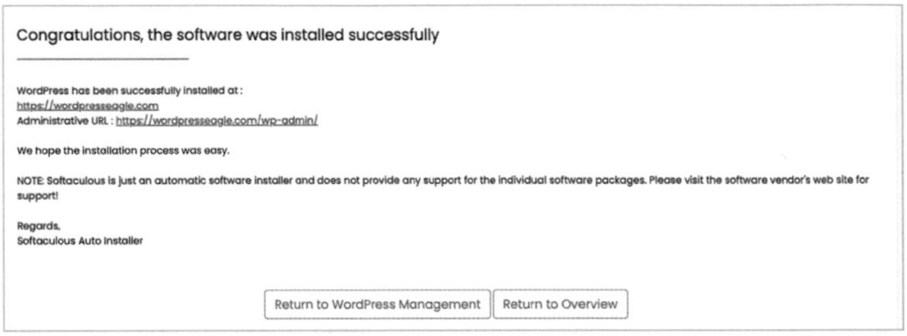
Congratulations, the software was installed successfully
WordPress has been successfully installed at :
https://wordpresseagle.com
Administrative URL : https://wordpresseagle.com/wp-admin/
We hope the installation process was easy.
NOTE: Softaculous is just an automatic software installer and does not provide any support for the individual software packages. Please visit the software vendor's web site for support!
Regards,
Softaculous Auto Installer
Return to WordPress Management
Return to Overview

8. You can now access WordPress by going to **http://www.yourdomain.com/wp-admin**
Remember to replace *yourdomain* with the domain you registered

Username or Email Address
Password
Remember Me
Log In
Lost your password?

This page is where you or any other members of your website will always log in. You can check the **Remember Me** box so that the website automatically logs you in.

Keep your login details in a safe place.

You can reset your password at the login screen. Click the **Lost your password?** button link at the bottom of the login panel.

Don't forget

It can take up to 24 hours for your domain to become active once registered with HostGator, so don't panic if you can't access the login screen right away.

Using WordPress.com

If you don't want to go through the WordPress installation stages with an external host, then you can use **WordPress.com** to host your site. There are currently six plans in place that range from free up to $45/£36 per month.

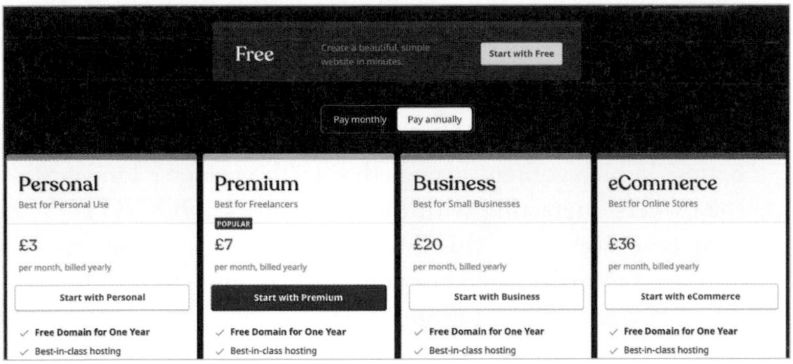

Quite a few of the packages of **WordPress.com** have limitations.

The package you choose depends on what functionality you need for your site. The free package holds quite a lot of limitations. For example, you don't get full control over the design, you will see ads appearing on your website, and you will also be limited to 1GB of storage. Bear in mind that you can only upload themes and install plugins if you have the **Business** or **eCommerce** plan. This is why I would recommend going through the installation process on pages 12-14 so that you get full control.

On **WordPress.com**, you can pick one of the WordPress domains or pay for a domain name. For example, if you were creating a website to do with antique cups, you might choose **antiquecups.wordpress.com**

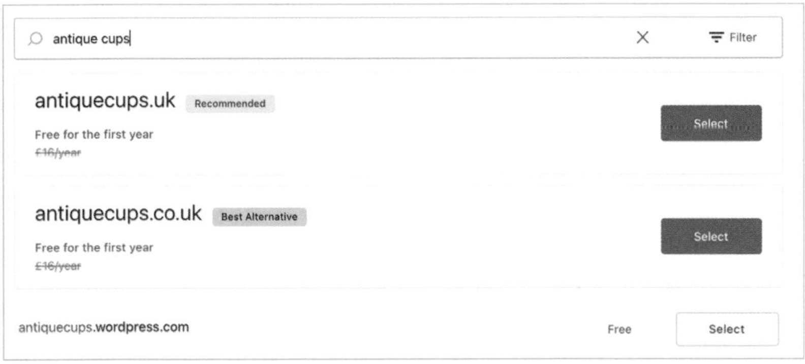

Once set up, you will be able to log in in the same manner as you would if your site were self-hosted, by going to **http://www.yourdomain.com/wp-admin**

Planning Your Website

Now we have gone through the installation stages, before we get our hands dirty with the interface, we are going to have a look at the important process of planning a WordPress website.

Don't forget

Planning is a key part of any project. You need to cover everything, all the way from design through to implementation.

- **Research**: The area you should start with is research. Have a look at websites similar to what you want to build. For example, if you are building a technology blog, you may want to look at other technology blogs. Compare the successful and unsuccessful ones. What are the successful ones doing better? Which content is engaging to the readers? How are the owners interacting with their customers? DO NOT copy other websites – this is key and will get you nowhere. You need to make sure your content is unique. Research is a valuable way to build a more successful site.

- **Brainstorming**: Now, it's time to sit down with a cup of coffee and a notebook and start brainstorming your website. What is going to go on there? Which pages are you going to have? How often is content going online? Will I use social media? How will my users interact with the website?

- **Page structure**: Will you have pages and subpages on your website? For example, an **About Us** section might have a jobs section as a subpage. You need to organize your page structure. Here is an example:

  - **Home**
  - **About Us**
    - Jobs
    - Our Office
    - History
  - **Services**
    - Web Design
    - Graphic Design
    - Web Hosting
    - Printing
  - **Events**
    - This Year
  - **Blog**
  - **Contact Us**

- **Plugins**: If you are looking to add functionality to your website, you may need to research which plugins you will need and find out what the best ones are. There are plenty of free plugins on the market but if you are going to spend any money on them, then you need to know what you are buying first (see Chapter 5).
- **Project management**: Do you have milestones or deadlines in mind? Make sure you keep a schedule, and stick to it. If you want to meet your goals you need to keep a tight schedule. It's the key to a successful website.
- **Web hosting**: Who am I going to host my website with? How much is it going to cost me? How reliable are the hosts? These are all important parts of planning your website.
- **Domain name**: A domain is a very important part of building a website; you want to have a catchy name. Don't make your domain too long; you want people to remember it. You can always point other domains to your website as well, which is another thing to bear in mind. Domain pointing allows you to direct multiple domains to the same website.
- **Website backups**: Make sure you are keeping backups of your site; daily would be ideal but if not, then every other day. You never know if the web server is going to go down or get hacked. You will sleep easier at night knowing you have a backup (see pages 175-178).
- **Payment methods**: If you are building a web shop, then you should think about which payment methods you want to offer. PayPal is probably the best and easiest one to set up, and most people are using it these days.
- **Social media**: Whichever website you are building, social media is a very important part of growing your audience. Be sure to share your content through as many social media channels as you can. Twitter, Facebook, Instagram, YouTube, and LinkedIn are the main ones.

This may seem like a long list, but it is important to keep each step in mind so that your web development will go smoothly.

Blog vs Website

Sometimes there is a lot of confusion when it comes to blogs and websites. Some people ask things like:

- Should I create a website or a blog?
- What's the difference between a website and a blog?

Let's clear this up before we start.

WordPress blog

Below is a screenshot of a blog built with WordPress. You will notice that the homepage lists a number of blog posts created by the user. Now, this may be fine with you, especially if you are wanting to document something like your hobbies, but what if you are building a website for your business?

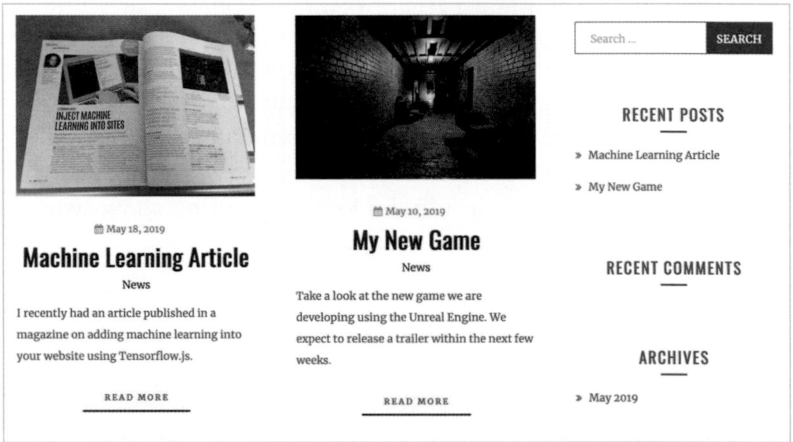

Example blog

Hot tip

We will be looking at themes in Chapter 3.

WordPress website

With WordPress you can install themes that will give your website a certain look. With some themes, it will even create pages for you (like an **About** or **Services** page) so that you can just enter your own content. A website is likely to have multiple pages and their services or products outlined on the homepage, and also inside the menu.

Business site menu

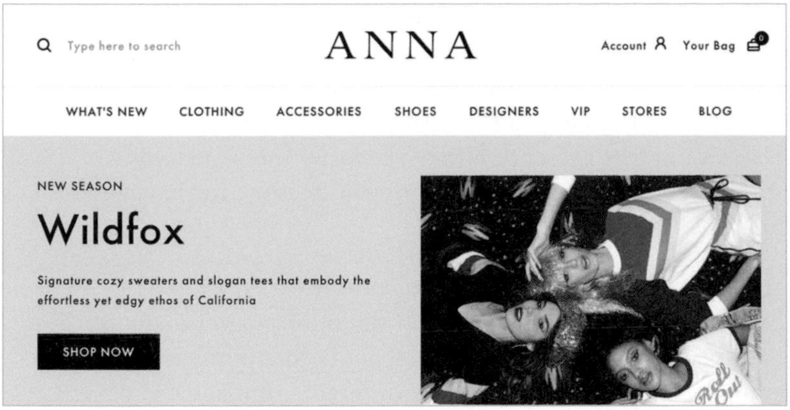

Example business website

Most companies or start-ups will have a blog on their website these days. It's a good way of interacting with their customers and providing extra value.

Website

- Content is mainly static apart from a blog or forum section
- More of a digital storefront eCommerce
- Professional look
- Much more functionality
- Pages about products and services

Also, remember that with a website, sometimes the only way for your customers to communicate with you is through the contact form.

Blog

- Content is updated more frequently
- Newest content appears near the top
- Usually arranged by category or date
- Google loves blogs because the content is fresh
- Not formal
- Users can interact via a commenting system

The last thing to bear in mind is that a blog is still a kind of website. Most people used to choose to set up a blog because they lacked the programming skills to build something bigger, but now WordPress makes anything possible!

Business Websites

The internet has revolutionized the world – it has become a global village and now everyone is linked by just a few mouse clicks. Businesses are taking advantage of a huge customer presence on the internet. Presently, 99% of successful businesses and industries have an internet presence either via social media networks or dedicated websites. There are several reasons for having a dedicated website for a business.

Huge number of potential customers

The internet user population is in the billions, and many of these users search a product on the internet before purchasing it. They compare the products offered by different companies and then make a decision about what to buy.

Cost-effective marketing tool

Websites are one of the cheapest marketing tools ever invented. A website can cost as little as $3-20/£2.50-£8 per month to start, depending on the web host. All you need to do to set up a live website is to buy a domain and hosting, and with little knowledge of any of the CMSs, you can create your very own website.

Easy customer interaction

Websites allow businesses to rapidly interact with their customers. Most websites now contain a **Contact Us** form where users can leave comments and queries whenever they want. Also, websites are live 24/7; therefore, potential customers can get information about products or services irrespective of the time zones.

Global presence

A company cannot open outlets in every corner of the world unless it generates billions of dollars of revenue, which is not the case with every company. The best possible way to have a global presence and reach potential customers located at diverse geographical locations is to have an international website.

Good first impression

Companies and businesses with an official and registered website are considered more authentic, credible and garner better customer trust, compared with businesses that do not have a website. A visually pleasing and easy-to-navigate website creates a good first impression and can be used to convince customers to stay on the website for longer periods of time, eventually resulting in business.

2 Dashboard & Users

This chapter introduces you to the WordPress dashboard and how to find your way around. You will also be introduced to the Users section.

Dashboard Overview

The WordPress dashboard is the Control Panel of your WordPress website. You can control every component of your WordPress website via this dashboard. You can change the theme of your site, manipulate various visible areas of your site, and change the behavior of posts and comments underneath the posts. You can also add users to your website through the dashboard and assign different roles to those users.

Hot tip

We will be using WordPress version 6.0 throughout this book.

This section presents a brief overview of various menu items on your dashboard, along with their functionalities. We will not dig deeper into the nitty-gritty of each menu item. However, after reading this chapter, you will be aware of what each individual item on the dashboard does and what functionality can be achieved through the item. So, let's jump straight to work!

Admin Bar

Once you log in to the dashboard of your website, you will see lots of menus and messages in different windows of your dashboard. Don't worry about them; we will explain everything.

After you log in, you should see a page similar to the screenshot below:

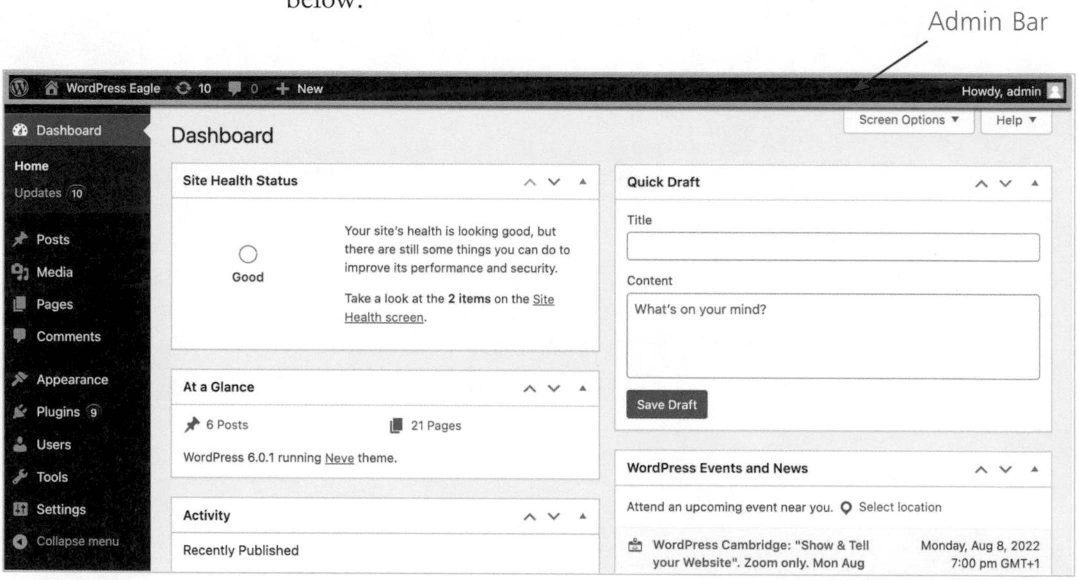
Admin Bar
WordPress Eagle
10
0
New
Howdy, admin
Dashboard
Home
Updates 10
Posts
Media
Pages
Comments
Appearance
Plugins 9
Users
Tools
Settings
Collapse menu
Screen Options
Help
Site Health Status
Good
Your site's health is looking good, but there are still some things you can do to improve its performance and security.
Take a look at the 2 items on the Site Health screen.
At a Glance
6 Posts
21 Pages
WordPress 6.0.1 running Neve theme.
Activity
Recently Published
Quick Draft
Title
Content
What's on your mind?
Save Draft
WordPress Events and News
Attend an upcoming event near you.
Select location
WordPress Cambridge: "Show & Tell your Website". Zoom only. Mon Aug
Monday, Aug 8, 2022
7:00 pm GMT+1

In the screenshot, at the top of the page, you should see some menu items (highlighted by a yellow rectangle). Collectively, these menu items are called the **Admin Bar**. Let us briefly discuss each of these menu items one by one, starting from the left.

Admin Bar Links

WordPress icon

Hovering your mouse over this icon opens a drop-down menu that contains links to WordPress resources such as **WordPress.org**, documentation resources and feedback, etc. If you want to have a look at the documentation, or you want to leave feedback, etc. you can use these links.

Visit Site

Displays the title of your website. A small house (home) icon is also displayed to the left of this item. If you click this item, you will be taken to the homepage of your website while logged in as an authorized user. If you hover your mouse over this icon, a drop-down list with one link appears, which shows **Visit Site**.

Updates

Usually this will appear with a number next to it, indicating how many updates there are available. Clicking this link will take you through to a page where you can update the WordPress version, plugins and themes.

Comment moderation

The fourth item from the left on the **Admin Bar** is the comment moderation menu. If you have specified that every post or comment needs to be moderated before publication, all comments awaiting moderation can be moderated from here.

New item

The last item on the **Admin Bar** on the left-hand side is the **New** item. This item contains links to pages where a new post, media file, page, link, etc. can be created. If you hover your mouse over this item, you will see these options appear.

Admin panel

If you look at the top right of the window, a link named **Howdy, admin** is displayed. This link contains information about the logged-in user. If you have assigned a different name to the admin, this link will display a different name. Basically, through this link, you can edit your admin profile. You can also choose to log out from here by selecting **Log Out** from the drop-down menu.

Hot tip

WordPress.org is a great place to find plugins, resources, support, and forums, and you can even download WordPress files from here. It is mainly for those who have used an external host for their WordPress setup.

Dashboard Menu Options

We have briefly explained all the menus on the top **Admin Bar**. Now, let's look at the menu options on the left-hand side of the dashboard.

Hot tip

Depending on which hosting provider you used, you may see a number of different menu links because of additional plugin installations. However the ones shown on this page are the main ones you will need to get used to.

Dashboard

If you hover your mouse on the dashboard menu items, a drop-down list will appear that contains two options: **Home** and **Updates**. Clicking on **Home** will take you back to the main dashboard, while clicking on the **Updates** link will take you to a new page where all pending updates will be displayed.

Posts

The **Posts** section in WordPress allows you to add, edit, delete and publish posts on your website. You can also put these into categories. The process of creating and publishing posts is explained in Chapter 4.

Media

This item is used to add any media file such as an image, an audio file or a video file to your website media library. You can also view your current library here. If you hover your mouse over this item, you will see two options appear: **Library** and **Add New**.

Pages

This option is used to add new pages to your WordPress site or to edit or update existing pages. Hovering your mouse over this option displays a new menu with two options: **All Pages** and **Add New**.

Comments

This section allows you to moderate comments posted on your website. If a user decides to post a comment on any of your posts or pages, then it will appear in this section. You can choose to approve, unapprove, mark as spam or move the comment to the bin.

Appearance

This is the section of WordPress where you can set out the look and feel of your website. Here, you can add new themes, customize your current theme, create menus and deal with widgets. This section is explained in more detail in Chapter 3.

Plugins

This menu item can be used to edit installed plugins, remove plugins, activate and deactivate them, and also add new plugins. If you hover your mouse over the **Plugins** menu item, you will see a new menu appear with three options: **Installed Plugins**, **Add New**, and **Editor**. Plugins are covered in Chapter 5.

Don't forget

When adding new plugins to WordPress, you might discover new links being added to your dashboard.

Users

This is the option that you can use to add, edit and update roles of the registered and authorized users of your website. You can update things like passwords and role types for each user. You can even make amendments to your own profile.

Tools

This option is basically used to import and export available tools that can be integrated into your website and enhance its functionality. Tools available here vary according to your host and domain provider.

Settings

The **Settings** panel is located at the bottom of the menu. It contains all the settings related to content writing, reading, commenting on posts, links and media settings, and – most importantly – the general settings of your website.

Collapse menu

This will collapse the dashboard menu options so that you can work without distractions.

Introducing Users

The **Users** section is where you can add and delete users, as well as edit their user privileges. This is extremely helpful if you have other users working on your website, whether it be writing content for you or developing the site further. To access the **Users** area, click **Users** from the menu on the left-hand side.

Before you start creating users, let's have a look at the various roles that you are able to assign to users of your website.

Administrator

Administrators have complete control over the WordPress site. They can perform all tasks in the WordPress dashboard, they have complete control over content, and they can do things like change themes, add plugins, etc.

Editor

The role of **Editor** is very much the same as it would be with a magazine. They can control all content and moderate comments. However, they can't change the appearance, add any plugins, etc.

Author

An **Author** can publish, edit or delete their own posts and upload their own media. However, they cannot access material created by other users. They are also unable to create or delete pages.

Contributor

Contributors can write and edit their own posts. However, the posts will need to be approved by an **Administrator** or **Editor** before being published.

Subscriber

This is the default role for all new user signups. **Subscribers** can read content and post comments but have no other privileges.

Adding Users

1. To add a new user, start by clicking **Users** > **Add New**

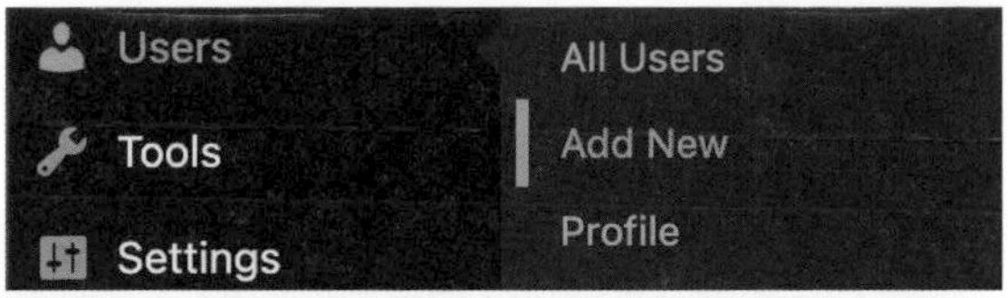

Users
Tools
Settings
All Users
Add New
Profile

2. You will be presented with a form to fill out for the user. Create a username for the new user, which they will log in with; also add in their email address, first name, last name, website, and a password. You can choose to send the login details to the user by checking the **Send the new user an email about their account** box

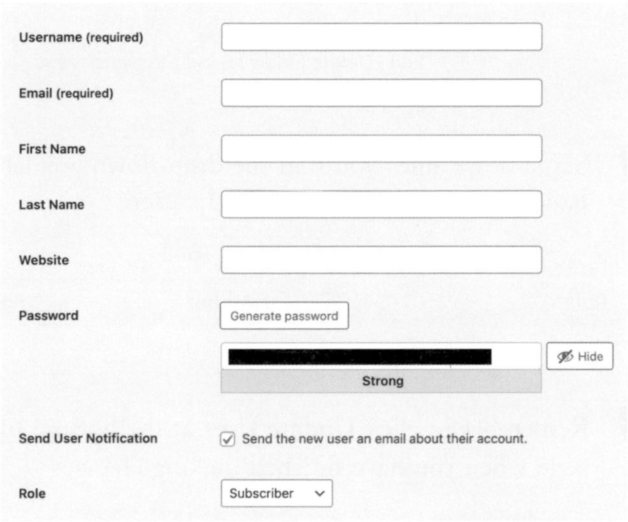

Username (required)
Email (required)
First Name
Last Name
Website
Password
Generate password
Hide
Strong
Send User Notification
Send the new user an email about their account.
Role
Subscriber

3. Make sure you select a role from the drop-down box

Role
Subscriber

4. Finally, click **Add New User**. The user can now log in to WordPress using the same login address (**www.yourdomain.com/wp-admin/**)

Add New User

Hot tip

WordPress will suggest a strong password for you, but you can choose anything you like. However, if you choose a weak password, then WordPress will prompt you to check a box to confirm the use of this.

Beware

Only give **Administrator** privileges to people who need it, and also make sure you trust them.

Changing User Roles

There may come a time where you want to give another user extra or restricted privileges. To change this, go to the **Users** page.

1. Start by clicking **Users** > **All Users**

Users
Tools
Settings
All Users
Add New
Profile

2. Click **Edit** underneath the name of the user you want to edit

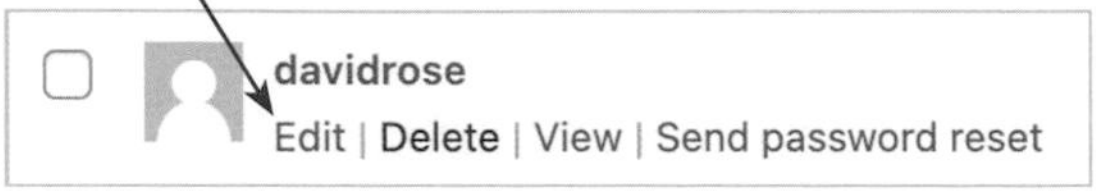
davidrose
Edit | Delete | View | Send password reset

3. Scroll down until you find the drop-down box labeled **Role** and select a new role for the user

Role
Author

4. Remember to click **Update User** at the bottom of the page when you have finished making changes

Color schemes

There are a number of other things you can change in this section for other users or even yourself – for example, you can change the color scheme for the dashboard.

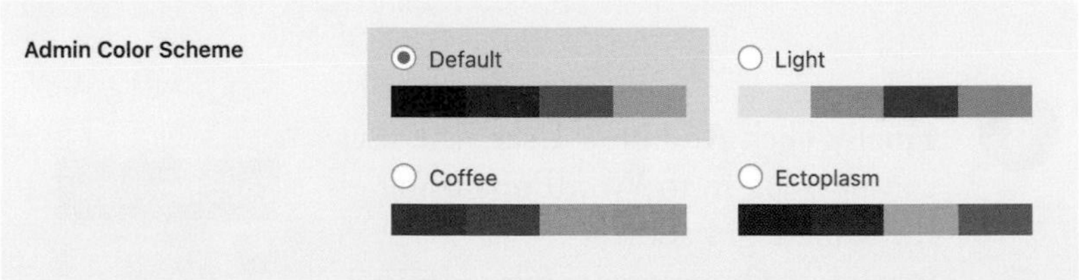
Admin Color Scheme
Default
Light
Coffee
Ectoplasm

3 Appearance & Themes

This chapter introduces you to themes, and how you can install, upload and customize them. Themes are an important part of how your website looks.

Introduction to Themes

Web development: from technical to user-friendly

In the early days of the internet, designing and developing websites was considered a complicated task. There was a common perception that only technical professionals and people with extraordinary IQs could dig into the world of website development. This perception was true to some extent since at that time, web development required writing down code and implementing algorithms in editors as simple as a word processor. However, it is said that change is the only constant. This rule applies to the web development industry as well.

Keeping in view the huge advantages associated with marketing and advertising through websites, web developers started developing platforms that could help people develop a website without much programming expertise. CMSs laid the foundation for such user-friendly web development platforms, and WordPress is one of those CMSs.

Where do themes fit in?

WordPress allows the layman user to develop sophisticated and professional-looking websites without any prior knowledge of programming, via themes.

Simply put, a WordPress theme is basically a pre-built, database-driven web template that can be tweaked and modified to fit the needs of a desired website. There are thousands of WordPress themes out there, some of which are free, but you can also pay extra for premium offerings. Experienced developers will create their own themes from scratch. This is something we will cover on pages 166-174.

A theme is composed of several components, some of which are common, while others are intrinsic to themes. Common components of a theme include menus, widgets and headers. You can change your theme at any time during the development of your website without having to worry about any content changing. Once a theme is activated, the look of your website will automatically change.

Adding Themes

To add a theme to a WordPress site:

1. Log in to the dashboard of your WordPress website or blog

2. In the dashboard, find **Appearance** and click **Themes**

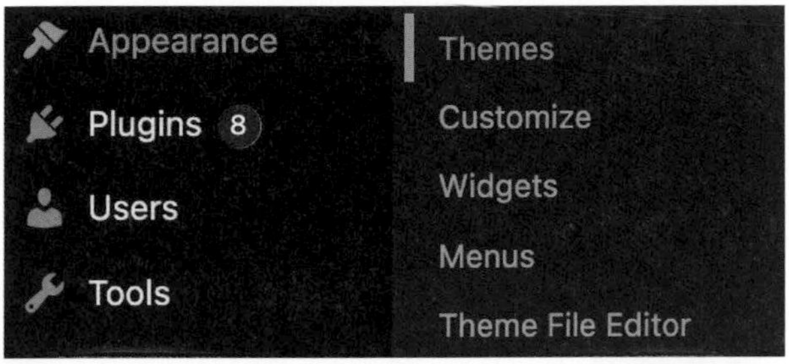

You should then be presented with a screen (similar to the one below) that shows themes already installed. At the top of the page there is a Search bar where you can search already added themes in your blog, as well as an **Add New** button where you can add new themes to WordPress.

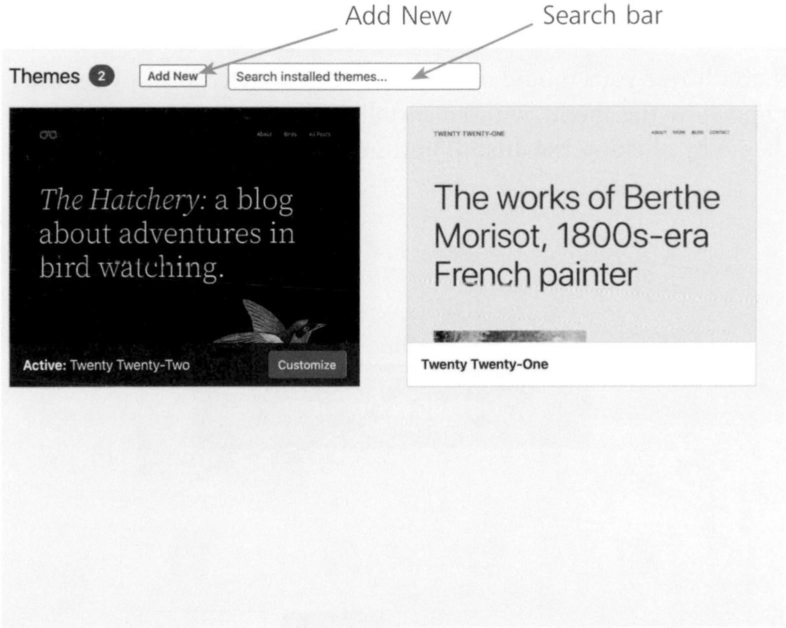

...cont'd

3. To begin adding a new theme, click **Add New**

You will then be presented with a screen where you can browse through a number of new themes. These include **Featured**, **Popular** and **Latest**. There is also a section called **Feature Filter** where you can browse for themes based on your feature requirements. There is also a Search bar where you can enter the name of a theme.

Theme categories

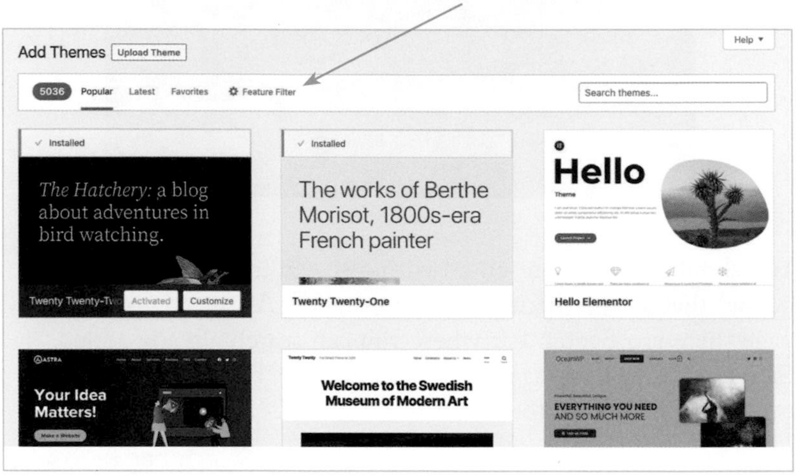

If you hover your mouse over one of the themes, you can choose to preview the theme without installing it, or you can install the theme by clicking the **Install** button.

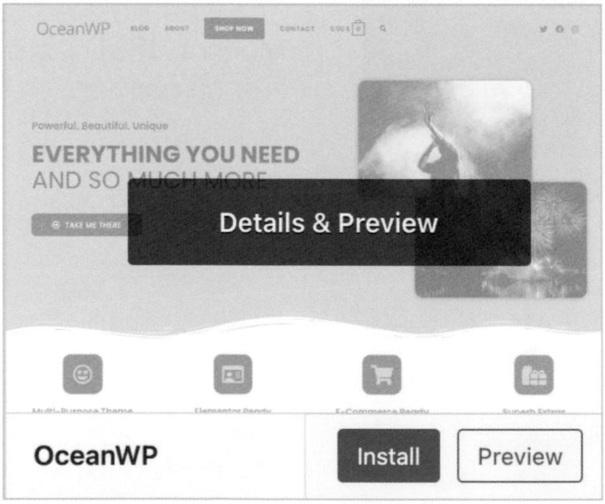

4. Once you click the **Install** button, the theme you selected will be installed and an **Installed** notice will appear

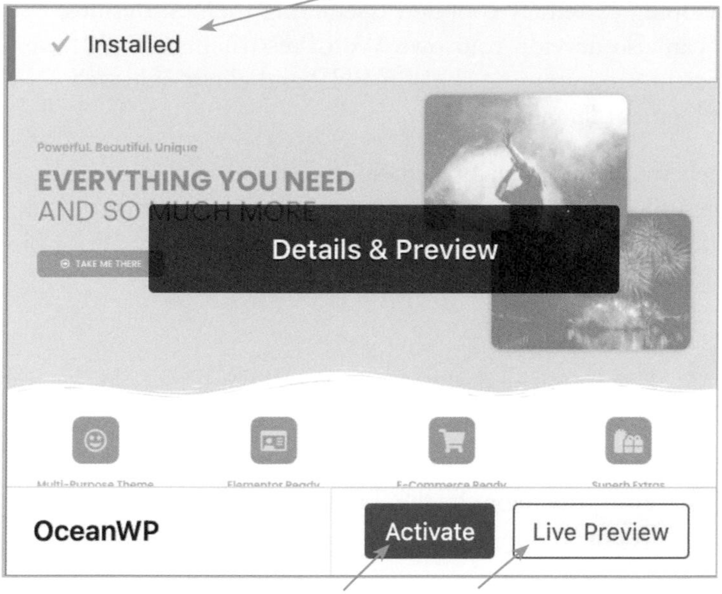

Activate Live Preview

Once installation has complcted, you have two options to choose from: **Activate** and **Live Preview**.

Clicking **Live Preview** will show you a live preview of your website with the theme you selected but it will not activate the theme, so it gives you a chance to decide whether or not you like the look of your theme with your current content. Clicking the **Activate** link will activate the theme. Now, if you visit your website, you will see the new theme applied to your site.

Deleting a theme

Deleting a theme is an extremely simple process. Go back to **Appearance** > **Themes** and click on a theme you wish to delete. A new page appears, displaying theme details. In the bottom right-hand corner, there is a link to delete the theme.

When you click **Delete**, you will be asked to confirm that you wish to delete the theme.

Don't forget

You can have more than one theme installed. However, only one can be activated at a time.

Beware

Activating themes can change the layout of your content, so make sure you are happy with the design before you decide to activate.

Uploading a Theme

Apart from installing built-in themes from **WordPress.org**, you can also buy themes from other vendors. WordPress has a huge developer community, and there are thousands of developers developing extremely cool and fascinating themes. Besides, you can also develop your own WordPress themes if you have sufficient programming skills in PHP and client-side web development languages.

When you buy or develop a theme, what you get is a simple zipped file that contains all the necessary files that make up a theme. This zipped file is then uploaded to your WordPress blog or site. To upload a new theme to WordPress:

1. Log in to the dashboard of your WordPress blog or website

2. From the menu in the dashboard, click **Appearance** > **Themes**

3. Click **Add New**

4. Click **Upload Theme** instead of selecting from any of the **WordPress.org** themes

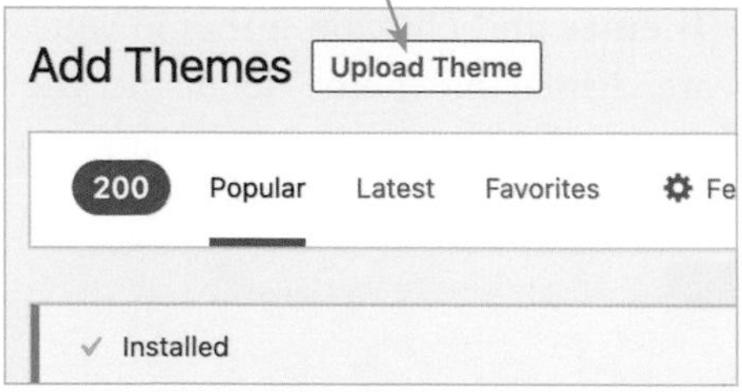

5. Click on the **Choose file** button. A new file dialog will open for you to locate the zipped file that includes your theme. Once you have located the file, click the **Open** button from the file dialog

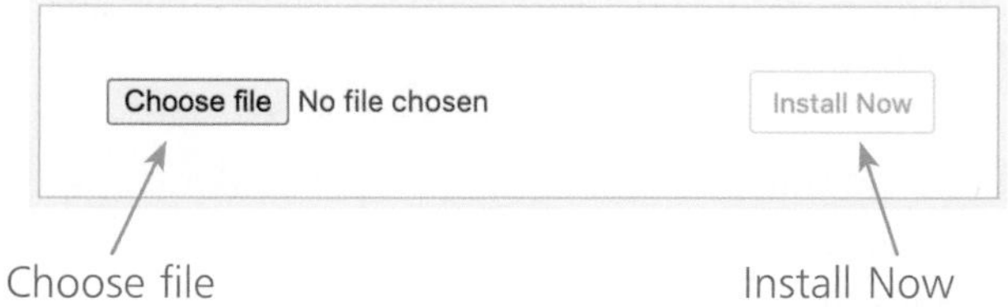
Choose file
No file chosen
Install Now
Choose file
Install Now

Favourites
Recents
Applications
Desktop
Documents
Creative Clo...
Locations
Macintosh...
Downloads
Today
ZIP
neve.3.3.4.zip

Selecting the zipped file from your PC

6. Once you click the **Install Now** button, the theme will begin uploading (this may take a few minutes). Once installation is complete, you will see the following screen:

Installing theme from uploaded file: neve.3.3.4.zip
Unpacking the package...
Updating the theme...
Removing the old version of the theme...
Theme updated successfully.
Live Preview | Activate | Go to Themes page

You will get three options – **Live Preview**, **Activate** and **Go to Themes page**. You simply have to click the **Activate** link to make the theme go live.

Customizing Your Theme

WordPress themes come with several default options such as tagline, header image, background color, etc. However, the default theme options can be customized via the WordPress admin dashboard. To customize WordPress theme options:

1. Log in to your WordPress dashboard

2. From the menu in the dashboard, click **Appearance** > **Customize**. You will notice a number of customizable options down the left-hand side, along with a web preview down the right-hand side

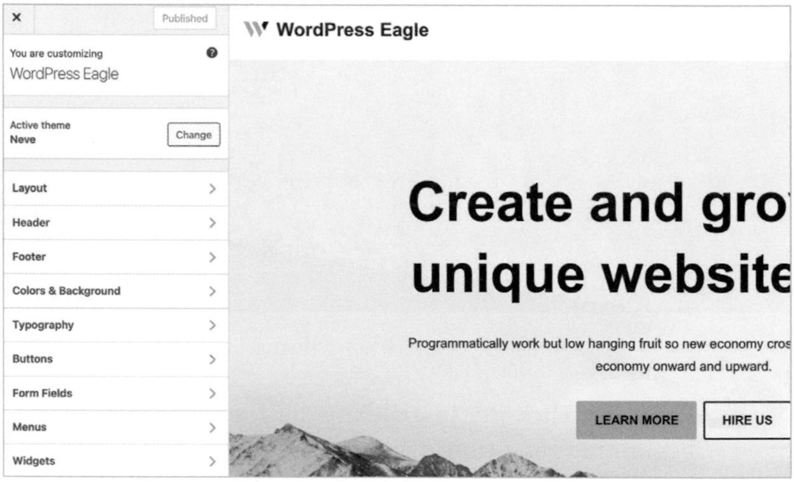
Published
You are customizing
WordPress Eagle
Active theme
Neve
Change
Layout
Header
Footer
Colors & Background
Typography
Buttons
Form Fields
Menus
Widgets
WordPress Eagle
Create and gro
unique website
Programmatically work but low hanging fruit so new economy cros
economy onward and upward.
LEARN MORE
HIRE US

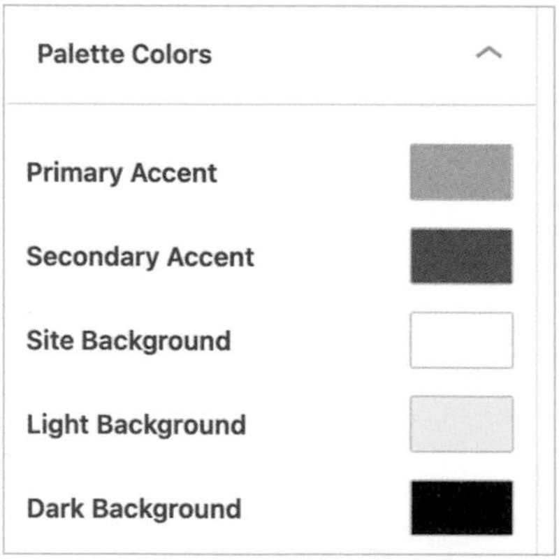
Palette Colors
Primary Accent
Secondary Accent
Site Background
Light Background
Dark Background

For example, here, you can customize the website color scheme.

There are many other elements you can customize without having to use any code.

Once you have finished, click **Publish** to update the live website.

Don't forget

The options you get will depend on the theme you have installed. The options shown in the screenshots on this page come from a free theme called **Sydney**.

Hot tip

The web preview will update when you change one of the element options.

Customizing Menus

Menus are usually located at the top of your page or sidebar, depending upon the theme you choose. They usually display a number of links, allowing the user to easily navigate through each page of your website. Always remember that your website can have multiple menus.

1. From the dashboard, click **Appearance** > **Menus**

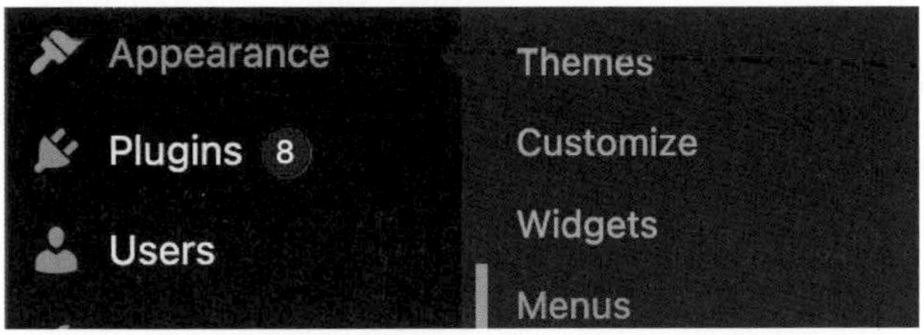
Appearance
Plugins 8
Users
Themes
Customize
Widgets
Menus

2. Click the **Create a new menu** link at the top of the page

3. Enter a name for your menu and click the **Create Menu** button

Menu Name
Menu 1

4. On the left-hand side will be a list of pages that you have already created. To select one or more of those, check the checkboxes next to them

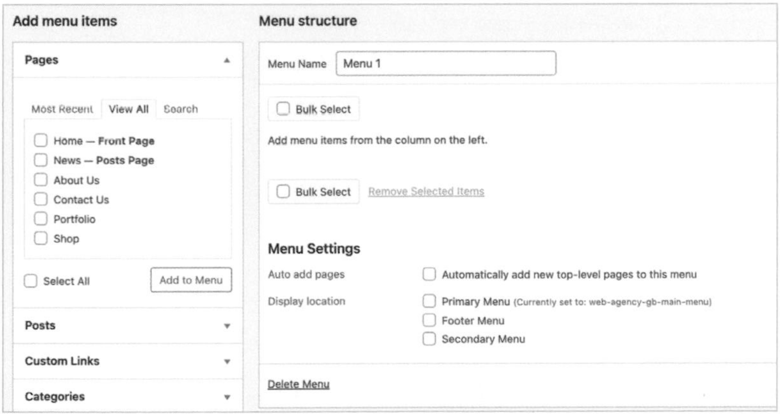
Add menu items
Pages
Most Recent
View All
Search
Home — Front Page
News — Posts Page
About Us
Contact Us
Portfolio
Shop
Select All
Add to Menu
Posts
Custom Links
Categories
Menu structure
Menu Name
Menu 1
Bulk Select
Add menu items from the column on the left.
Bulk Select
Remove Selected Items
Menu Settings
Auto add pages
Automatically add new top-level pages to this menu
Display location
Primary Menu (Currently set to: web-agency-gb-main-menu)
Footer Menu
Secondary Menu
Delete Menu

...cont'd

Hot tip

You are not just restricted to one menu on your website. You are not just restricted to one. Some themes will already have a second one built in.

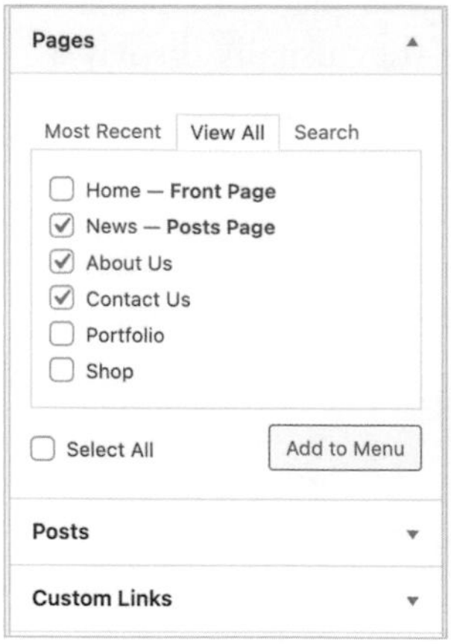
Pages
Most Recent
View All
Search
Home — Front Page
News — Posts Page
About Us
Contact Us
Portfolio
Shop
Select All
Add to Menu
Posts
Custom Links

Once you have selected the pages you wish to add, click the **Add to Menu** button. This will add the pages to the menu structure.

In this example, I have selected three pages, which means these items will be added to the menu.

You may have a different list of items, depending on which pages have been created.

5. Your pages will now appear in the **Menu structure**. You can reorder the pages by selecting an item and dragging it above or below another menu item

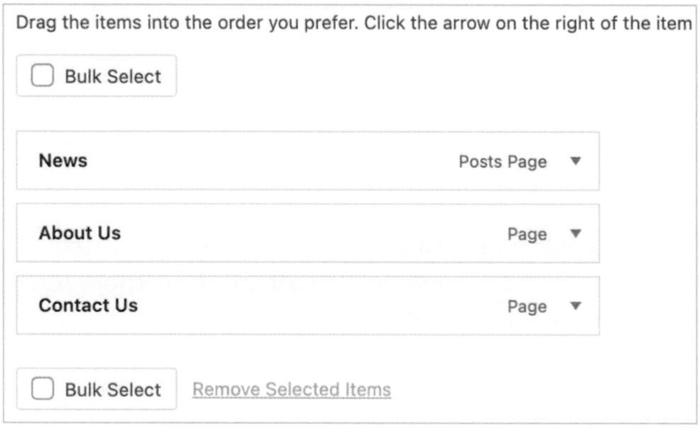
Drag the items into the order you prefer. Click the arrow on the right of the item
Bulk Select
News
Posts Page
About Us
Page
Contact Us
Page
Bulk Select
Remove Selected Items

6. Under **Menu Settings**, make sure you have selected a location for the menu. This will vary depending on the theme

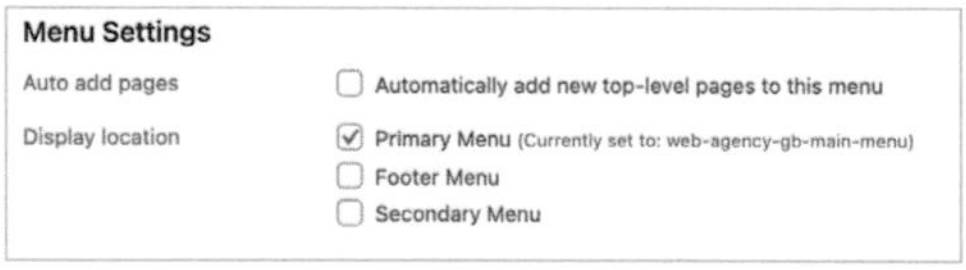
Menu Settings
Auto add pages
Automatically add new top-level pages to this menu
Display location
Primary Menu (Currently set to: web-agency-gb-main-menu)
Footer Menu
Secondary Menu

7. Click the **Save Menu** button and head to your website or blog. You will see that your items have been added to the menu

Hot tip

You can also add external links to your menu. All you need to do is select the **Custom Links** section on the left-hand side then fill out the following options:

URL: The URL of the page you want to link to.

Link Text: This is how you want the link name to appear.

Adding Widgets

Widgets are small applications that enhance user experience and responsiveness and provide additional functionalities other than built-in theme features. A really cool demonstration of a widget is a Facebook Like Box, which is often displayed on the homepage of a website. A Facebook Page plugin box displays the number of people who have liked the page, and the user can also like the page directly from the Like Box instead of finding the page on Facebook and then liking that.

1. From the dashboard, click **Appearance** > **Widgets**

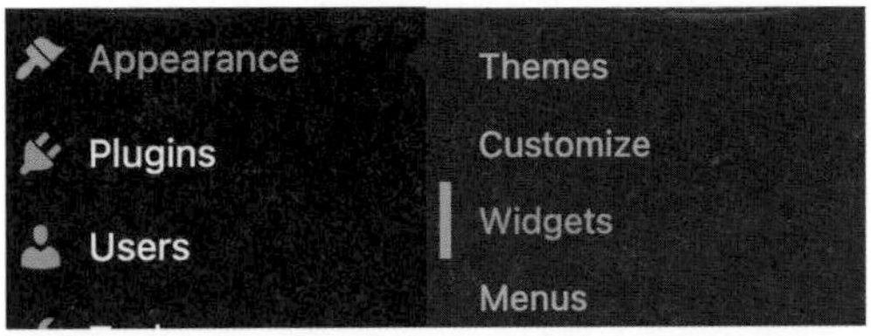
Appearance
Plugins
Users
Themes
Customize
Widgets
Menus

Something very similar to the screenshot below will appear. This again will vary by theme. You may find you have more widget areas to choose from.

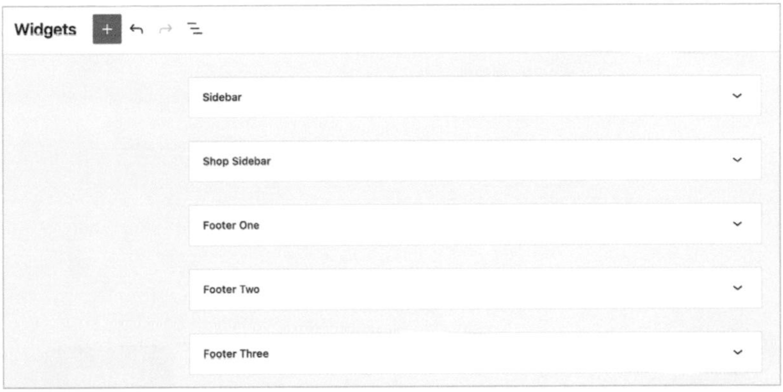
Widgets
Sidebar
Shop Sidebar
Footer One
Footer Two
Footer Three

2. Click the **+** button, which is located on the top left-hand side

3. This will bring up a number of different widgets you can add to your website. Drag the **Latest Comments** widget from the left-hand side and put it into the **Sidebar** section

Don't forget

When adding new plugins (see Chapter 5), you will sometimes have new widgets appear relevant to that plugin. For example – if you add a Twitter plugin, then you may see a Twitter widget appear allowing you to display Tweets.

...cont'd

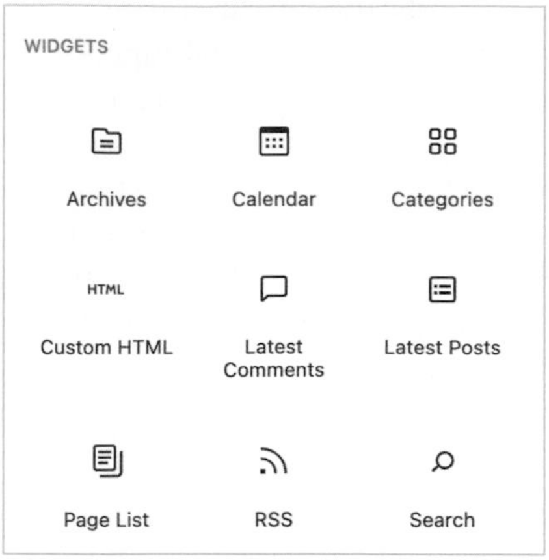
WIDGETS
Archives
Calendar
Categories
HTML
Custom HTML
Latest Comments
Latest Posts
Page List
RSS
Search

Widget selection

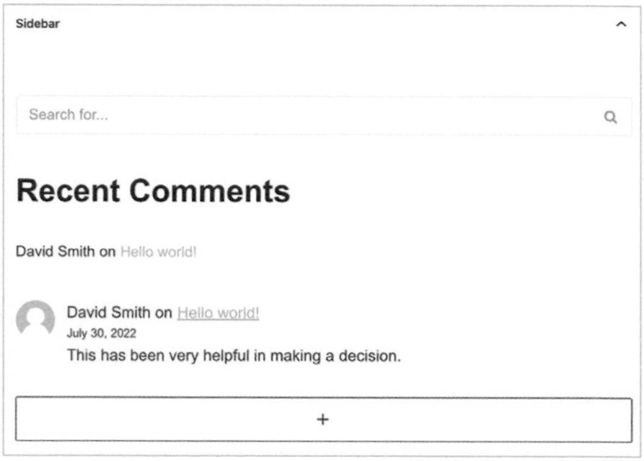
Sidebar
Search for...
Recent Comments
David Smith on Hello world!
David Smith on Hello world!
July 30, 2022
This has been very helpful in making a decision.
+

Sidebar widget section

Don't forget

Depending on which theme you select, the widget areas that you get are going to vary.

4. Click the **Update** button on the top right-hand side to save the changes you just made

Update

You will now notice on the live site that **Recent Comments** has appeared in the sidebar. This is a very basic example – you can get some very good widgets, many of which are already installed, or you can get extra ones through plugins (see Chapter 5).

To add a Facebook Page plugin inside a widget:

1. Visit **https://developers.facebook.com/docs/plugins/page-plugin**

2. You can customize the height, width and URL of a Facebook widget. It will give you an instant preview of how your box will look

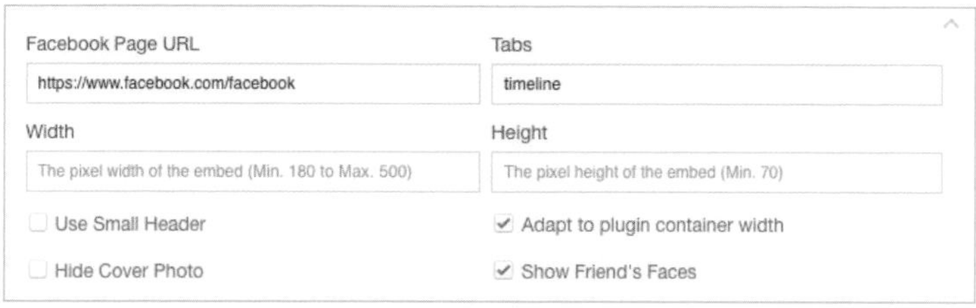
Facebook Page URL
https://www.facebook.com/facebook
Tabs
timeline
Width
The pixel width of the embed (Min. 180 to Max. 500)
Height
The pixel height of the embed (Min. 70)
Use Small Header
Adapt to plugin container width
Hide Cover Photo
Show Friend's Faces

3. Once you are finished, click **Get Code** right at the bottom of the page

Get Code

4. Copy both sets of code you are given

5. Now, go back to the **Widgets** page, and drag a **Custom HTML** widget over to one of the widget areas. Feel free to use the **Sidebar** section, like you did on pages 39-40

6. Paste both sets of code into the box shown below

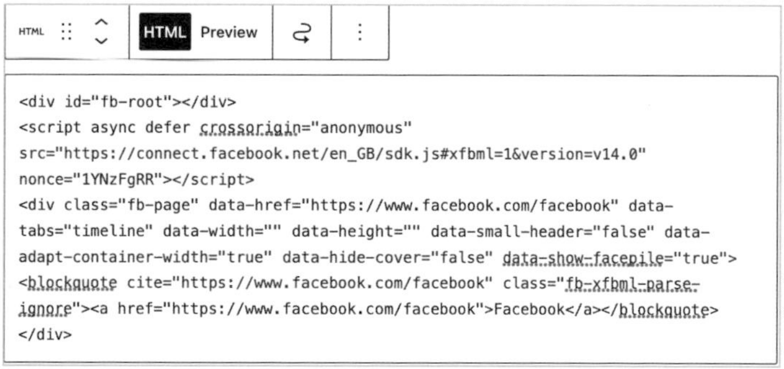
HTML
HTML
Preview
<div id="fb-root"></div>
<script async defer crossorigin="anonymous"
src="https://connect.facebook.net/en_GB/sdk.js#xfbml=1&version=v14.0"
nonce="1YNzFgRR"></script>
<div class="fb-page" data-href="https://www.facebook.com/facebook" data-
tabs="timeline" data-width="" data-height="" data-small-header="false" data-
adapt-container-width="true" data-hide-cover="false" data-show-facepile="true">
<blockquote cite="https://www.facebook.com/facebook" class="fb-xfbml-parse-
ignore"><a href="https://www.facebook.com/facebook">Facebook</a></blockquote>
</div>

7. Click the **Update** button to save the changes

Hot tip

You can go back to Facebook to edit your Like Box at any time. There are various Facebook plugins on offer too.

The Editor

With sufficient programming knowledge of CSS, HTML, JavaScript and PHP, you can easily edit already developed CSS themes. WordPress provides built-in functionality for editing themes via the Editor. To edit WordPress themes:

1. From the menus in the dashboard, click **Appearance** > **Theme File Editor**

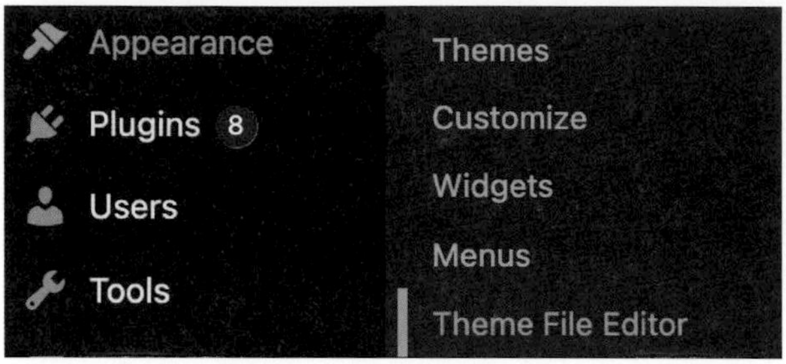
Appearance
Plugins 8
Users
Tools
Themes
Customize
Widgets
Menus
Theme File Editor

The page that appears contains all the pages, styles, functionalities and virtually every component of the theme.

Theme Files
Comments
(comments.php)
Theme Footer
(footer.php)
Theme Header
(header.php)
Image Attachment Template
(image.php)
inc
Main Index Template
(index.php)
Single Page
(page.php)
Search Results
(search.php)
Single Post
(single.php)
template-parts

The pages, style sheets and script appear on the right-hand sidebar. You can choose any page to edit from the right-hand sidebar. Once you click any page, the content of the page will appear in the center window where you can make changes in the code.

2. Once you have made your changes, click the **Update File** button at the bottom of the document and your file will be updated. This area is more for experienced developers – if you consider editing any templates, then it is best to have a File Transfer Protocol (FTP) account set up so that you can constantly back up and make changes very easily

Beware

Be careful when altering PHP files, as you could end up causing damage to your website. Proceed with caution!

Don't forget

If you are using a block-based theme, you will find the editor under **Tools** > **Theme File Editor**.

Hot tip

Any theme can be edited from this area. This adds flexibility, giving experienced developers the opportunity to extend their website even further.

4 Creating Content

This chapter introduces you to pages and posts. It will also walk you through adding content, such as text, images, videos, custom HTML, and sliders.

Pages & Posts Differences

What is the difference between a WordPress page and a post? This is one of the most common questions asked by entry-level WordPress developers, but it's not hard to understand. Once you log in to your WordPress blog or website, you will see two separate options on your dashboard for posts and pages.

The screenshot below highlights both **Pages** and **Posts** and their location in the dashboard.

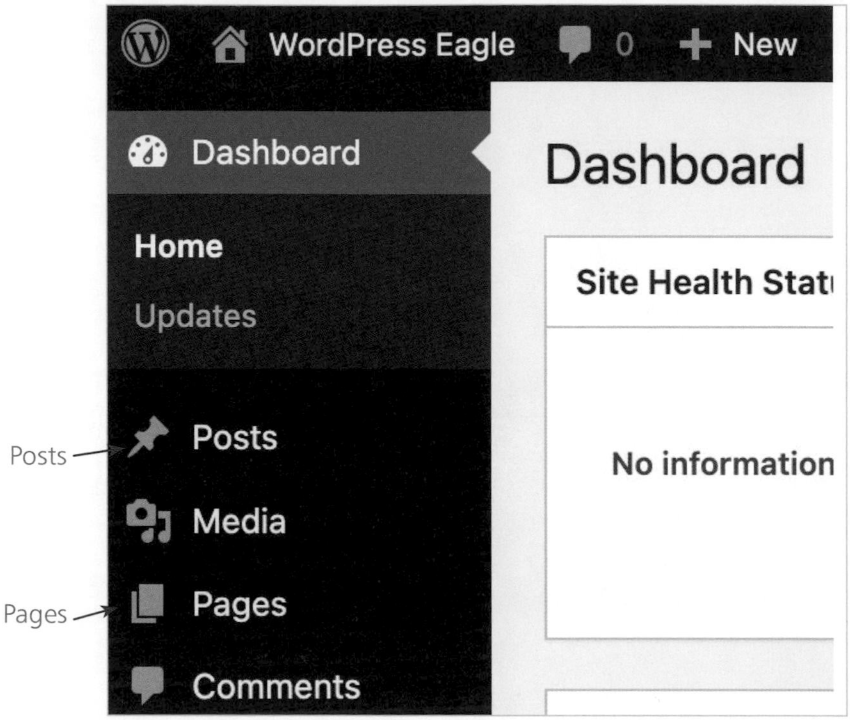

Let us have a look at the major differences between a WordPress page and a post.

What is a page?

Whenever you visit the homepage of a website, you see multiple options on the menu bar, which is mostly located at the top of the page. The menu bar contains options such as **Home**, **About Us**, **Services**, **Contact Us**, etc.

When you click any of these options, you are taken to another page that contains details of the option you selected.

For instance, if you select the **Services** option from the menu bar, you will be taken to a page that contains details of the services offered by the company. The same holds true for **Contact Us** and other options. Basically, these options represent an individual, dedicated page.

Usually, a page contains static content that is not likely to change for long periods of time. The content of the page is usually not required to be updated too often.

For instance, your **About Us** page is unlikely to change frequently. In simple words, it can be said of pages that they are timeless entities. Though the backend database stores the date of publication of the page, you will not usually see the publication date of a page's content.

A page usually doesn't contain social media buttons. For instance, you might prefer that your privacy policy is not shared on Facebook or Twitter, etc. Also, comments are disabled on pages.

What is a post?

Posts are entries on your website that are listed in reverse order of time of publication. The latest posts appear at the top of the page and older posts appear down the page. Posts are bound with time. Therefore, posts can be retrieved based on year and month. Since posts are time-bound entities, they can be delivered via RSS feeds to the subscribers.

Another important consideration regarding posts is that comments are allowed under the posts. Posts are meant to foster healthy discussions. Therefore, social media icons are also enabled alongside posts so that readers can directly share the content of the post on their social media profiles. When viewing a post, you will see the following information:

- Post title
- Category
- Author
- Date posted

Don't forget

RSS stands for Really Simple Syndication. It's a way for you to easily distribute a list of headlines and update notices and – sometimes – content to a wide number of people.

Creating a Page

Creating a page in WordPress is a simple process. Here are the steps that need to be performed in order to create a page in WordPress:

1. Log in to your WordPress blog/website with admin credentials

2. On the dashboard, hover your mouse over the **Pages** option. A new menu appears containing two options: **All Pages** and **Add New**. Click on the **Add New** option

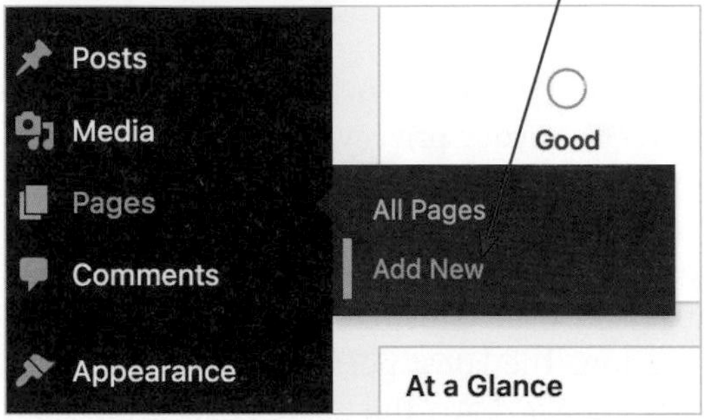

3. A new window appears where you can enter a title for the page, and you can also begin writing some text below it. In the screenshot below, **My First Page** is the title of the page, followed by some text

4. On the right, choose your **Status & visibility** settings

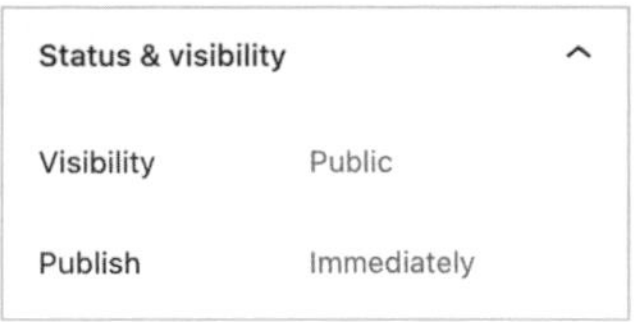
Status & visibility
Visibility
Public
Publish
Immediately

Visibility: Choose whether you want your page to be **Public**, **Private** (visible to site admins and editors only) or **Password Protected**.

Publish: Choose whether you want your page to go live immediately, or at a chosen date and time.

5. Click on the **Publish** button on the top right-hand side of the page to make your newly created page go live. You can also choose to save a draft of your work by clicking **Save draft**. If you wish to preview your current page at this time, click on the **Preview** button

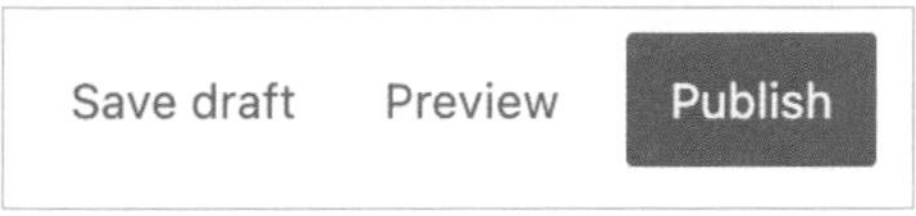
Save draft
Preview
Publish

6. Now, if you go to **Pages** > **All Pages**, you will find that your newly created page has been added to the list of pages contained by your website/blog, as shown in the screenshot below

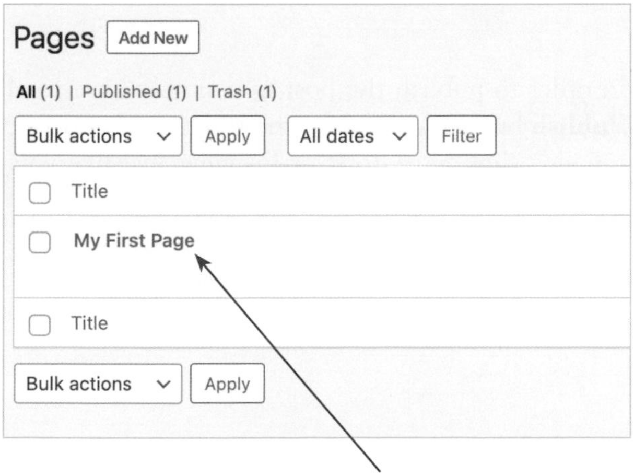
Pages
Add New
All (1) | Published (1) | Trash (1)
Bulk actions
Apply
All dates
Filter
Title
My First Page
Title
Bulk actions
Apply

Your page

Hot tip

You can save a draft of your page instead of publishing instantly, so you can finish the page at a later date if you wish.

Hot tip

The **Publish** button will turn to **Schedule** if you select a different publish time under **Status & visibility**.

Creating a Post

Creating a post is very similar to creating a page. Follow the steps below to create a post in WordPress:

1. Log in to the dashboard of your blog and hover your mouse over **Posts**. This will expand a menu toward the right. Click on **Add New** from the expanded menu

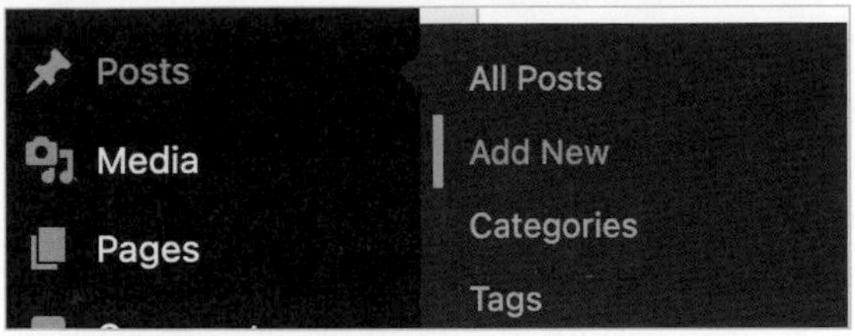

2. In the window that appears, enter the title of the post, and enter some text below it. In this example, **My First Post** is the title of the post, followed by **Here is my first ever post!**

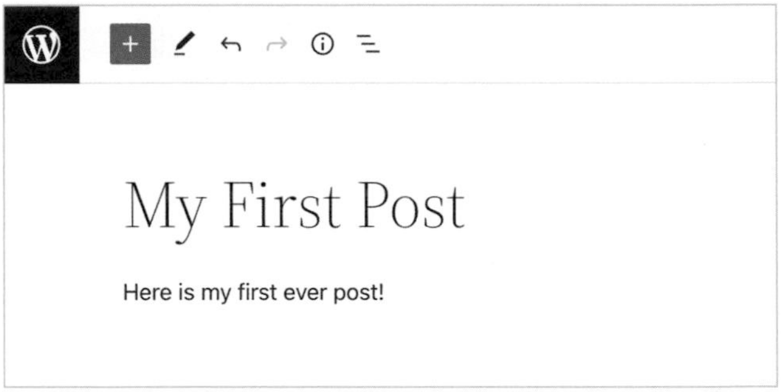

3. In order to publish the post, you simply have to click the **Publish** button located on the top right-hand side. You can also click **Save draft** or **Preview**, just like you did when you created a page

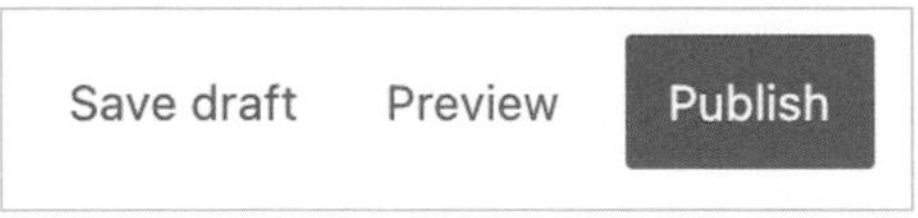

Try to keep backups of your pages and posts on your local machine in a Word document or text document.

Text Blocks

Now that you have learned how to create pages and posts, you are ready to start adding content. In WordPress 5, you use blocks to add content to your pages. We are going to start by looking at the main text blocks.

Paragraph block

When you created both your first page and post, there was a paragraph block already waiting for you to enter text. Let's look at how you can add these in yourself.

1. Let's start by loading up the post we just created. Click **Posts** and then click **My First Post**

My First Post
Here is my first ever post!

2. Click the + button on the top left-hand side. This gives you a selection of blocks available to you

3. Select **Paragraph** under **TEXT**

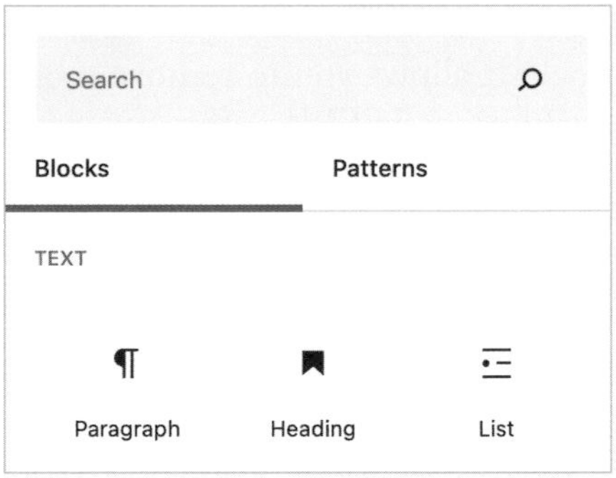
Search
Blocks
Patterns
TEXT
Paragraph
Heading
List

4. A new paragraph block will appear below the last block. You can now enter some text

...cont'd

If you click inside the block, you will notice some formatting options appear above the box:

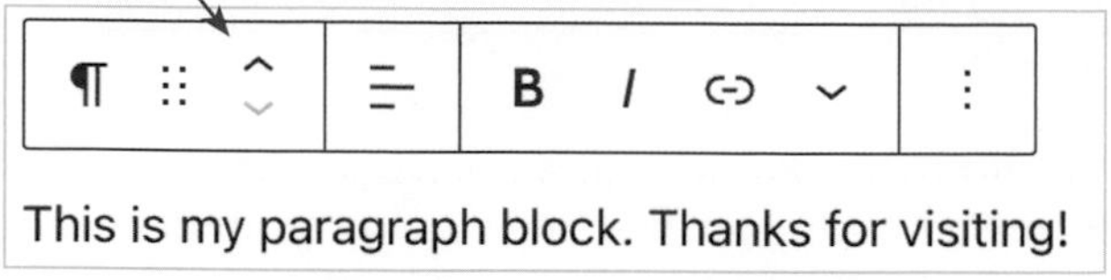
This is my paragraph block. Thanks for visiting!

Here is an explanation of each of the elements:

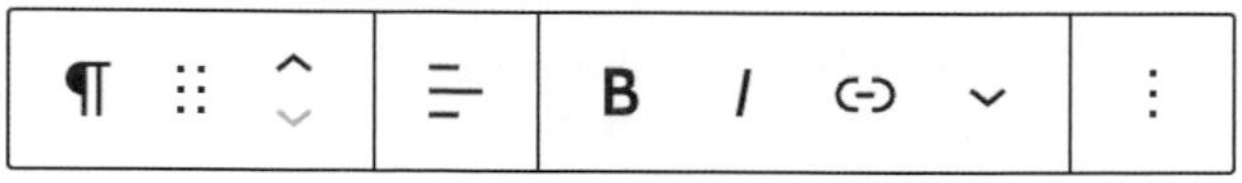

1 2 3 4 5 6 7 8 9

1. This lets you transform a paragraph block to a similar style of block. For example, you could change it to a header or a list block. We will cover these on page 51.
2. If you hold down the left-click button on your mouse on this element, it will allow you to drag the block to a new location.
3. Move the block above or below another block.
4. Align the text to the left, right or center.
5. Make text bold.
6. Make text italic.
7. Create a link.
8. This drop-down section will allow you further formatting options like strikethrough text or adding an inline image. We cover images on pages 52-54.
9. This will appear on all blocks that you add, not just a paragraph block. It allows you to remove a block, duplicate a block, edit a block as HTML, etc.

Don't forget

Block options will only appear on the right-hand side when your block has been selected. Different block types will have different options.

On the right-hand side of the editor, you will notice some options for your paragraph block:

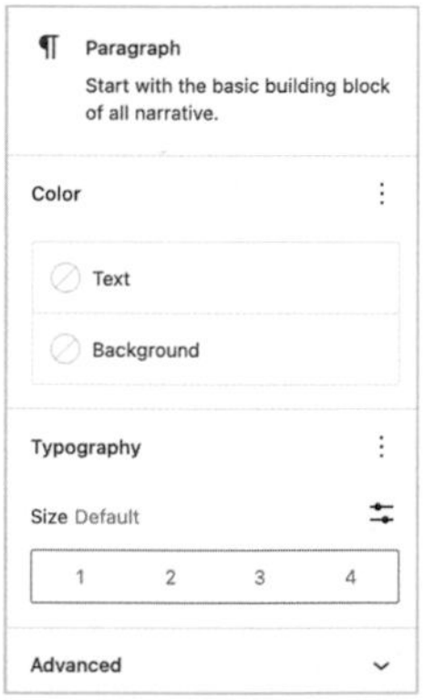
Paragraph
Start with the basic building block of all narrative.
Color
Text
Background
Typography
Size Default
1
2
3
4
Advanced

Color: Choose text and background color.
Typography: Here, you can choose font size, appearance, letter case and letter spacing.
Advanced: You can assign a CSS class to the block.

Header block

Header blocks are useful if you want to create a title above a section of text. If you want to add a header block, follow these steps:

1. Click the + button on the top left-hand side

2. Select **Heading** under **TEXT**

3. Enter your text

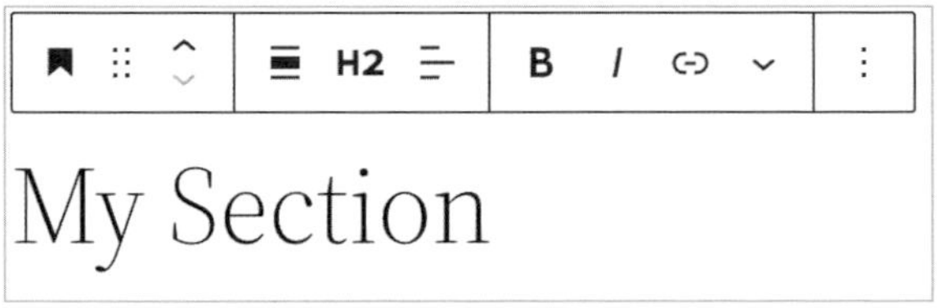

A header block will have very similar options to a paragraph block. The main difference is that you can choose H1, H2 H3, H4, H5, and H6, which are all different heading types.

List block

List blocks are useful if you want to create bulleted lists or numbered lists.

1. Click the + button on the top left-hand side

2. Select **List** under **TEXT**

3. Create your list

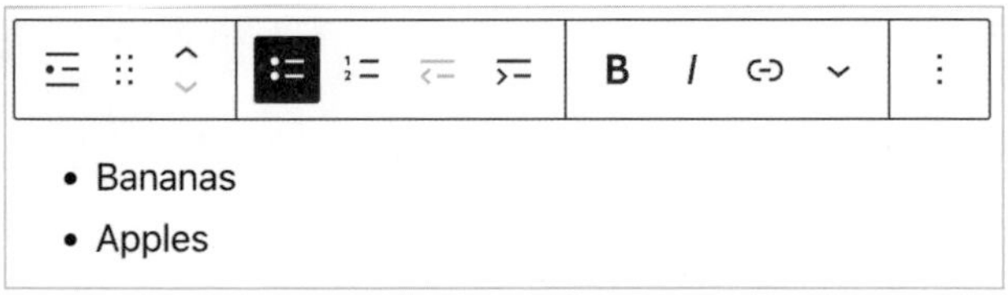

The list block formatting options allow you to choose between a bulleted list or a numbered list, and indent particular items.

Adding Images

We all want our websites to look great, and what better way to tell a story than by adding media to your pages? Adding images to a page is extremely straightforward.

1. Click the + button on the top left-hand side
2. Select **Image** under **Media**

The following block should appear inside the editor:

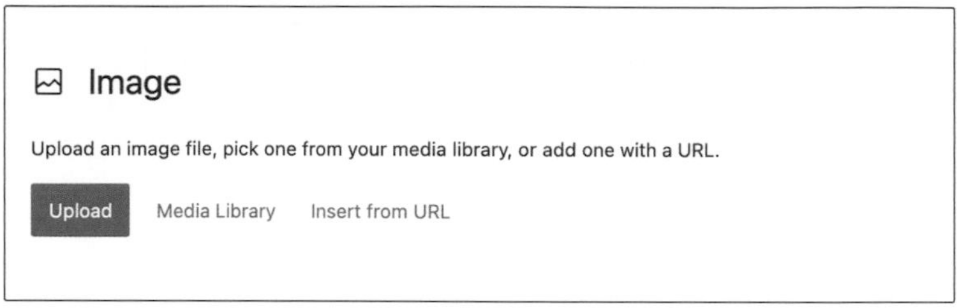

- **Upload**: This allows you to upload media you have saved on your computer.
- **Media Library**: This will allow you to select media that you have already uploaded to WordPress.
- **Insert from URL**: This allows you to type in the URL of an image that's already on the internet.

Uploading an image

1. Click the **Upload** button inside the **Image** block
2. Choose an image from your computer

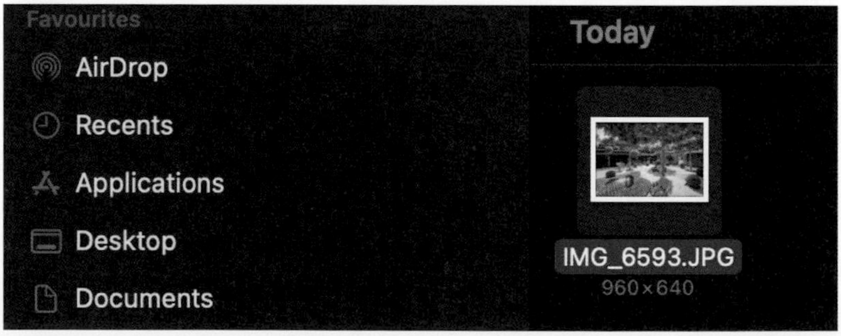

Your image will now appear inside the **Image** block.

B
I
Add caption

You can add a caption to describe the image, which you can format or link to another web page.

If you select your **Image** block by clicking on it, you should see some options appear on the right-hand side of the editor:

Alt text: If the image does not load on your website, then it will display this text. This is an effective way of telling Google the topic of your page, which will boost your search rankings.

Image size: Select the size of your image or specify custom dimensions and percentages.

Advanced: Here, you can set up things like a title attribute (describe the role of image), HTML anchor and any additional CSS classes.

Image settings
Alt text (alternative text)
Describe the purpose of the image Leave empty if the image is purely decorative.
Image size
Full Size
Image dimensions
Width
Height
960
640
25%
50%
75%
100%
Reset
Advanced

Hot tip

Alt text is also a good way to provide an audio description for those who are visually impaired and use audio describe to hear what is on the screen.

Hot tip

Why not check out **CSS in easy steps** to learn more about CSS?

...cont'd

Media Library

At some point, you may want to select an image that you already have inside your Media Library.

1. Click the **Media Library** button inside the **Image** block
2. Select the **Media Library** tab

3. Choose an image

4. Click **Select,** and the image will appear inside the **Image** block

Inserting from a URL

You can also insert an image from another website.

1. Click the **Insert from URL** button inside the **Image** block
2. Insert the URL where your image is located and press the arrow button

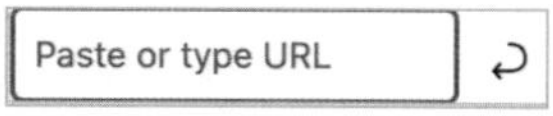

3. The image will now appear inside the **Image** block

Make sure you ask permission or check image rights before using images from other websites.

Other image blocks

There are a couple of other **Image** blocks inside **Common Blocks** that you might want to check out. You can upload images in the same way as you did on pages 52-53 or add them from the Media Library, as we explained above.

- **Gallery**: This block allows you to create a gallery of images. You will be able to select multiple images inside the Media Library.
- **Cover**: This is useful if you want to have a full-width image and add some text over the top (like a title).

Adding Videos

You will be amazed at just how simple it is to embed YouTube videos onto your WordPress website. Videos are becoming much more popular, and video blogging is on the rise!

1. Copy the URL of the YouTube video from your browser

https://www.youtube.com/watch?v=MhXiKZW7y2Y

2. Open up the page or post where you want the video to go, and click the **+** button on the top left-hand side

3. Select **YouTube** under **Embeds**

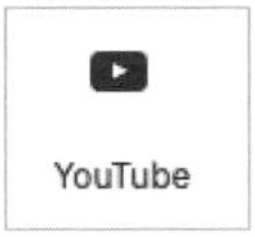
YouTube

YouTube URL
Paste a link to the content you want to display on your site.
Enter URL to embed here...
Embed
Learn more about embeds

A YouTube block should now appear inside your editor.

4. Paste in the YouTube video address and click **Embed**. A thumbnail of the video should appear

My AR Demo
Watch later
Share
Watch on YouTube
Add caption

5. Then, click **Publish** or **Update** to save your changes. The YouTube video will then be embedded onto your page or post

Adding Custom HTML

If you are familiar with HTML code, then you can add code to your pages and posts. HTML is a great way of adding functionality and style to your web pages.

Hot tip

Learn more about HTML with **HTML in easy steps**.

1. Open up a page or post that you have created
2. Click the **+** button on the top left-hand side
3. Select **Custom HTML** under **Widgets**
4. You will now be presented with a block where you can start entering HTML code

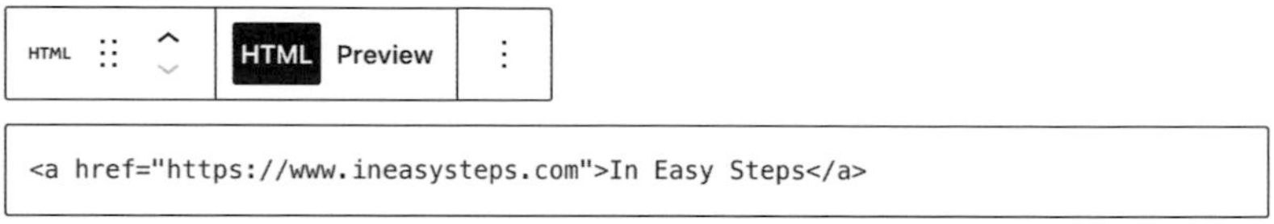

You can add your own code inside the **HTML** tab if you wish. You can use the **Preview** tab to see your code in action.

Don't worry if you don't understand the code here. You can always learn HTML at a later stage if you wish to advance your skills.

Below are a few examples of HTML for you to try out:

Links

<a href ="https://www.ineasysteps.com">In Easy Steps</a>
This will create a hyperlink on the page called "In Easy Steps", which will link to the https://www.ineasysteps.com page

Text color

<p style="color: blue;">House</p>
This code will write the word "House" in the color blue.

Aligning text

<p style="text-align: center;">Hello</p>
This code will align the word "Hello" in the center.

Adding Shortcodes

Shortcodes are going to be very useful when building your website. You won't need them right now, but as you progress through the book, there will be times where you will need shortcode blocks so that you can enter shortcodes provided by a plugin. For example, on page 118 you will need a shortcode block to display an Instagram feed created by a plugin. Here is a quick look at how to add a shortcode block.

1. Open up a page or post that you have created

2. Click the + button on the top left-hand side

3. Select **Shortcode** under **Widgets**

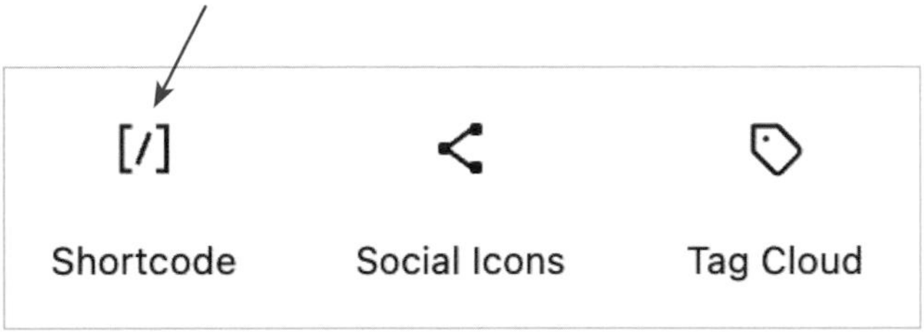
[/]
Shortcode
Social Icons
Tag Cloud

4. You will now be presented with a **Shortcode** block

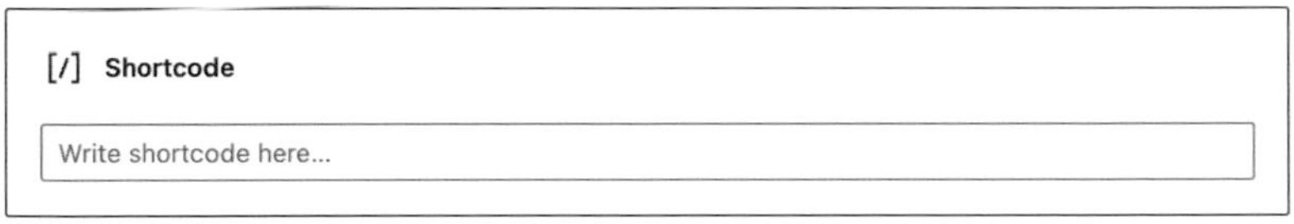
[/] Shortcode
Write shortcode here...

Now, when you get a shortcode from a plugin, all you need to do is paste it inside the text box. Then, you will need to click **Publish** or **Update** to save your changes to the page or post.

Adding Audio

Adding audio to websites has become more popular over the last few years, especially with those trying to get their music noticed. Adding audio to your page or post is as simple as adding an image.

1. Load up the page or post where you want to add your audio

2. Click the **+** button on the top left-hand side

+

3. Select **Audio** under **Media**

Audio

An **Audio** block should now appear inside your editor.

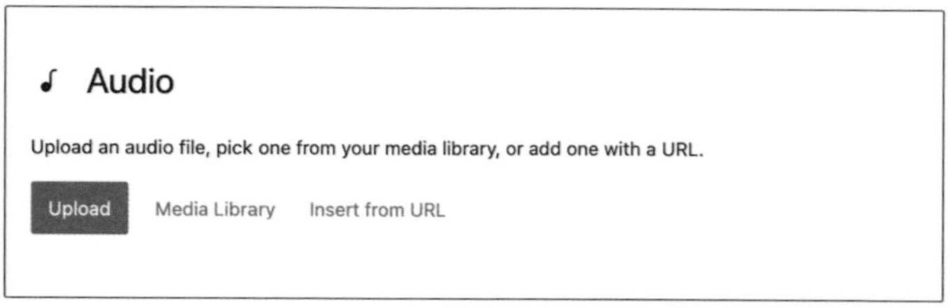
Audio
Upload an audio file, pick one from your media library, or add one with a URL.
Upload
Media Library
Insert from URL

4. Click the **Upload** button inside the **Audio** block, and choose an audio file from your computer

5. Your audio file will be added to the page/post. Click **Publish** or **Update** to save your changes

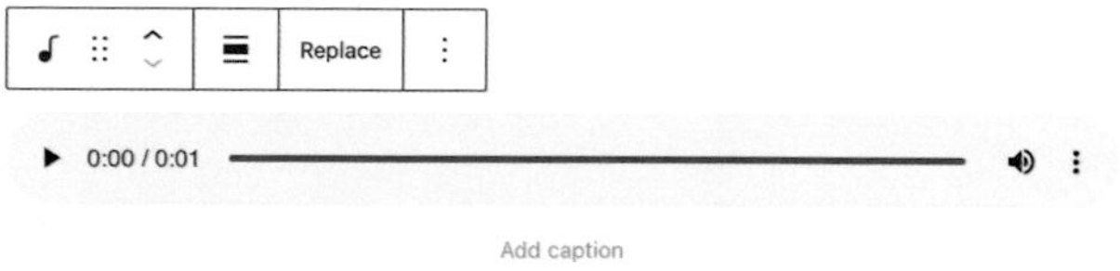
Replace
0:00 / 0:01
Add caption

In the **Audio settings** section on the right-hand side, you can choose whether you want the audio to start as soon as the page opens, and whether or not you want it to loop.

Audio settings
Autoplay
Loop

Hot tip

You can also choose **Audio** from the **Media Library** or **Insert from URL** using the same steps as you did with an image on page 54.

Creating Categories

Posts can be added to categories or subcategories. Categories are basically a way to group posts. For instance, you can create a category named **Web Development** on your blog and add all your web development posts to that category. Usually, if you create a post and don't create a category, then it will go into the **Uncategorized** category. Creating a category is a simple process.

1. Click **Posts** > **Categories**, as shown below

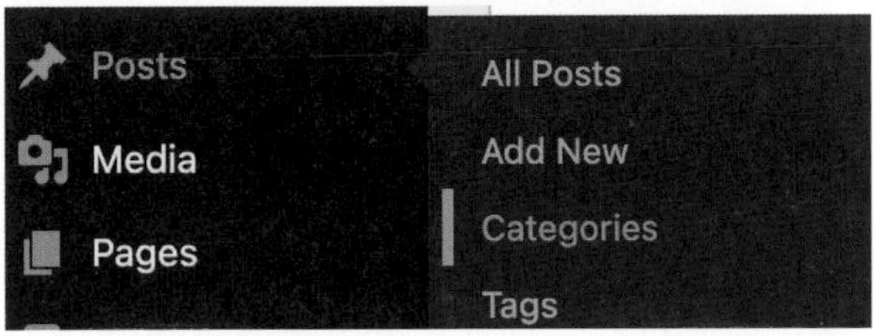

2. A new window appears where you can add the particulars of the new category

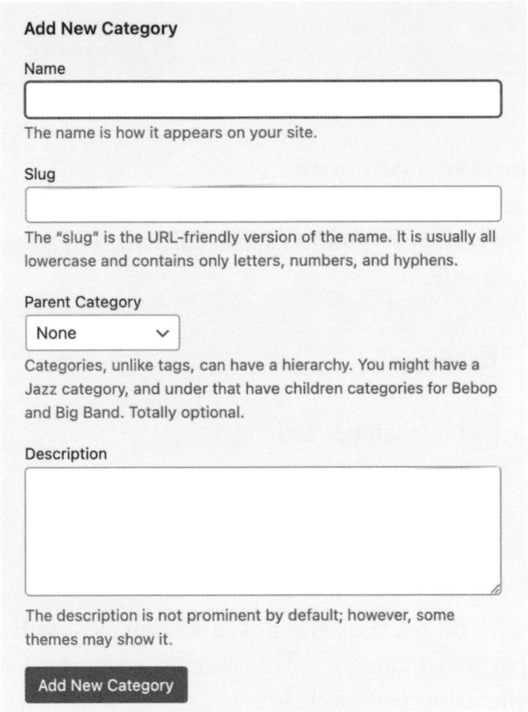

3. In the **Name** field, enter the name of the new category

...cont'd

4. Enter the **Slug** value, which is a URL-friendly version of the category name – usually lowercase letters, numbers and hyphens. Don't add any spaces

5. From the **Parent** category drop-down list, choose **None** as this is your first category. You would only add a parent if you were creating a subcategory. For example, if you had already created a category called **Games Consoles** and you were creating a new category called **Xbox**, then you might select **Games Consoles** as a parent

6. Finally, click the **Add New Category** button at the bottom of the window to create a new category. The newly added category will show straight away in the list of categories on the right

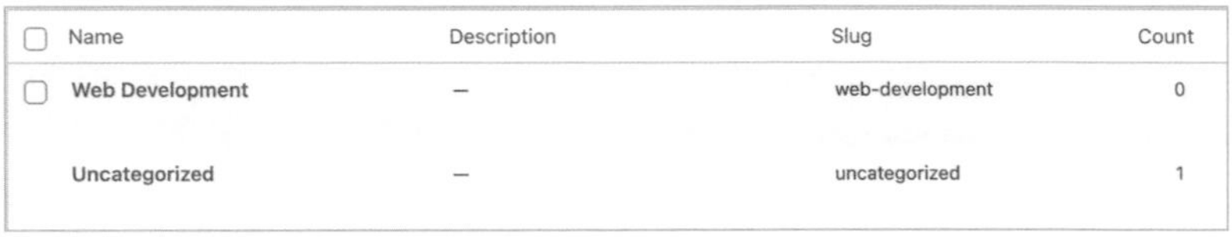

Name	Description	Slug	Count
Web Development	–	web-development	0
Uncategorized	–	uncategorized	1

Adding a post to a category

When you are creating a post, as explained on page 48, you will notice that the category you have created will now appear down the right-hand side.

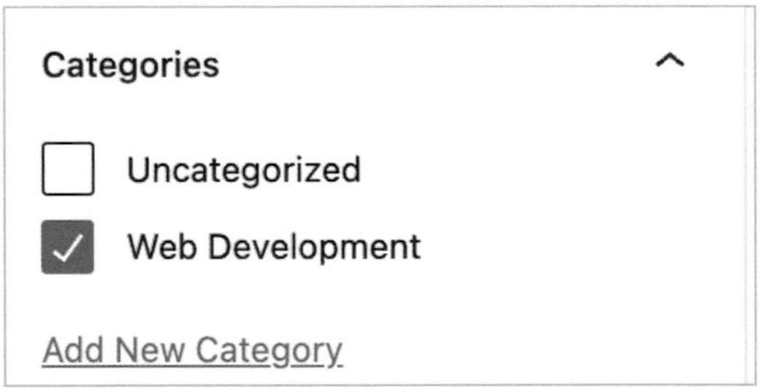

All you need to do is check the box, and that post will appear under that particular category. This is really important when it comes to structuring your website.

You can also add categories right there in the post, by clicking **Add New Category** inside the **Categories** box.

Sliders

Homepage sliders can give a professional look to your website, and it isn't complicated to create them. There are plenty of WordPress slider plugins to help you create the look you want. Soliloquy Lite is probably the best slider plugin out there. There is a free Lite version and several paid options.

Hot tip

Sliders are usually found at the top of the homepage, and they come in various sizes. They use a slideshow-style format and a mixture of different types of media.

1. From the dashboard, click **Plugins** > **Add New**
2. Search for "Soliloquy" and click **Search Plugins**

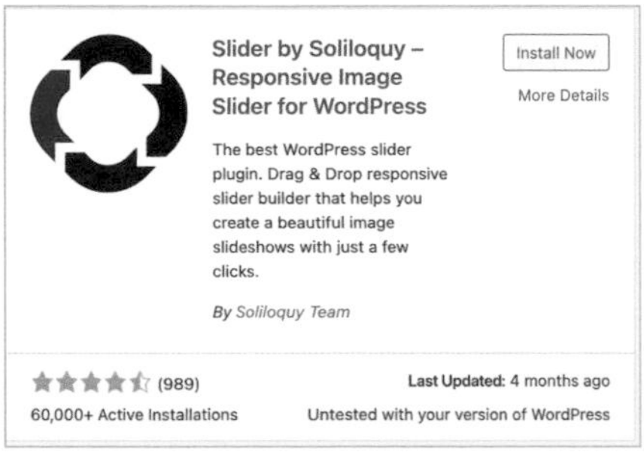

3. Click **Install Now** and activate the plugin

You will notice **Soliloquy** will have appeared in your dashboard links.

4. Click on **Soliloquy** from the dashboard and then click **Add New**

5. Start by adding a title to the first text box, as shown below. This will not be shown on the slider itself

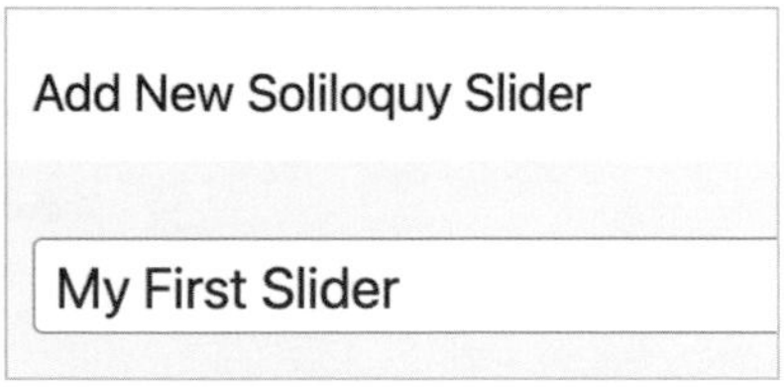

...cont'd

Hot tip

The default dimensions for Soliloquy sliders is 960 x 300 pixels. You can change this in the slider configuration, which is explained on pages 65-66. Try to make sure the slider dimensions and image sizes are the same.

6. Next, start adding images to the slider. Select **Select Files from Your Computer** or just drop images into the center

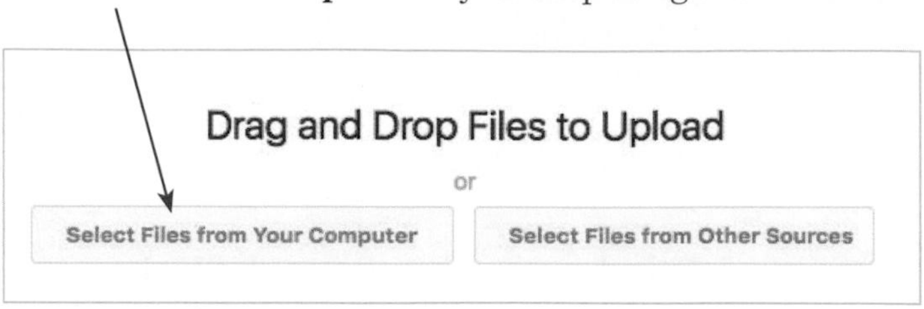
Drag and Drop Files to Upload
or
Select Files from Your Computer
Select Files from Other Sources

7. Upload photos, as shown on pages 52-54. Once you have chosen images, they will appear at the bottom, ready to publish

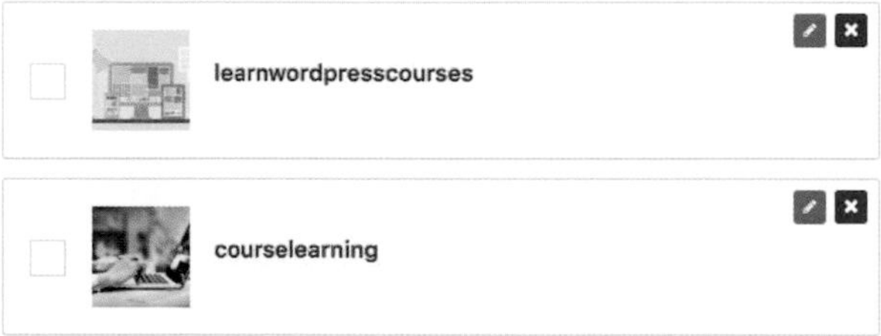
learnwordpresscourses
courselearning

Don't forget

You can add as many slides as you want but try to keep the file sizes of the images low so that it doesn't affect website performance.

8. Click **Publish**, which gets your slider ready for the website

9. Now, go to a post or page and click the + button on the top left to add a new block

10. Search for "Soliloquy" in the Search box

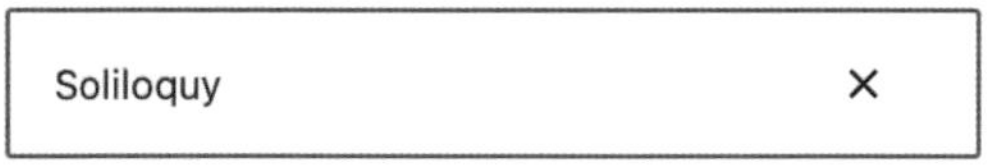
Soliloquy
×

11. Select the **Soliloquy** icon

Soliloquy

...cont'd

12 Select your slider from the drop-down menu on the **Soliloquy** block that has been added to the page/post

SOLILOQUY
Search for a slider.
My First Slider

13 Click **Publish** or **Update**

Update

14 Now, if you visit your page, you will see that your slider appears

15 Next, you need to add text to your slider. Go to **Soliloquy** on the dashboard and select your slider from the list

Title
Shortcode
My First Slider
[soliloquy id="522"]
Copy to clipboard

...cont'd

16 This time you need to click the pencil icon, at the far right of one of your images

17 You will now be presented with a form to fill out that looks similar to the one below

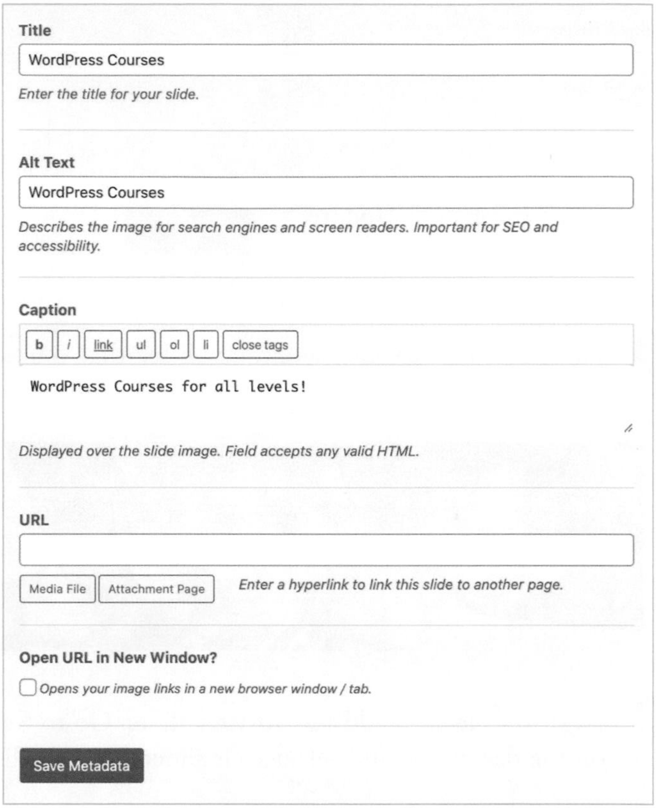
Title
WordPress Courses
Enter the title for your slide.
Alt Text
WordPress Courses
Describes the image for search engines and screen readers. Important for SEO and accessibility.
Caption
b
i
link
ul
ol
li
close tags
WordPress Courses for all levels!
Displayed over the slide image. Field accepts any valid HTML.
URL
Media File
Attachment Page
Enter a hyperlink to link this slide to another page.
Open URL in New Window?
Opens your image links in a new browser window / tab.
Save Metadata

Title: Give a title for your image.

Alt Text: This is what will display if the image fails to load.

Caption: This is where you get to enter some text for this particular slide.

URL: If you want the user to be directed to another page when they click on the slide, then enter the link in this box.

Open URL in New Window?: If you want the link to open in a new browser tab, then check this box.

Hot tip

Try to keep your slider text short and sweet. All you need is just enough information to encourage the viewer to visit that particular page.

18. Remember to click **Save Metadata**. You will need to make sure you repeat the process for each slide

Visit your live website and check out how your slider looks. Since you have already added the shortcode, you won't need to do this again.

WordPress Courses for all levels!

You can also add PHP code to your theme files using the editor if you want to, as we discussed on page 42.

```
if ( function_exists(
'soliloquy' ) ) { soliloquy(
'522' ); }
```

Soliloquy slider settings

There are various settings you can change that allow you to style the slider the way you want – without programming.
To access the settings for your particular slider:

1. Go to **Soliloquy** from the dashboard and select your slider from the list

Title	Shortcode
My First Slider	[soliloquy id="522"] Copy to clipboard

2. Select the **Configuration** option from the menu down the left-hand side

Configuration

...cont'd

Below are some of the various settings you can change:

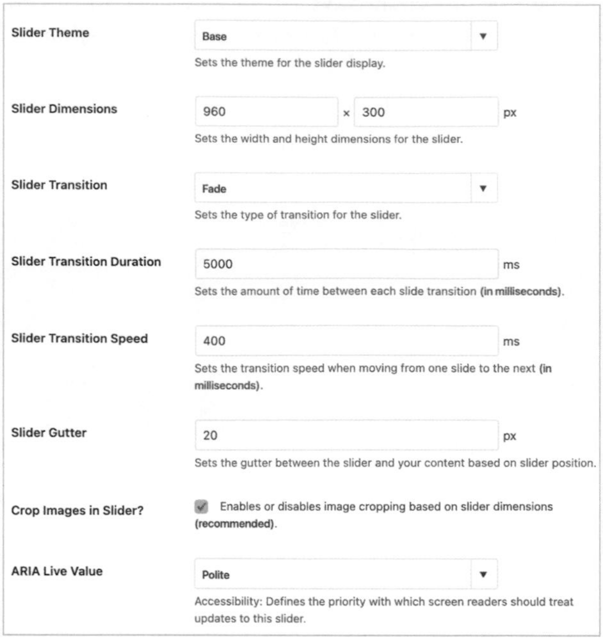
Slider Theme
Base
Sets the theme for the slider display.
Slider Dimensions
960
×
300
px
Sets the width and height dimensions for the slider.
Slider Transition
Fade
Sets the type of transition for the slider.
Slider Transition Duration
5000
ms
Sets the amount of time between each slide transition (in milliseconds).
Slider Transition Speed
400
ms
Sets the transition speed when moving from one slide to the next (in milliseconds).
Slider Gutter
20
px
Sets the gutter between the slider and your content based on slider position.
Crop Images in Slider?
Enables or disables image cropping based on slider dimensions (recommended).
ARIA Live Value
Polite
Accessibility: Defines the priority with which screen readers should treat updates to this slider.

Slider Theme: Here, you can choose from two particular themes – these are **Base** and **Classic**.

Slider Dimensions: Here, you can set the height and width.

Slider Transition: You can choose the transition type for your slides. These include **Fade, Scroll horizontal** and **Scroll vertical**.

Slider Transition Duration: Sets the amount of time between each slide transition (in milliseconds).

Slider Transition Speed: Sets the transition speed when moving from one slide to the next (in milliseconds).

Slider Gutter: This sets the gutter (in pixels) between your slider and your content. This is based on your slider position. By default, this is set to 20 pixels.

Crop Images in Slider?: This option enables or disables image cropping based on slider dimensions. This is enabled by default.

ARIA Live Value: Defines the priority with which screen readers should treat updates to this slider. You can choose between **Off**, **Polite**, and **Assertive**. It is set to **Polite** by default.

5 Plugins

This chapter will introduce you to plugins. You will learn how to find, install, update, and even edit plugins.

Finding & Installing

Plugins are a great way to expand the functionality of your WordPress website. There are literally thousands available and your options are limitless, which is another reason why WordPress is one of the leading platforms for web development.

There are many reasons why you may look for a plugin. For example, you may want a plugin so that you can turn your website into an eCommerce website, or you may want a plugin so that you can create a contact form for your website. There are loads of free ones available and also ones that come at a cost. We will start by looking for plugins within WordPress itself.

1. Click **Plugins** > **Add New** on the dashboard

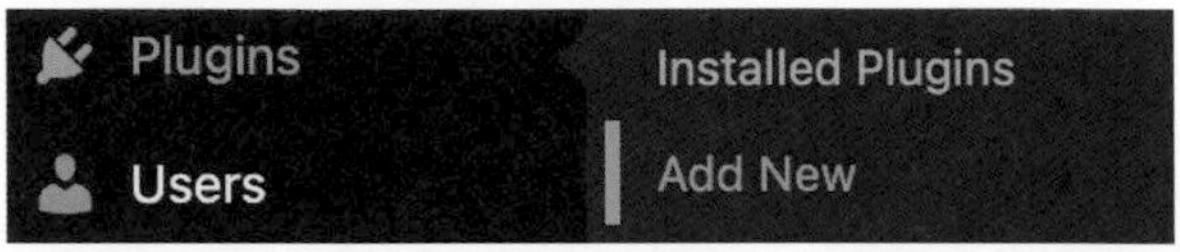

2. You will be presented with a Search box that allows you to search for terms relevant to the kind of plugin you are looking for. For example, if you are looking for a plugin that can set up contact forms, type "contact form" inside the Search box, and plugin results will start to automatically appear

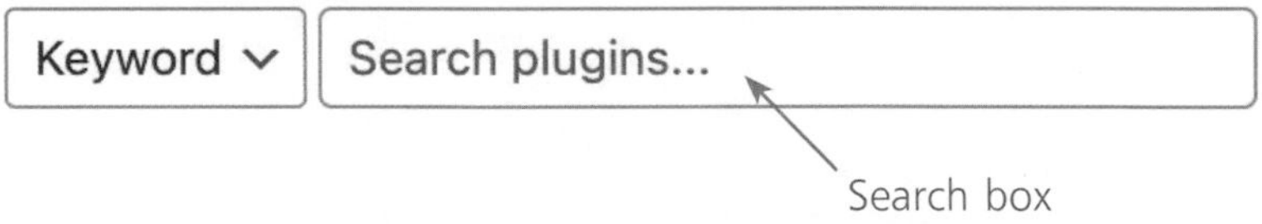

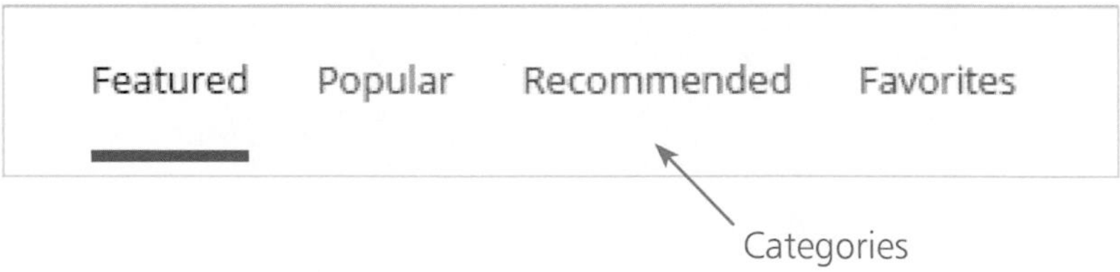

If you just want to look for the current featured plugins, most popular or newest, then you can choose from one of those categories at the top.

3. After searching for "contact form", you will then be presented with a number of search results relevant to contact forms. Most plugins will have some kind of rating – this is the best way to judge which one will be best for your website. You can find out more details about each individual plugin by clicking **More Details**

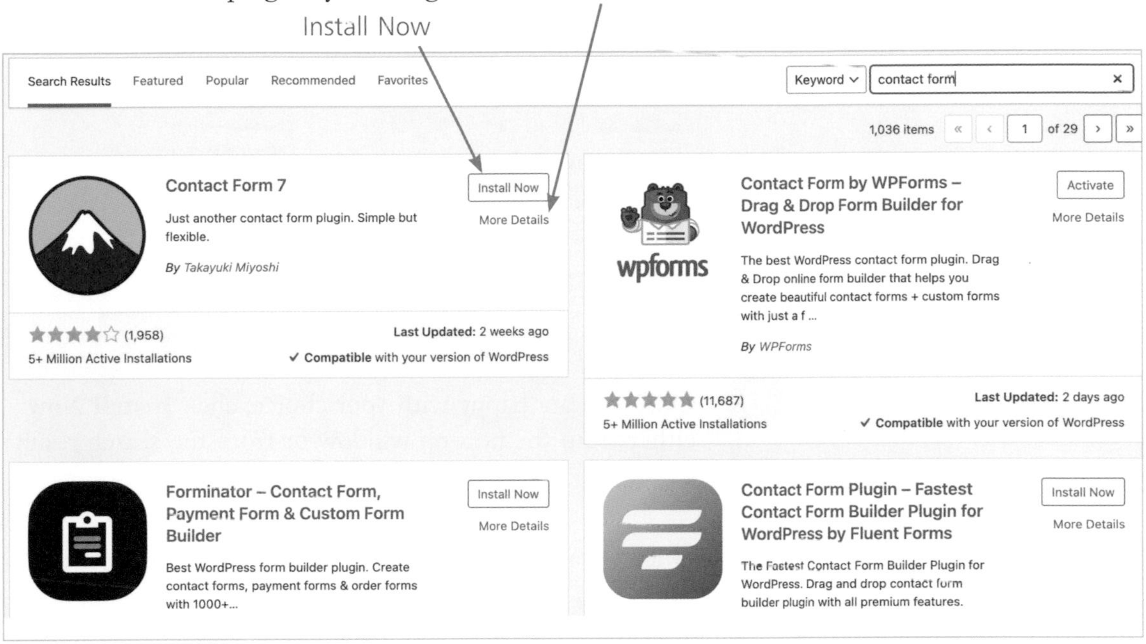

This will bring up a pop-up with more information on the plugin, along with installation details and screenshots.

4. Read the installation steps carefully for that particular plugin. It would also be helpful to make a note of the author's website as it is likely that further documentation will be available there

5. Make sure you take a look at the reviews, and when the plugin was last updated. The more support you can get for the plugin, the better. You ideally want to choose one that has regular updates, especially since WordPress has a lot of updates

Don't forget

There are dozens of choices. Make sure you take your time when selecting your plugin. Reviews are a good way to find out about the best ones.

...cont'd

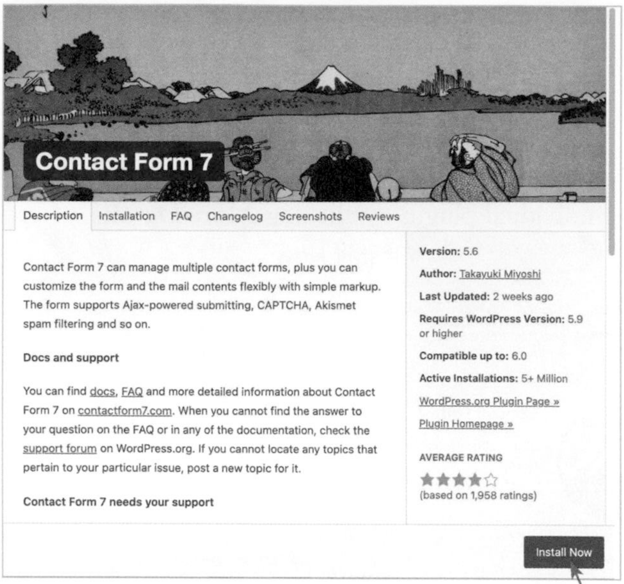

6. Once you are happy with your choice, click **Install Now** either from the pop-up window or from the search result window

7. Once installed, it should give you the option to activate the plugin there and then

8. If you miss the screen, then you can easily go to **Plugins** > **Installed Plugins**. Scroll down until you find the plugin, and select **Activate** just underneath the title

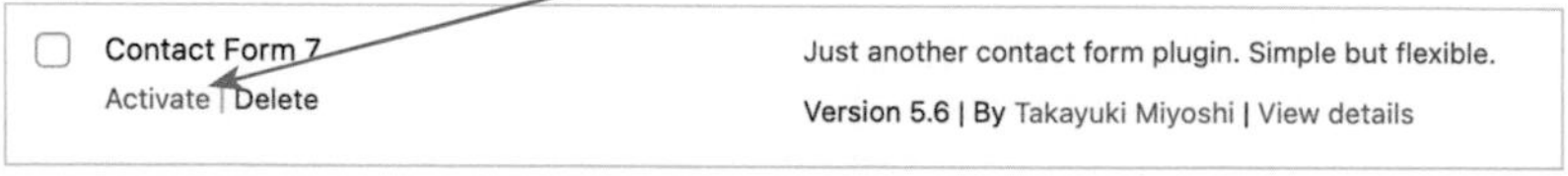

After this point, each plugin will have its own unique setup. Some will require you to configure some settings right from the start. Generally you can find these settings by going to your **Installed Plugins** page, scrolling down to your plugin and selecting **Settings** under the plugin.

If not, your installed plugin will appear somewhere on the dashboard, usually on the menu down the left-hand side or under **Settings**.

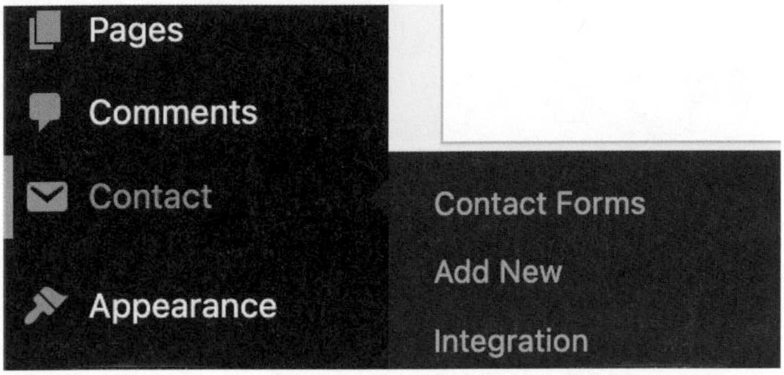

Finding plugin documentation

Remember: each individual plugin setup will be different once it is installed. This makes it extremely important for you to read the documentation. To find the documentation for your plugin:

1. Select **Plugins** > **Installed Plugins** from the dashboard
2. Select **View Details** on the chosen plugin
3. Select the **Installation** link. Most developers use this area to provide steps on how to use it, or give a link to an external website for full documentation

Uploading a Plugin

You might find a really nice WordPress plugin on an external website that you want to upload. Some developers will let you try a Lite version of their plugin and then want you to upgrade to a Pro version for more features. If you have downloaded or purchased from an external source, then it is pretty easy to upload the plugin file (usually a zipped file).

Beware

Make sure you are buying plugins from a trusted source. You should do your research before purchasing by finding reviews for the plugin or by finding out more about the developer.

1. Click **Plugins** > **Add New** in the dashboard

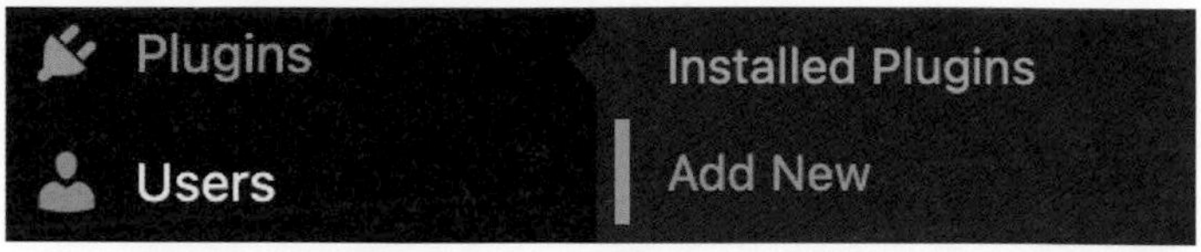
Plugins
Users
Installed Plugins
Add New

2. Select **Upload Plugin**

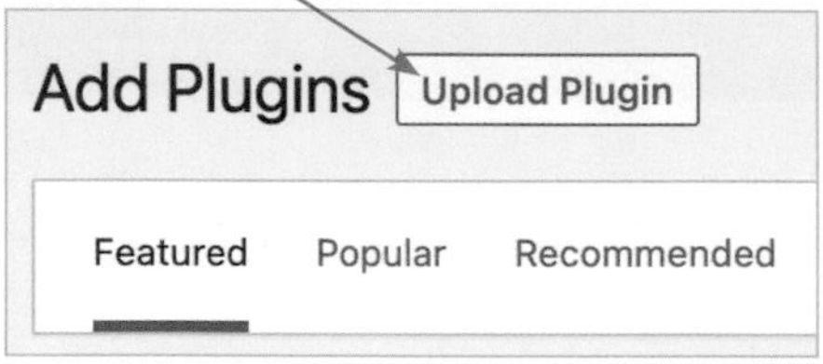
Add Plugins
Upload Plugin
Featured
Popular
Recommended

3. You will now be asked for the plugin in .zip format. When you purchased or downloaded the file, you should have been given a zipped file to upload. Select **Choose file** and then locate your plugin .zip file. Once you have found your file, click **Install Now**

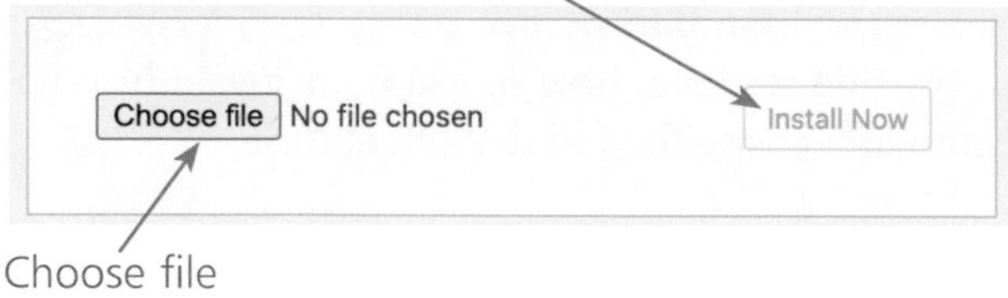
Choose file
No file chosen
Install Now
Choose file

4. Once it has finished installing, you will still need to activate the plugin, like you did before when you selected a plugin from the search results (see page 70)

Installed Plugins

The **Installed Plugins** page is where you can view all your currently installed plugins, and you can also deactivate and delete them from here. Try to keep a note of all the plugins you install. Make sure you deactivate any you are not using, as they can slow down your website. The bigger your website gets, the more plugins you are likely to use. To access the **Installed Plugins** page:

1. Select **Plugins** > **Installed Plugins**

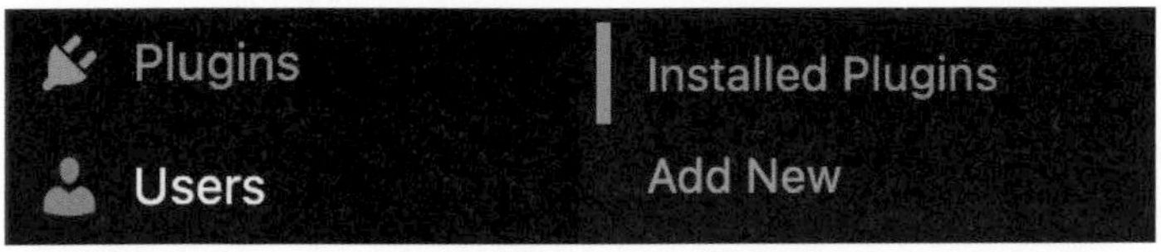
Plugins
Users
Installed Plugins
Add New

Deactivating a plugin

To deactivate a plugin, find the appropriate plugin and select **Deactivate**.

Contact Form 7
Settings | Deactivate

Deleting a plugin

To delete a plugin, find the appropriate plugin and select **Delete**. You will need to deactivate the plugin before you have the option to delete.

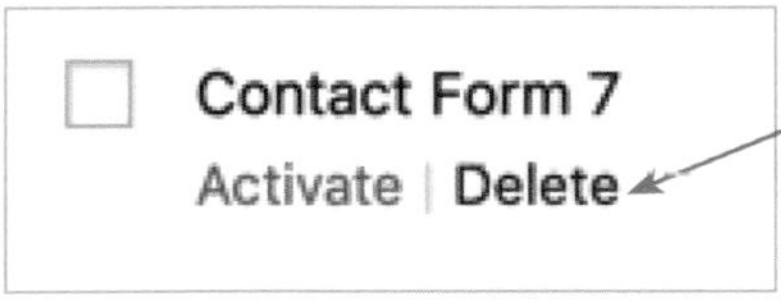
Contact Form 7
Activate | Delete

You can also visit the website for a particular plugin by clicking **Plugin Homepage** under the plugin details section.

Hot tip

Try to deactivate and delete any plugins you are not using so that there are no conflicts. Having too many plugins may slow your website down.

Updating Plugins

Now and again, you will need to update your plugins. Developers will constantly make improvements to their plugins so that your website can function effectively.

The signs

You will know when a plugin needs to be updated when a number appears next to **Plugins** on the dashboard.

For example, if there is a 1 next to **Plugins**, then it means one plugin needs to be updated.

1. Click on **Plugins** > **Installed Plugins**

2. Now, select **Update Available** along the top

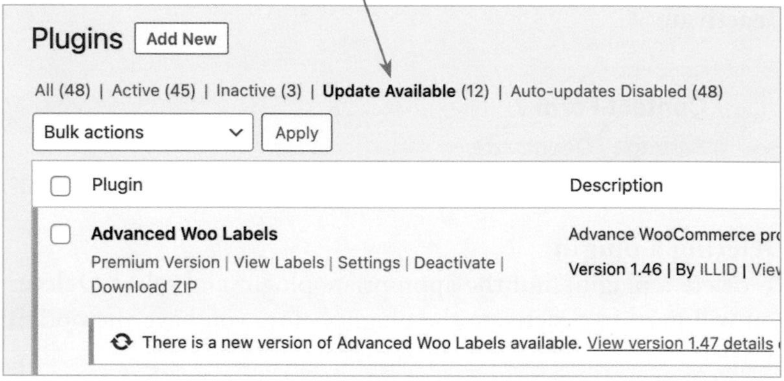

3. Now, select the checkbox next to the plugin and select **Update** from the drop-down box and click **Apply**, and this will update the plugin

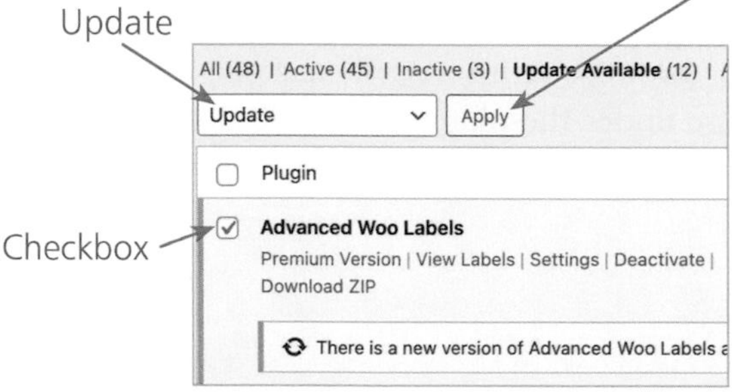

Must-have Plugins

There are lots of great plugins out there to get you started and more are being developed every day, so you will never be short of ways to boost the functionality of your website. Here are some of the most credible ones:

WooCommerce

This plugin is FREE and allows you to build an online shop for your website. This is very handy if you are planning to sell your products online to customers. We will be having a look at this plugin in more detail in Chapter 6.

Contact Form 7

All websites need a contact form so that customers and readers can get in touch with you. This plugin makes it very easy to set one up (see pages 129-130).

Yoast SEO

This is a great plugin that optimizes your WordPress blog/website for search engine optimization (SEO). SEO has become vital for ranking on search engines, so this plugin will really help you maximize your website's potential (see pages 106-110).

bbPress

If you are looking to set up a forum for your website, then look no further. This does all the hard work for you. It is very simple to set up and has become the top choice for setting up forums on WordPress websites (see pages 123-128).

Akismet

This is a good plugin to consider if your website or blog is going to have user interaction. It checks comments on your website to see if they look like spam. It should be installed by default.

XML Sitemaps

Sitemaps will help index your website better with search engines. This plugin is great for generating an XML sitemap (see pages 157-158).

Smash Balloon Social Photo Feed

Social media is crucial nowadays, especially if you are running a business. This plugin allows you to add your Instagram photo feed to your website (see pages 117-118).

Plugin File Editor

Just like with themes, you are able to edit plugins if you have knowledge of PHP. There might be a functionality you want to extend or edit inside WordPress or maybe add a feature that was not included in the original plugin. To edit plugins:

Beware

Do not edit code unless you have a good knowledge of PHP.

1. Click **Plugins** > **Plugin File Editor** in the dashboard

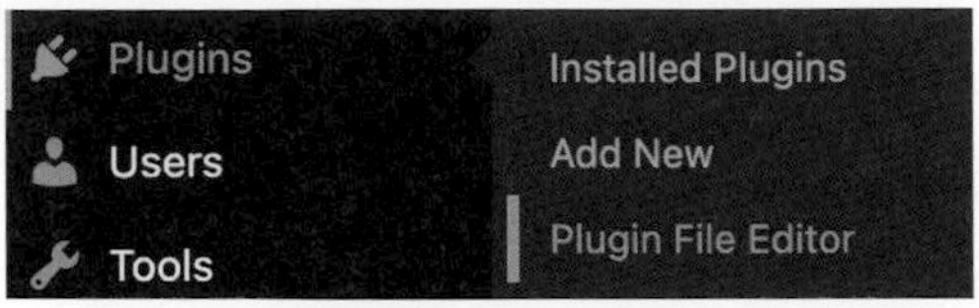

Hot tip

Check out **PHP in easy steps** to learn more about PHP!

2. Select a plugin you want to edit from the drop-down menu on the right-hand side

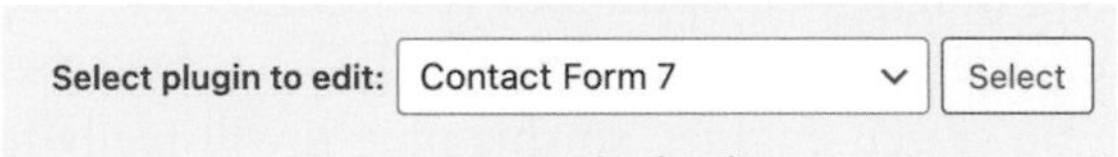

Don't forget

If you are using a block-based theme, you will find the editor under **Tools** > **Plugin File Editor**.

3. From the list of files on the right-hand side, select the one you want to edit
4. Make the changes in the code window
5. Click **Update File** when you are finished

Don't forget

Make sure you keep backups of files in case something goes wrong (see pages 175-178).

Code window

6 Creating an Online Store

This chapter will introduce you to a plugin called WooCommerce that will allow you to build your own online store with WordPress.

WooCommerce Setup

You might think that creating an online store would be difficult. However, WordPress makes it very easy. Now that you have a better grasp of WordPress, let's have a look at how you can build your online store with ease.

Hot tip

It would be handy to have a payment method set up. If you already have a PayPal account then you are good to go!

Installing WooCommerce

WooCommerce is a free but very powerful plugin that allows you to set up a shop and easily configure it using the WordPress dashboard. To install WooCommerce:

1. Navigate to **Plugins** in the WordPress dashboard
2. Now, click **Add New**
3. In the search box type **WooCommerce** and click **Search Plugins**. It should appear as the first search result

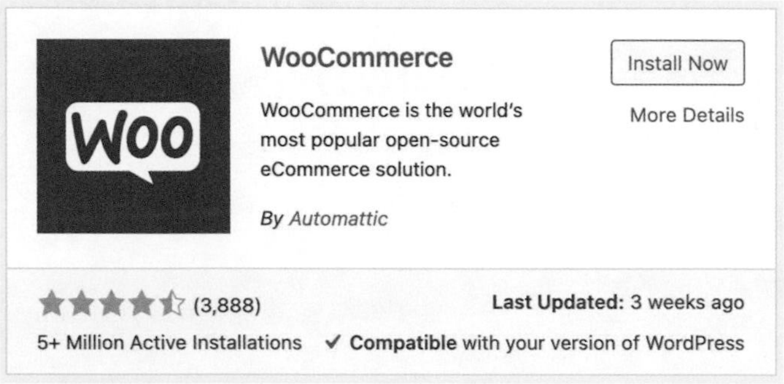
WooCommerce
Install Now
WooCommerce is the world's most popular open-source eCommerce solution.
More Details
Woo
By Automattic
(3,888)
Last Updated: 3 weeks ago
5+ Million Active Installations
✓ Compatible with your version of WordPress

4. Click **Install Now** to install the plugin
5. Click **Activate** and WooCommerce is all ready to go!

Activate

Now that WooCommerce has been installed, you will be asked to walk through a short setup wizard. This will include things like store details, industry, product types, business details, etc.

You will only see this setup screen once, but most of the details can be updated at any time, so don't worry too much if there are some details you are unsure about.

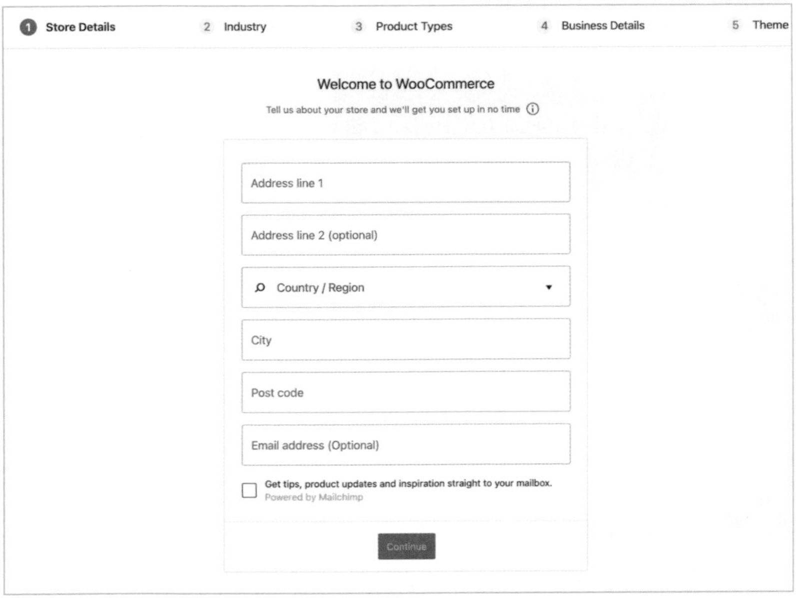

You should now notice that four new pages have been added to your website:

- **Cart**: This will eventually display everything that the user has added to their shopping cart.
- **Checkout**: This is where the user will go to start the process of buying the products they want.
- **My Account**: This is where the user can change their buying or account details, billing address, etc.
- **Shop**: This page will display all the products you have for sale.

These are the basic pages needed to get your online shop off the ground. If you check out the **Shop** page (**http://www.yourdomain.com/shop**), you will find there are no products currently on display.

Adding Products

There can be no shop without products, so let's begin by showing you how to add a product to the store.

1. Select **Products** from your WordPress dashboard. It should be right underneath **WooCommerce**

2. Click **Create Product**

You can also use the **Add New** button.

3. Add an item title and an item description, as shown below:

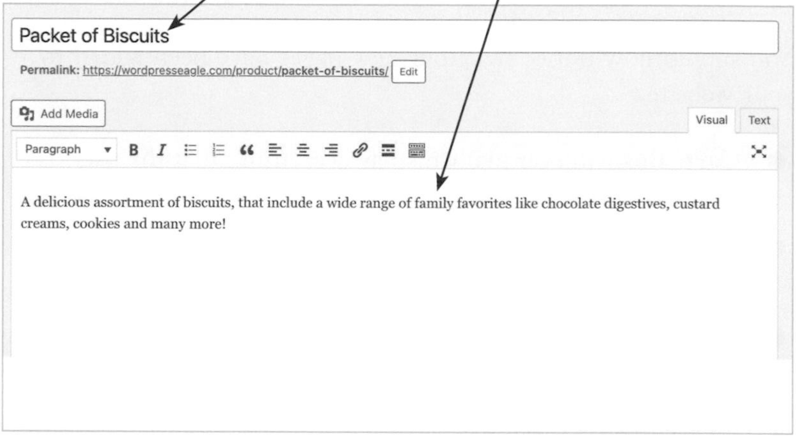

4. You will notice on the right-hand side that you can create a product category. In the example above, a packet of biscuits would fit well in a **Biscuits** category. Click the **+ Add New Product Category** button and then type in "Biscuits" in the text box that appears (see the next page). Finally, click the second **Add new category** button to complete the setup. Your product will now automatically be part of the **Biscuits** category

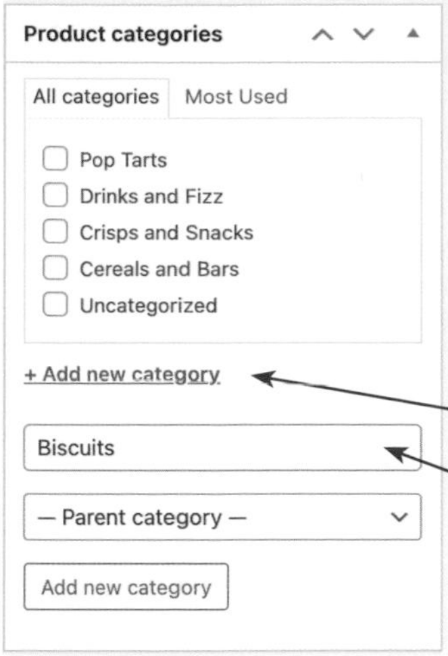

You can add as many products to each category as you like. Once a category has been created, you can then just check the product category box rather than having to add a new one.

Don't forget

Try to keep your products in relevant categories so that the customer can easily find items.

5. Scroll down to the **Product data** section where you need to add in more information about your product

You will see a drop-down box. Choose **Simple product**, for this example, and complete the sections as follows:

Virtual checkbox: Check this if your item is a virtual item.
Downloadable checkbox: If your item is a downloadable item like an ebook, then this would be appropriate.
Regular price: This is the standard price for the item.
Sale price: If the item is on sale, then you would put the sale price here.

Hot tip

We will cover advanced product options later in the book (see pages 90-94).

...cont'd

Adding a product image

The last thing to do is add a product image so that the customer can see what they are buying.

1. On the right-hand side of the **Product data** section, you will see a box that says **Product image**. Select **Set product image**

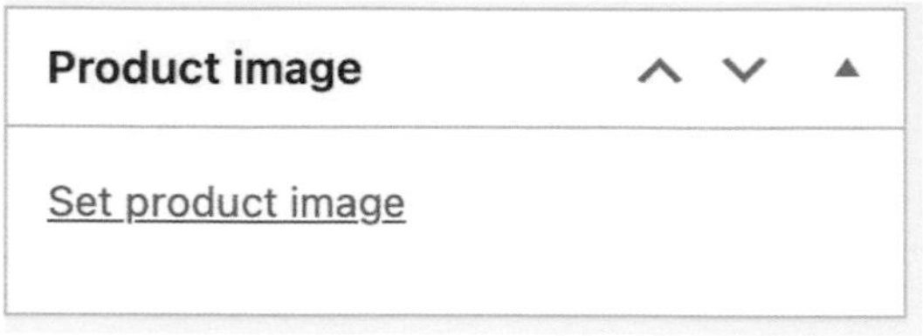
Product image
Set product image

2. Upload your product image or select from the **Media Library**, just like you did in Chapter 4

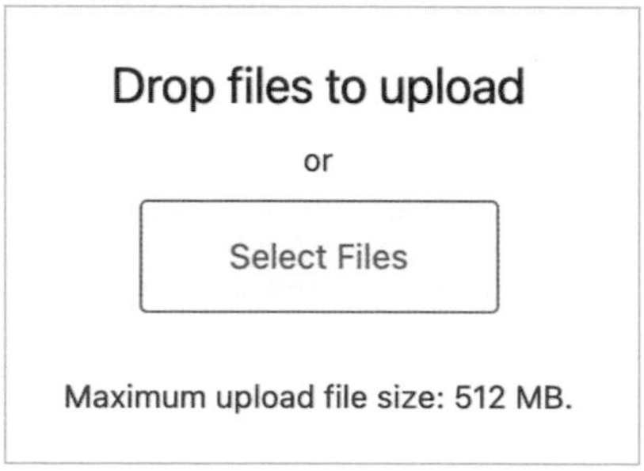
Drop files to upload
or
Select Files
Maximum upload file size: 512 MB.

Product image
Click the image to edit or update
Remove product image

3. Select **Set product image**

Set product image

4. Click **Publish** at the top right of your page to update your product

5. Go to the **Shop** page on your website; you can now see your item is there!

Packet of Biscuits
£2.99
Add to basket

You will notice that the image is showing, along with the title and price, and an **Add to basket** button has automatically been added so that users can purchase straight away!

Don't forget

Your prices may be set in your local currency. See page 84 for WooCommerce settings.

6. If you click on the title, you will be sent through to the product page where it also shows a description along with the same **Add to basket** option

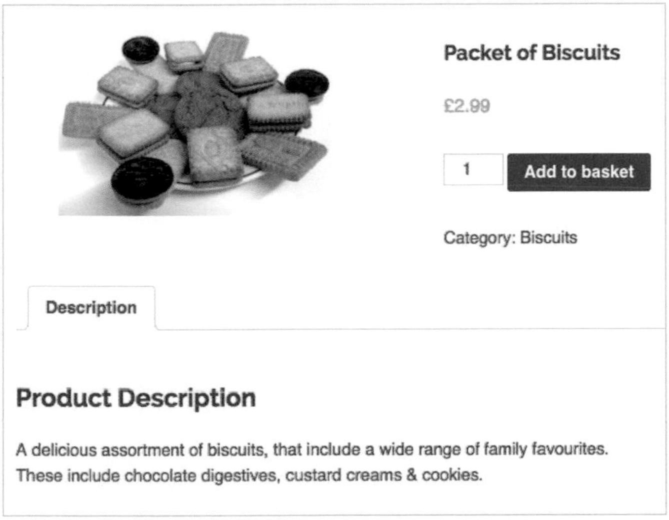
Packet of Biscuits
£2.99
1
Add to basket
Category: Biscuits
Description
Product Description
A delicious assortment of biscuits, that include a wide range of family favourites.
These include chocolate digestives, custard creams & cookies.

7. You can now go ahead and add more products to your store – there is no limit to the number of products you can add. Every time you add a product, it will automatically appear in the **Shop** page

Settings & Payments

Now that you have products set up, you need to set up your shop settings as well as a payment method.

1. Select **WooCommerce** > **Settings**

2. You will now be presented with a number of tabs. Let's go through the most important options in this section:

- **Selling & Shipping Locations**: Here, you can choose which countries you wish to sell and ship to (**General** tab).
- **Enable Coupons**: Check this box to allow the use of coupons on your website (**General** tab).
- **Currency**: Select the currency you are selling in (**General** tab).
- **Enable Reviews**: Check this box if you want to let customers review your products (**Products** tab).
- **Guest Checkout**: Here, you can choose whether or not you want to allow the customer to place an order without an account. You can also allow the user to log in to an existing account during checkout (**Accounts & Privacy** tab).
- **Page Setup**: Here, you can select which pages you want to use for things like **Checkout**, **My Account**, **Cart**, and **Terms and Conditions** (**Advanced** tab).
- **Checkout Endpoints**: Endpoints are appended to your page URLs to handle specific actions during the checkout process. For example, for order received, it might be **order-received**. This would make your domain: **www.domain.com/order-received/** (**Advanced** tab).

Setting up PayPal

PayPal is a very popular choice with online customers, as it's safe and secure. Let's set up your checkout so that the customer can pay funds into your PayPal account during checkout.

1. Click the **Payments** tab from the top menu, and then click **Discover other payment providers**

2. This will open up the external WooCommerce website; select **PayPal Payments** and click the **Free Download** button

3. You will need to upload the zipped file just like a plugin. If you need guidance, then refer back to page 72

4. Head back to the **Payments** tab under **WooCommerce** > **Settings** and select **Set up** next to **PayPal**

5. You will need to select the type of card processing you require before clicking **Activate PayPal**. You will then be prompted to sign in to your PayPal account to complete the setup

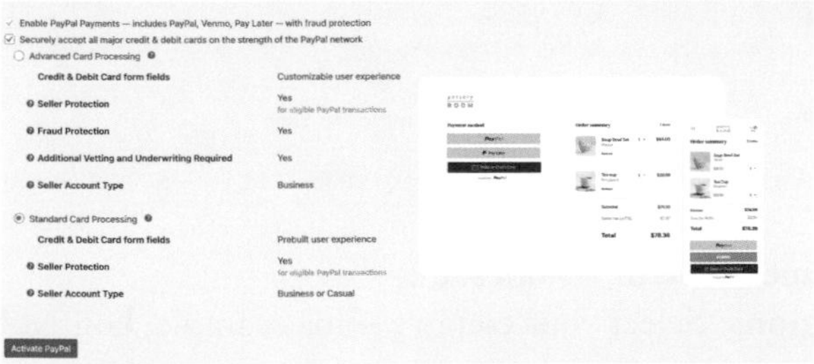

Don't forget

PayPal is one of the most commonly used online payment methods. You will need to set up an account online at www.paypal.com

Don't forget

Standard Card Processing is selected by default, and is probably the best option to get started with PayPal payments.

Shipping

Another important part of owning an online store is the shipping process. WooCommerce handles this well, and it is not too complicated.

1. Select **WooCommerce** > **Settings**
2. Select **Shipping** from the top bar

Shipping zones

Shipping costs will be down to your own preference. However, to get started you need to set up a flat-rate cost for domestic buyers.

1. Select **Shipping zones** from the second menu under the top bar

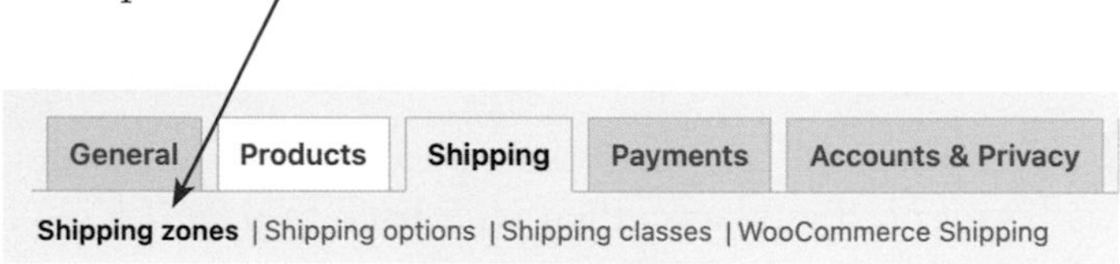

2. Click the **Add shipping zone** button

3. You now have three areas to fill out. Let's start out with the zone name and region:

Zone name: Type in "Domestic".
Zone regions: Select your country – for example, United States.

4. Click the **Add shipping method** button underneath **Shipping methods**

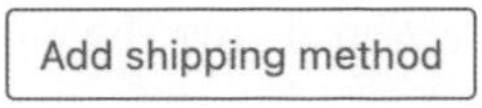
Add shipping method

5. This will open up a pop-up. Select **Flat rate** from the list box and click **Add shipping method**

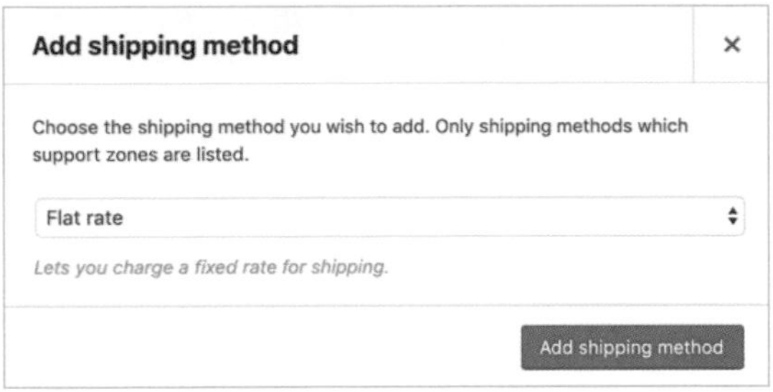
Add shipping method
×
Choose the shipping method you wish to add. Only shipping methods which support zones are listed.
Flat rate
Lets you charge a fixed rate for shipping.
Add shipping method

6. Click **Flat rate** under **Shipping methods** for your shipping zone

Title
Flat rate

7. Finally, fill out the form for your flat rate:

   Method title: This is set to **Flat rate** but you can change the name if you wish.
   Tax status: Select **Taxable** if you wish to charge tax for this rate.
   Cost: Enter the shipping cost here.

Method title
Flat rate
Tax status
None
Cost
1.99

Shipping
Flat Rate:
$1.99

Shipping rate appearing at checkout

Don't forget

Remember to save your changes after completing the form.

Viewing Orders

Once you get orders coming in, you need to know how to view them and sort through them efficiently. WooCommerce offers a dedicated section to manage your orders easily.

1. Select **WooCommerce** > **Orders**

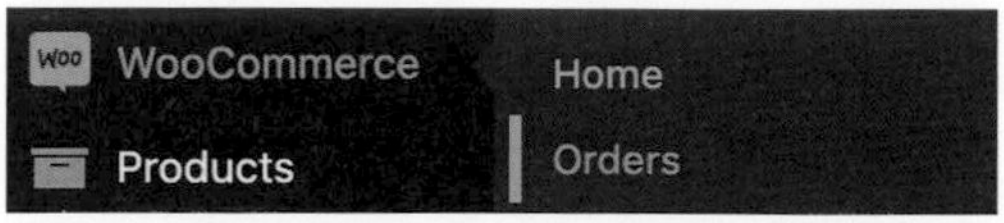
WooCommerce
Products
Home
Orders

You will now see a page that displays all your current orders. You will see in the example below that there is just one order here:

Order
Date
Status
Total
#35 John Davids
Jul 10, 2022
Completed
£2.99
Order
Date
Status
Total

Hot tip

You can filter your orders by using the links at the top of the **Orders** section.

2. If you click on the order number, you will see a more detailed breakdown of the order

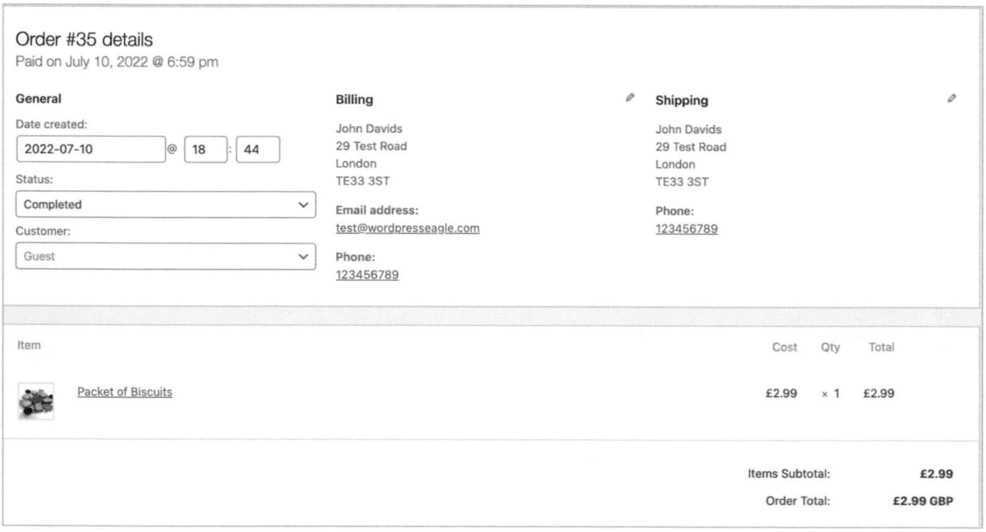
Order #35 details
Paid on July 10, 2022 @ 6:59 pm
General
Date created:
2022-07-10
@
18
44
Status:
Completed
Customer:
Guest
Billing
John Davids
29 Test Road
London
TE33 3ST
Email address:
test@wordpresseagle.com
Phone:
123456789
Shipping
John Davids
29 Test Road
London
TE33 3ST
Phone:
123456789
Item
Cost
Qty
Total
Packet of Biscuits
£2.99
× 1
£2.99
Items Subtotal:
£2.99
Order Total:
£2.99 GBP

Order details

At the top you will see your order status, and it will display order date, billing address, shipping address, and – of course – payment method. You can edit the address too.

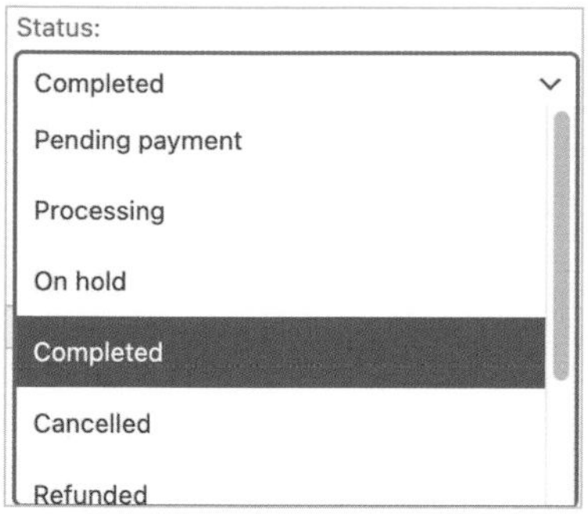

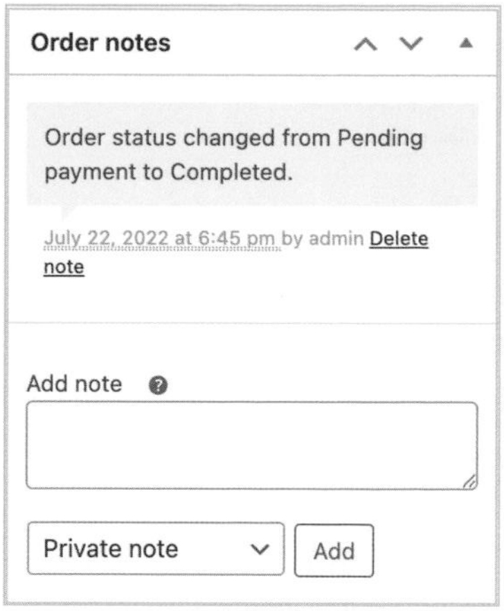

You will also notice the **Order notes** box, which will make automated notes based on the order. You can, however, add your own if you need to.

If your product is a downloadable product, then you can grant access at the bottom by typing in the name of the product and clicking **Grant access**.

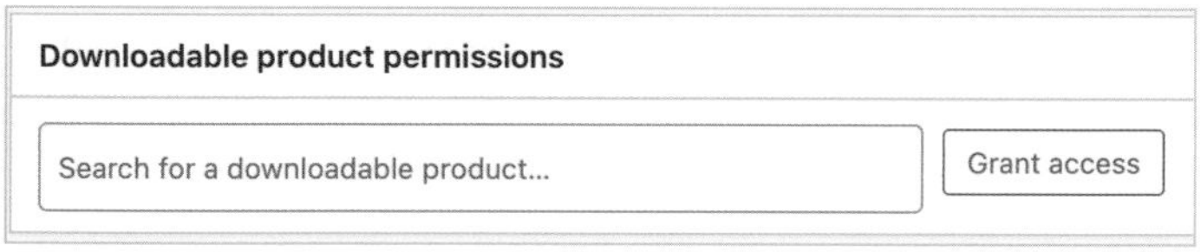

Manual order

If you want to add a manual order from within WordPress, then it's pretty simple to do.

1. Select **WooCommerce** > **Orders**

2. Select **Add order** from the top

3. A new form is presented for you to fill out. Of course, this is a longer process and requires you to fill out everything

Use a plugin called **WooCommerce Print Invoice & Delivery Note** if you want to print order invoices and delivery notes. Just search for it in the WordPress dashboard and install and activate the plugin.

Advanced Product Options

Let's go through some of the advanced options you can set when creating a product.

Product data —
Simple product
Virtual:
Downloadable:
General
Inventory
Shipping
Linked Products
Attributes
Advanced
Regular price (£)
2.99
Sale price (£)
Schedule

In the example shown on pages 80-83, the **General** options were already set when you added the price, but let's look through some of the other options.

Inventory

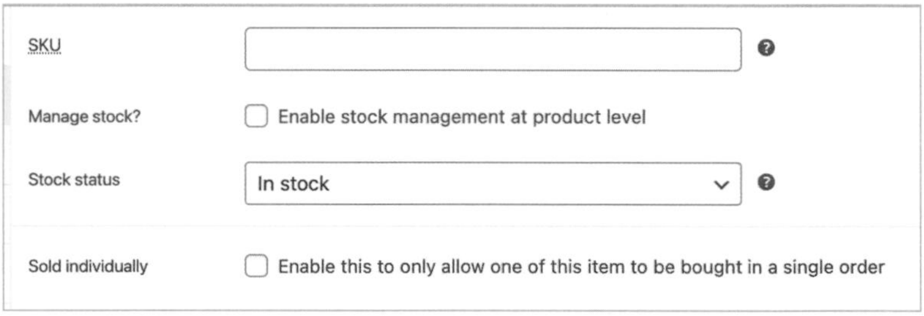
SKU
Manage stock?
Enable stock management at product level
Stock status
In stock
Sold individually
Enable this to only allow one of this item to be bought in a single order

SKU: This stands for stock-keeping unit. Here, you can put a unique identifier (UID) for your product.
Manage stock?: If you check this box, it will allow you to set a quantity of how many of the item you have in stock. It will then continue to keep an accurate count of the stock left. You can also choose to allow backorders from here. A backorder allows a customer to order when an item is out of stock.
Stock status: You can select whether or not an item is currently in stock.
Sold individually: If this is selected, then the customer can only buy one of these in a single order.

Shipping

This section will allow you to set dimensions and weight for a particular item. You can also assign a shipping class to it.

Linked products

Upsells: Here, you can add items that you want to recommend to the customer rather than the currently viewed item. For example, the customer may be viewing a standard wallet, and you want to recommend a leather one to them.
Cross-sells: Here, you can add other products that you might recommend to the customer based on their current order.

Attributes

This allows you to set up various attributes for your product, like size and color (see page 92).

Advanced

Purchase note: Here, you can enter a note that will be sent to the customer after they purchase that particular item.
Menu order: This is the position you want your item to appear in. For example, the items will appear numerically (1, 2, 3, 4, etc.).
Enable reviews: Checking this box will enable customers to leave reviews for the product.

Most of the extra extensions will have a fee.

Get more options

This tab will give you a list of recommended extensions you can install for WooCommerce. These include things like **One Page Checkout** and **Additional Variation Images**.

Setting up a variable item

The options above will give your simple products extra detail, but let's say you are selling T-shirts in multiple colors or sizes. This is where variable products come in handy.

1. Firstly, you need to change the item from a simple product to a variable product. You can start by creating a new product and then selecting **Variable product** under the **Product data** section

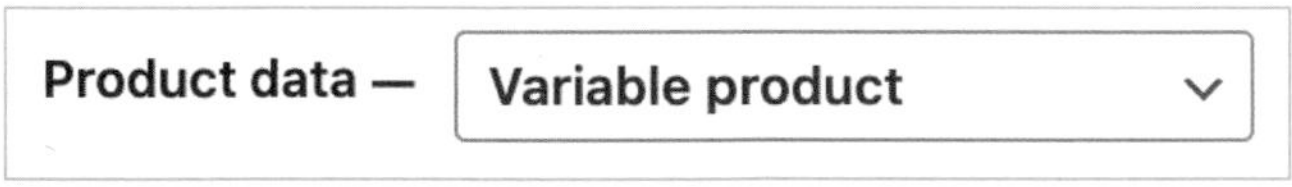

...cont'd

Don't forget

You can add as many variations as you like, which allows you to add several different options for your customers.

2. Select the **Attributes** tab. This will allow you to create separate attributes for your product, like color or size

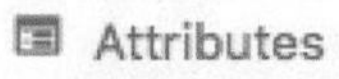
Attributes

3. Click **Add** to bring up a new form

Size
Name:
Size
Value(s):
Small | Medium | Large
Visible on the product page
Used for variations
Save attributes
Expand / Close

- **Name**: In this example, "Size" has been entered in this box, because you are setting up three sizes for the item.
- **Value(s)**: Here, you will put the sizes of your item. Each size needs to be separated by "|". For example, here, you would put "Small | Medium | Large".
- **Used for variations**: It is important to check this so that your variations are set up correctly for the next stage.

4. Click the **Save attributes** button

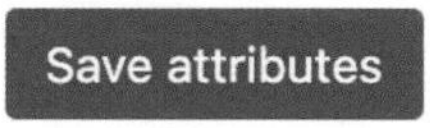
Save attributes

5. Click the **Variations** tab, as your variations will now be ready to set up

Variations

6. Select **Create variations from all attributes** from the drop-down **menu** and click **Go**

7. Your variations will now appear in order down the center of the page. You can click on each one to expand the options for that particular variation

Click to expand

8. Enter the regular price for each of your variations (**Small**, **Medium**, and **Large**)

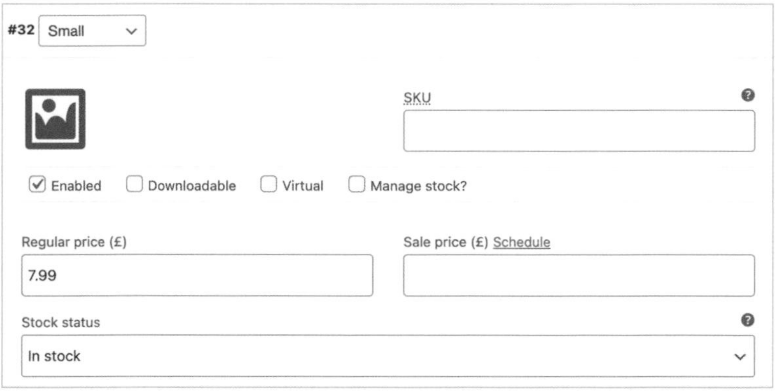

9. Click **Save changes** to update your variation changes

...cont'd

10 Once you have finished, you will still need to update the product by clicking **Update** at the top of the page

You will now notice you can select from the three variations – **Small**, **Medium** and **Large**.

When your customer lands on the T-shirt page, you might want to have a default selection. To do this, you need to go back to your product page.

1 Click the **Variations** tab inside **Product data**

2 Select one of the variations from the **Default Form Values** drop-down box

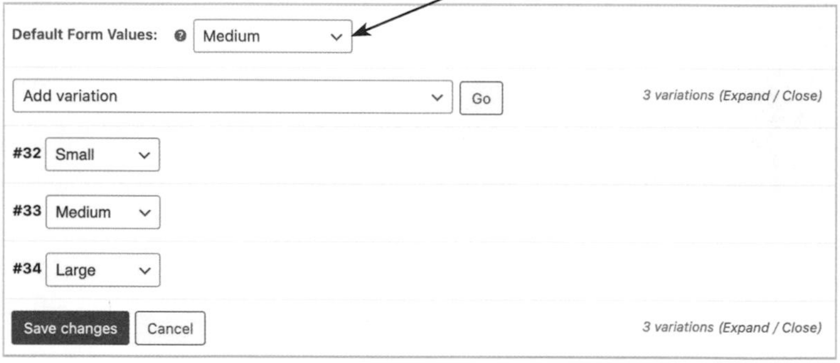

You should now be on your way to creating your own online store. WooCommerce has a lot of add-ons to help you enhance your store even further!

7 Settings & Tools

This chapter explains the different settings sections and will guide you through what each change will do. You will also learn more about the Tools section.

General Settings

Hot tip

The **Settings** section is probably the most important area of WordPress. It controls the basic foundations of your website.

We are now going to take a look at the **Settings** section of the WordPress dashboard. This is where you will configure your WordPress website. Let's start by taking a look at the **General** section. Go to **Settings > General**.

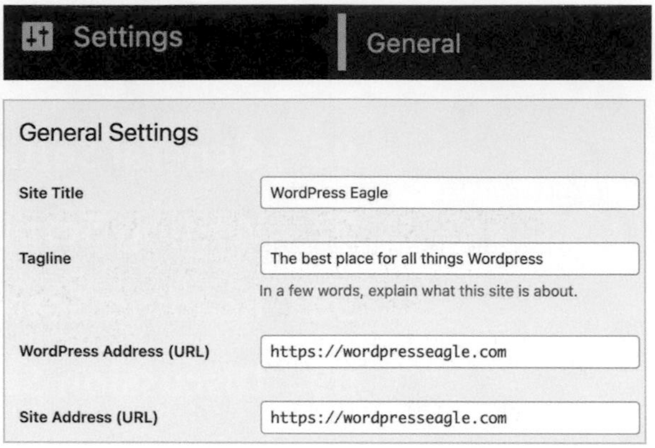
Settings
General
General Settings
Site Title
WordPress Eagle
Tagline
The best place for all things Wordpress
In a few words, explain what this site is about.
WordPress Address (URL)
https://wordpresseagle.com
Site Address (URL)
https://wordpresseagle.com

Site Title: This is basically the name for your website. Name it as you wish!

Tagline: This is used to explain what your website is about.

WordPress Address (URL): This is most likely going to be the same as the Site Address (below). The WordPress URL is the location of your WordPress files.

Site Address (URL): This is the URL for your website homepage.

Administration Email Address: This should contain the email address you entered when you installed WordPress. It is mainly used for user notifications or password reset.

Membership: Check this box if you want anyone to be able to register for this website.

New User Default Role: If you checked the Membership box, then this drop-down box defines the types of privileges that you want new users to have.

Site Language: This sets the language for the WordPress dashboard.

Timezone: Choose your current time zone.

Date Format: Choose how you want the date to display on your website.

Time Format: Choose how you want the time to display on your website.

Week Starts On: The default setting is Monday. However, you can select your preferred start date for WordPress calendars.

Writing Settings

The **Writing** settings are used for posts and interface settings, as well as things like post via email. You can access these by clicking **Settings** > **Writing**.

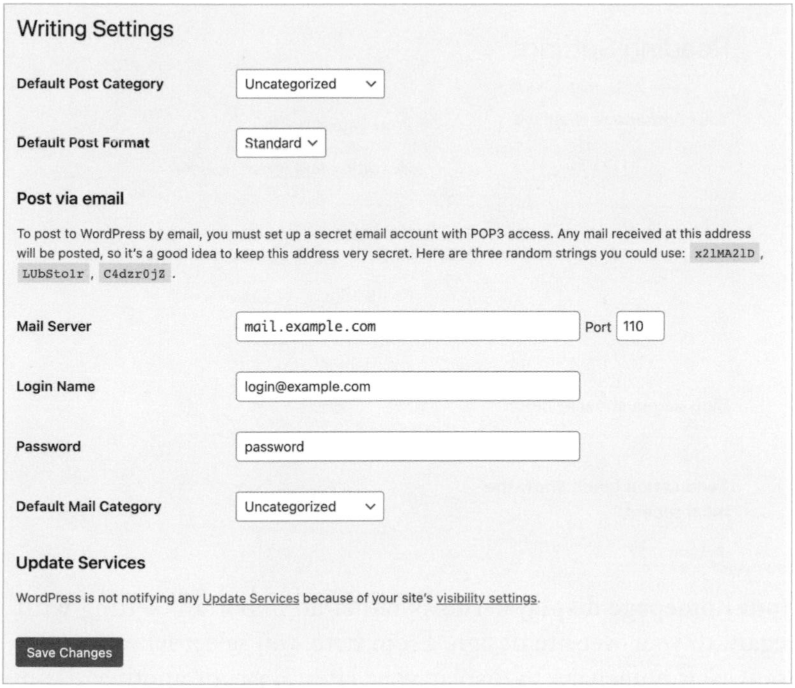
Writing Settings
Default Post Category
Uncategorized
Default Post Format
Standard
Post via email
To post to WordPress by email, you must set up a secret email account with POP3 access. Any mail received at this address will be posted, so it's a good idea to keep this address very secret. Here are three random strings you could use: x21MA21D, LUbStolr, C4dzr0jZ.
Mail Server
mail.example.com
Port
110
Login Name
login@example.com
Password
password
Default Mail Category
Uncategorized
Update Services
WordPress is not notifying any Update Services because of your site's visibility settings.
Save Changes

Default Post Category: We talked about post categories on pages 59-60. WordPress will automatically assign a post to this category if none is assigned.

Default Post Format: There are various different post formats that can be used depending on the theme – for example, Standard or Image. When creating a post, if nothing is selected for Post Format, then the post format will automatically be assigned to the default selected here.

Post via email: This is a little feature that will allow you to publish emails as blog posts. However, to achieve this you will need help from your email host to provide you with settings. If you are not using this setting, then leave the defaults in place.

Update Services: In this section, you can choose to notify various services when you add a new post. All you need to do is add the URL into the text box.

Hot tip

Unless you are building a blog, try to set your homepage as a static page.

Hot tip

To add an RSS feed to your website, go to Appearance > Widgets.

Drag the **RSS Feed Widget** from the left-hand side (**Available Widgets**) to one of your widget areas on the right.

Fill out the details in the RSS Feed Widget Box:

Enter the RSS feed URL here: *This will be http://www.yourdomain.com/feed/*

Give the feed a title.

How many items would you like to display?

Display item content? *Check this box if you want the story to display some of the content underneath.*

Display item author if available?

Display item date?

Click **Save**.

Reading Settings

The **Reading** settings are there to display how you want things to appear to the user of your website.

To access these, select **Settings** > **Reading**.

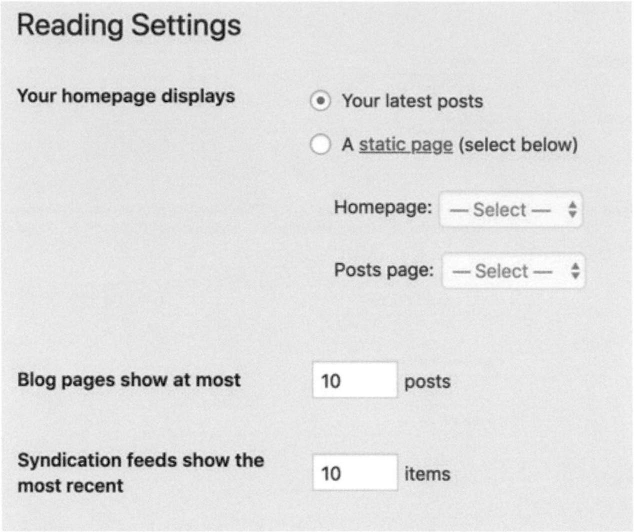
Reading Settings
Your homepage displays
Your latest posts
A static page (select below)
Homepage:
— Select —
Posts page:
— Select —
Blog pages show at most
10
posts
Syndication feeds show the most recent
10
items

Your homepage displays: This is rather an important setting with regard to your website design. From here, you select whether you want your homepage to display your latest posts or another static page that you have created. If you select a static page, then you must select which page you want to use for the homepage. You must also select the page you want to use as your posts page.

Blog pages show at most: This is the maximum number of posts you want to display per page. The default is 10. However, you can change this to whatever you like.

Syndication feeds show the most recent: This is the number of posts that the user will see if they download one of your feeds. The default is 10.

For each article in a feed, show: This will determine whether or not you show the full text from your post or just a summary on your blog/post page.

Search Engine Visibility: You might want to use this while your website or blog is still in development. It will stop search engines from indexing the site.

Discussion Settings

The **Discussion** settings are there for you to control how other users interact with your website or blog.

These can be accessed by selecting **Settings** > **Discussion**.

Default post settings: There are three checkboxes here:

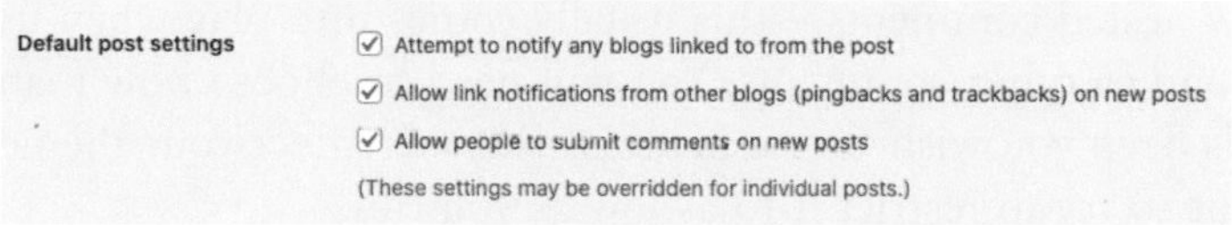

Attempt to notify any blogs linked to from the post: If you choose to check this box, then your blog will send out pings and trackbacks to other articles.

Allow link notifications from other blogs (pingbacks and trackbacks) on new posts: If you check this box, then your blog will accept trackbacks from other blogs.

Allow people to submit comments on new posts: This checkbox is self-explanatory. If you have the box checked, then it will allow users to add comments on any new posts on your website.

Other comment settings: This small section will control your comment settings for your website.

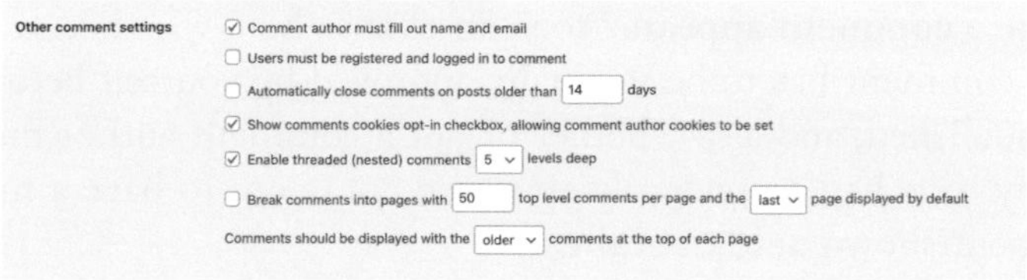

Comment author must fill out name and email: This first checkbox will determine whether or not the user has to fill out their name and email address when posting a comment.

Users must be registered and logged in to comment: This checkbox determines whether or not the user has to be registered or logged in to comment – this all depends on how you feel is best to monitor your comments.

Automatically close comments on posts older than ... days: This checkbox, if selected, will automatically close comments on articles or posts older than a certain number of days. You can choose the number of days yourself.

Hot tip

Trackbacks and pingbacks are methods for alerting websites that you have linked to them.

...cont'd

Show comments cookies opt-in checkbox, allowing comment author cookies to be set: This allows a cookie to be set so that the user doesn't need to enter their details every time they post a new comment.

Enable threaded (nested) comments ... levels deep: This checkbox will allow nested comments – this usually comes into play when users respond to other comments. You will need to choose how many levels deep you wish to use for this. This can affect your theme layout so try to restrict it to as low as you can.

Break comments into pages with...: If your website is getting a lot of comments, then this option lets you break your comments section up by placing a set amount over a number of pages. Choose how many top-level comments you want per page and whether or not you want the first or last comment page displayed by default.

E-mail me whenever: You will receive an email whenever anybody posts a comment or when a comment is held for moderation if you choose to select both checkboxes.

Before a comment appears: You can choose here whether or not a comment has to be manually approved by yourself before it is published, and also whether or not a comment author must already have had a previously approved comment to have a further comment shown automatically.

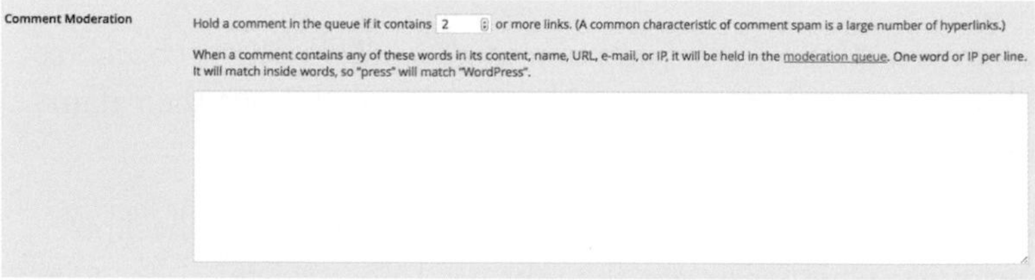

Comment Moderation: You can choose here to hold comments if they contain a certain amount of links. You can type keywords in the box, and if the user who comments has one of those keywords in the comment, then it will be held in moderation.

For example, if you put "biscuit' in the word box, and a user posted a comment saying "I like biscuits", then the comment would be held in the moderation queue and would need to be approved.

Disallowed Comment Keys: This box works in a similar fashion to the Comment Moderation box. However, in this case, you can put keywords into the Disallowed Comment Keys box, and if a user comments with one of those words, then it will be put in the trash.

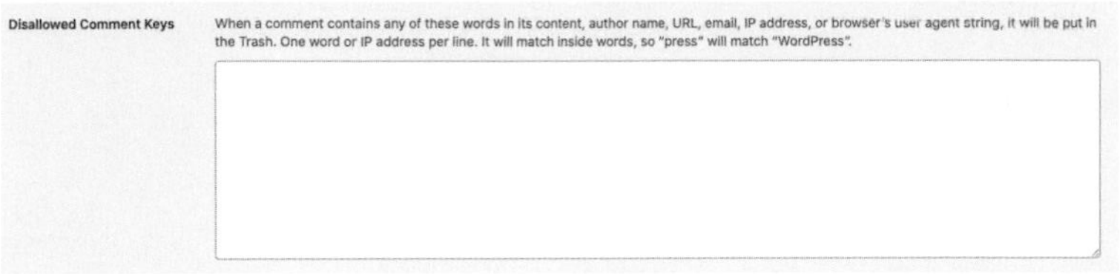

For example, if you put "jam" in the comment blacklist, and a user made a comment on a post saying "I like jam", then that comment would be put in the trash.

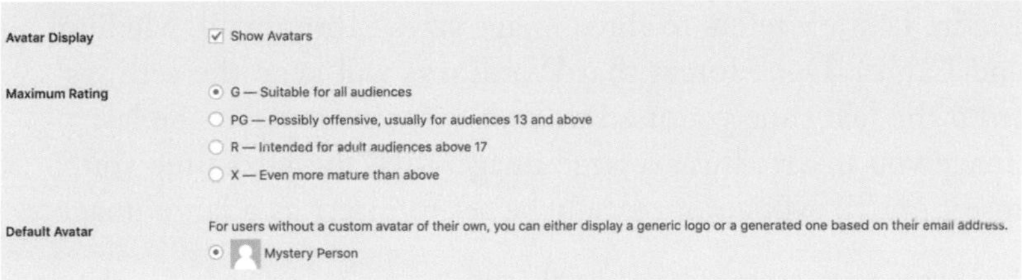

Avatars

An avatar is something that appears by your name on a blog or website. You might have noticed them on forums.

Avatar Display: You can choose to show avatars on your website or blog.

Maximum Rating: We all know about movie ratings; right? Well, this works in the same way with avatars. Choose the maximum rating level of avatars for your website. This is all going to depend on your audience.

Default Avatar: This is for users who have not chosen their own custom avatar. You are able to select a generic logo for them until they decide to use their own.

Media Settings

These settings will control how media is displayed on your WordPress website. You can access **Media** settings by going to **Settings** > **Media**.

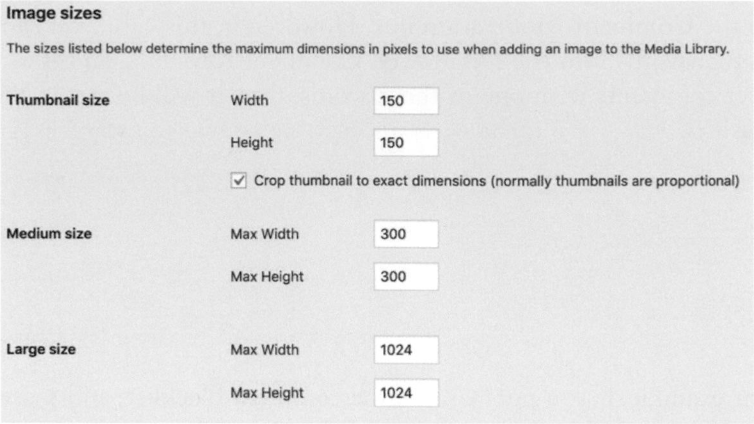

Image sizes:
We discussed adding media and images back in Chapter 4. The Media Library refers to three image sizes (Thumbnail, Medium, and Large). Don't forget that WordPress will keep the settings from the last time you used them. So, for example, if the last image you inserted was a large image, then the next time you insert one, it will automatically be set to insert as a large image.

In this section, you can select the dimensions in pixels for those three sizes. It is a good idea to check the **Crop thumbnail to exact dimensions** box (normally, thumbnails are proportional).

Most of us will usually insert an image as a full-size image, as you can then set it to the correct scale.

Uploading Files: If you check the box below this heading, it will organize your uploads into month- and year-based folders.

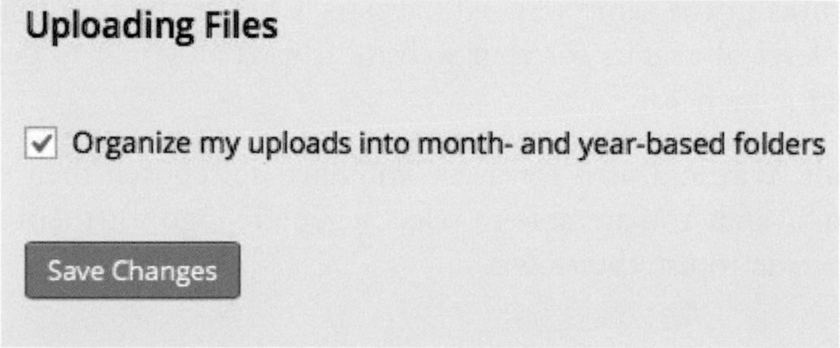

Permalinks Settings

This section allows you to set up the structure for your WordPress URLs. You can access these settings by clicking **Settings** > **Permalinks**.

Common Settings: You have six options here for the structure of your URLs. Most people will choose **Post name**, as this keeps the URL much simpler. You can see the examples set out in the screenshot below, and choose from there which one you want to use.

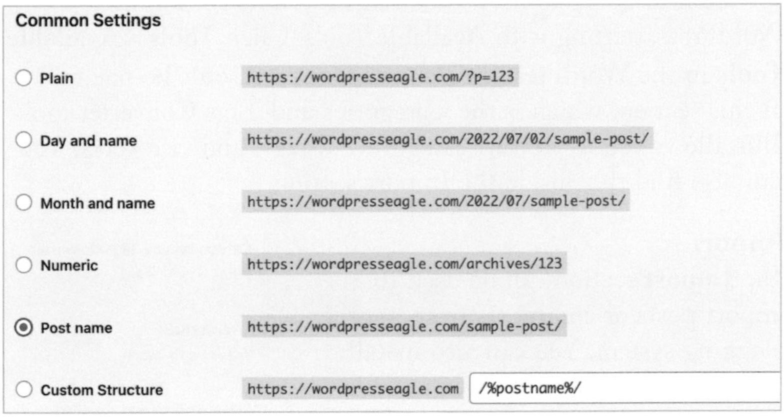

Common Settings
Plain
https://wordpresseagle.com/?p=123
Day and name
https://wordpresseagle.com/2022/07/02/sample-post/
Month and name
https://wordpresseagle.com/2022/07/sample-post/
Numeric
https://wordpresseagle.com/archives/123
Post name
https://wordpresseagle.com/sample-post/
Custom Structure
https://wordpresseagle.com
/%postname%/

Hot tip

Try to use **Post name** for your permalinks settings, as it will do better for your SEO.

Optional: This gives you the opportunity to create custom structures for category and tag URLs. The default structure will be used if you leave these blank. The default structure for the category will look something like the URL below:

http://yoursite.com/category/WordPress

Category base
Tag base
Product category base
product-category
Product tag base
product-tag
Product attribute base

Privacy & Tools

Privacy

WordPress recently introduced a **Privacy** section, which you can access by going to **Settings** > **Privacy**. This is so that you can create a privacy policy for your website. It is really important that you have a privacy policy in place to follow both national and international laws. WordPress has a draft in place for you to get started.

Available Tools

We are now going to have a look at the **Tools** section in WordPress, starting with Available Tools. Click **Tools** > **Available Tools** in the WordPress dashboard. There will only be one tool in this section, which is the Categories and Tags Converter tool. This allows you to convert categories to tags, and vice versa. You can also find this inside the Import section.

Import

The **Import** section can be used to import posts or comments from another blogging system. You can also install content from a WordPress export file.

For example, if you have posts that you want to import from Tumblr, then you can click **Tumblr** and it will bring up a Tumblr importer.

Categories and Tags Converter
Install Now | Details
LiveJournal
Install Now | Details
Movable Type and TypePad
Install Now | Details
RSS
Install Now | Details
Tumblr
Install Now | Details
WordPress
Install Now | Details

Export

Export can be used to export your WordPress content to an XML file. You can choose to export everything or just certain sections like Posts or Pages. This can then be imported into another WordPress installation. For example, if you want to export your posts, then select **Posts** and click **Download Export File**.

Export Personal Data & Erase Personal Data

WordPress has also added two new tools that allow you to erase and export personal data that you may have collected. These are to comply with General Data Protection Regulation (GDPR) guidelines.

Hot tip

You can learn more about the GDPR by going to **https://ec.europa.eu/justice/smedataprotect/index_en.htm**

8 SEO & Social Media

This chapter explains how to make your WordPress website more SEO-friendly, and explains how you can add social media elements.

WordPress SEO by Yoast

One of the top reasons for developing websites with WordPress is the SEO aspect. There are dozens of amazing SEO plugins out there to help you optimize your website. This helps Google rank these websites higher compared with the sites developed in contemporary CMSs.

One such plugin is Yoast SEO. The Yoast SEO plugin can be used to improve the on-page SEO of any WordPress website.

Installing the Yoast SEO plugin

1. Download directly from the developer's site at **https://yoast.com/WordPress/plugins/seo/**

   Or, go to the WordPress dashboard, then go to the **Plugins** menu and install it from there

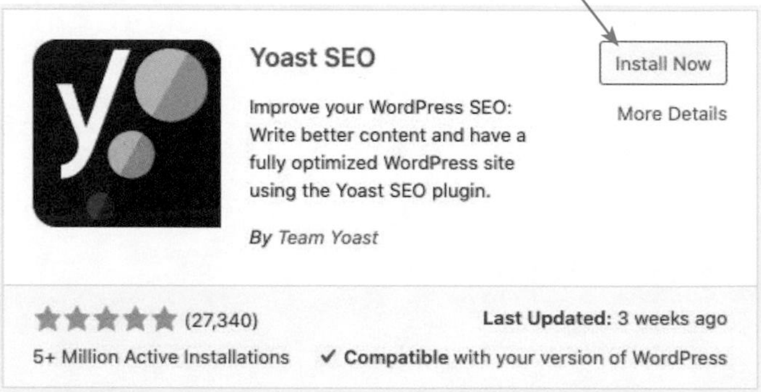

Once the plugin is installed, if you add a new post or page to your website, you will notice that a **Yoast SEO** window appears below the post or page. This section is broken down into four tabs: **SEO**, **Readability**, **Schema**, and **Social**.

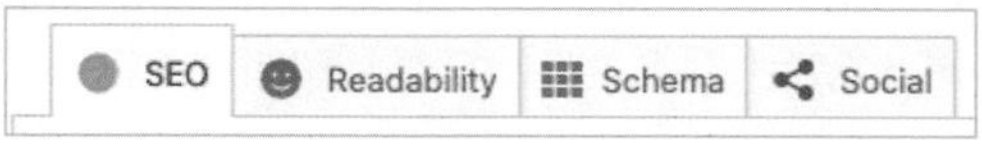

SEO

This section focuses on your keyphrase, SEO analysis and cornerstone content.

Google Preview shows how your website will appear in Google's search results.

Hot tip

Search engine optimization (SEO) is a technique to help your website rank higher on search engines, such as Google, for particular keywords.

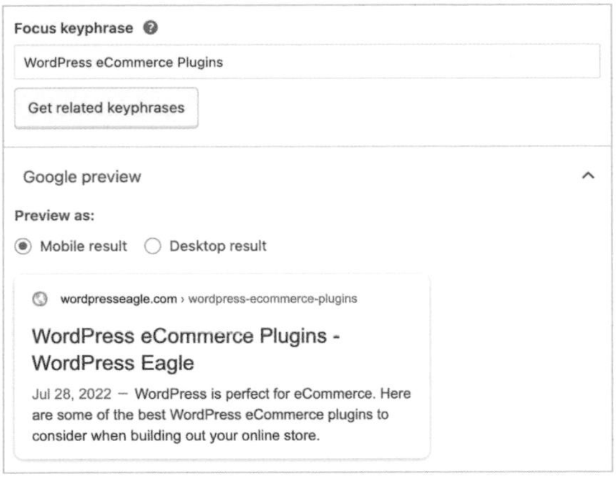

The **Focus keyphrase** is the keyphrase that you want your page to rank for so that when people search for that keyphrase, they'll find you. For instance, in the above screenshot, the keyphrase "WordPress eCommerce Plugins" has been entered.

Underneath, there are three sections: **SEO analysis**, **Cornerstone content**, and **Advanced**.

SEO analysis

This area contains an SEO analysis of your focus keyphrase in areas like the title, URL, content, etc. and provides you with feedback on what needs to be changed. It can be seen from the screenshot below that the page analysis report contains some comments and recommendations that are categorized by different-colored circles. Red means that you need to pay particular attention to this item – these are all problems. Orange depicts an area for improvement, and the green circles will display all the things you have done well.

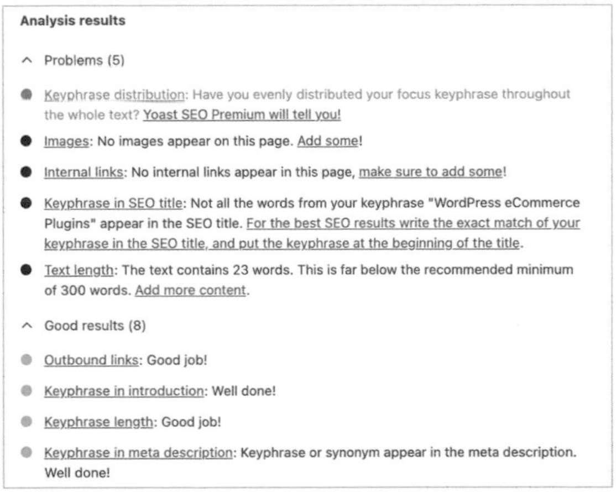

...cont'd

Cornerstone content

These are pages or posts on your website that are considered the most important. If you think of four or five pages that you would like someone to read when they first visit your website, these would be your cornerstones. These should be the ones you want to rank high on search engines, and they should be well written and updated frequently. Any other posts that have a similar topic should link back to your cornerstone articles. You can choose your cornerstone content by changing the switch to **On** under the **Cornerstone content** section.

Cornerstone content
Cornerstone content should be the most important and extensive articles on your site. Learn more about Cornerstone Content.
Mark as cornerstone content
On

Advanced

The **Advanced** section contains some of the most advanced and powerful SEO options. These settings are usually done at a website level. However, the Yoast plugin allows you to perform these functionalities at a post or page level.

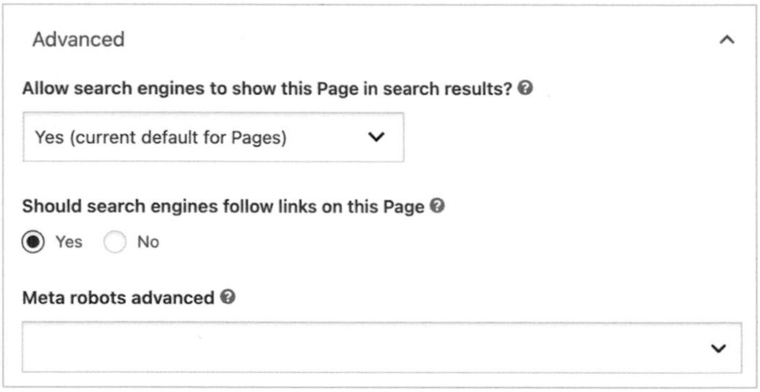
Advanced
Allow search engines to show this Page in search results?
Yes (current default for Pages)
Should search engines follow links on this Page
Yes
No
Meta robots advanced

Allow search engines to show this Page in search results?

By default, this will be set to **Yes**; however, if you don't want search engines to display this page, then you can set it to **No**.

Should search engines follow links on this Page?

Here, you can set whether or not you want search engines to follow links on your page. You might set this to **No** if you can't or don't want to vouch for the content on another site you are linking to, or if it's a paid link.

Hot tip

Don't forget to check out **https://yoast.com** as SEO is a very broad topic.

Meta robots advanced

Here, you can choose some advanced values for meta robots:

None: This is set by default. It just means no extra settings.

No Image Index: Disallow search engines from spidering images on that page.

No Archive: Prevents search engines from showing a cached copy of the page.

No Snippet: Prevents search engines from showing a snippet of this page in the search results.

Canonical URL

You might have two pages with very similar content on the same URL, so you need to decide which is the preferred version so that search engines can understand which is the preferred one when it comes to rankings.

Readability

The **Readability** section consists of several readability checks. This includes things like: sentence length, paragraph length, reading ease and consecutive sentences, etc. This section will provide you with feedback in a similar fashion to the **SEO analysis** section (using red, orange and green comments).

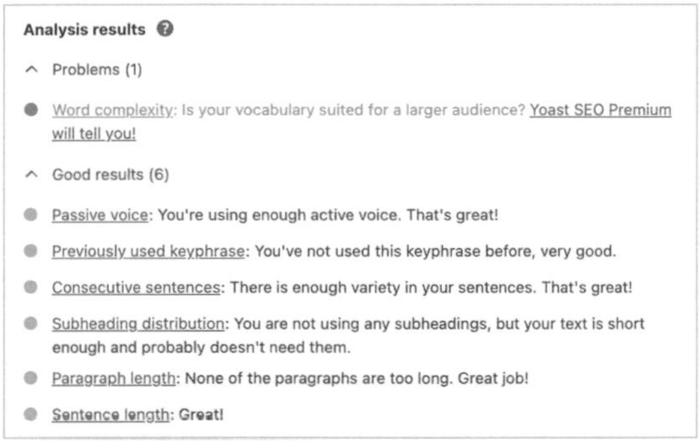

If you go to **Dashboard** > **Pages**, you should see the color for both **SEO** and **Readability analysis**, on the very end columns for each page.

Schema

This section will help you describe your website content to search engines. This is particularly useful if you have different types of content (e.g. product pages, service pages, etc.). Having this set as **Default for Pages** or **Default for Posts** works fine for most websites.

Hot tip

Meta robots tell search engines what content to follow and what not to follow. This gives you control over what content you want to hide from search engines and what you want them to look at.

Hot tip

You can learn more about Schema settings here: **https://yoast.com/help/selecting-content-types-in-schema-settings/**

...cont'd

Social

The last section of the **Yoast SEO** WordPress plugin is the **Social** section. Here, all social media-related options are specified. Below is a screenshot of this section:

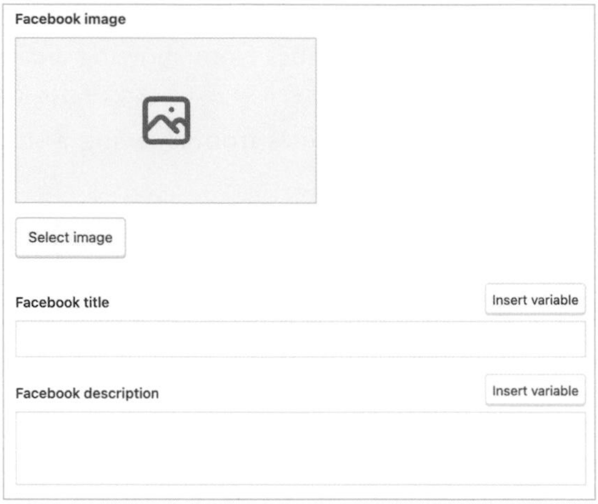

Don't forget

When people share your content on Facebook, you want to make sure the content is attractive, so try to make the description as appealing as possible.

These options specify the behavior of a page or post when they are shared on social media platforms. For instance, you can set a Facebook title and description for posts. This title will appear on Facebook when a post is shared there, along with the description. You can also upload an image to be displayed alongside a Facebook post.

If you entered "WordPress eCommerce Plugins" as the page title name, but in the **Social** section you put "eCommerce Plugins for WordPress" in the **Facebook title** box, then on Facebook it would appear as **eCommerce Plugins for WordPress** rather than the page title. The same applies with the description.

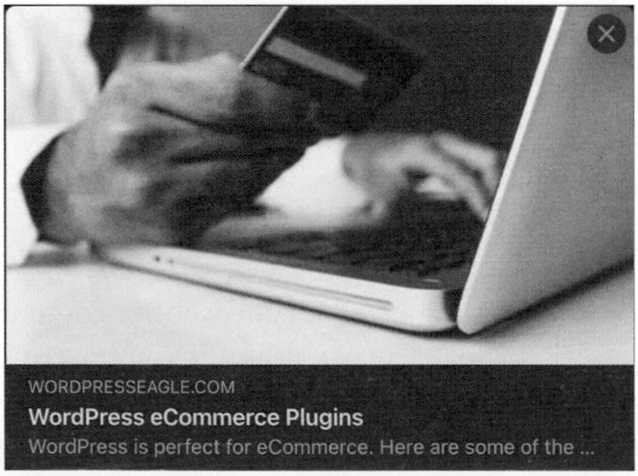

Social Media Overview

Social media is everywhere these days. Whether you are browsing an online magazine or watching a video on YouTube, you will be sure to see a **Share** button of some kind. Most people will now have some kind of social media account, whether it be Facebook, Twitter, LinkedIn, or one of the other sites. This is why it is even more important for you and your users to be able to share content.

Here are some interesting statistics (source: **hootsuite.com**) that show just how important social media is:

- Social media platforms gained 424 million users in 2021 (10.1% increase on the previous year).
- 4.62 billion people use social media around the world.
- The average user spends 2 hours 27 minutes on social media every day.
- Facebook has 2.91 billion monthly users. 2.11 billion of those users can be reached with Facebook Ads.

These statistics are changing all the time, even while you read this book.

Improving social media presence

When building a website, it is important to think of ways that users can discover and share your content. Users find a lot of good articles in their Facebook, Twitter and Instagram feeds. Here are some ways your social media presence can be improved:

- Add sharing buttons to your content so that users only need to click a button to share the content via their social media account.
- Create social media accounts for your own organization.
- Add **Follow**, **Like Us** buttons, etc. on your page so that users can start following your feeds.
- Interact with your users by answering their questions or queries.
- Create great content for users to read, as they will keep coming back for more.

Hot tip

Check out Digital Marketing for Businesses in easy steps for more on social media marketing.

Share Buttons

Share buttons are a good way for users to be able to share content from your WordPress website. We suggest a great plugin called **Social Share Buttons & Analytics**, which will make it easy for you to add these **Share** buttons to your posts.

To install this:

1. Go to **Plugins** > **Add New**
2. Search for "Social Share Buttons & Analytics Plugin"
3. Install and activate the plugin

GetSocial
Social Share Buttons & Analytics Plugin – GetSocial.io
Install Now
More Details
Free share buttons for 30+ of your favorite social networks. Increase traffic through social sharing...
By Getsocial, S.A.
(154)
7,000+ Active Installations
Last Updated: 5 months ago
Untested with your version of WordPress

4. Now it's installed, go to **GetSocial** on your dashboard to set up your buttons

GS GetSocial

5. Enter your URL and email address to activate your account

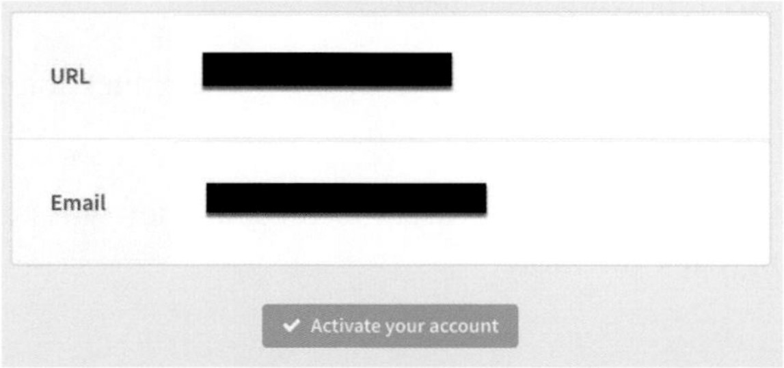
URL [redacted]
Email [redacted]
Activate your account

6. Scroll down to the **Horizontal Sharing Bar** box and click **Install App**

7. Fill out the form to set up your buttons

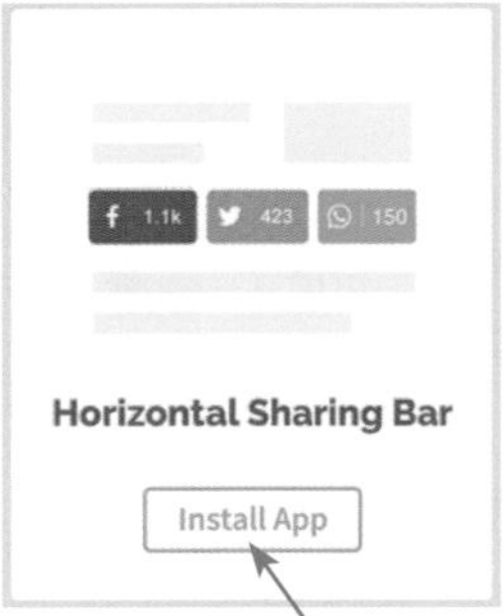

Install App

Form

There are a number of options that allow you to customize your social sharing bar. Here are the free ones:

Social Networks: Select social networks that you want your visitors to be able to share content on.
Share Label: This allows you to add some text next to your buttons.
Size: Choose the size of the buttons.
Position: Choose the position of the buttons (left, center, right).
Counter: If you choose to have a counter, it will display a number next to each social button. This number will let visitors know how many times the content has been shared.
Location in Page: This allows you to place your bar at the top or bottom of the page.

As you fill out the form, you will be shown a preview of how the social buttons will look on your website.

8. Finally, click **Save and Activate** to make your social buttons live

Hot tip

It is best to keep your social buttons at the bottom of your content. This way, you will be keeping the page tidy and the user can share straight after they have read the content.

Twitter Feed

Hopefully, you have set up a Facebook or Twitter page by now for your blog/website. If not – what are you waiting for? We demonstrated adding a Facebook page plugin when we were talking about widgets on pages 39-41. This is a great way to get users to like your page. We are now going to have a look at adding a Twitter feed to your website so that users can see your latest Tweets and get the chance to follow you.

1. Open up a post or page
2. Click the + button on the top left-hand side 
3. Select **Twitter** under **Embed** 

4. Inside the Twitter block, enter your Twitter handle and click **Embed**

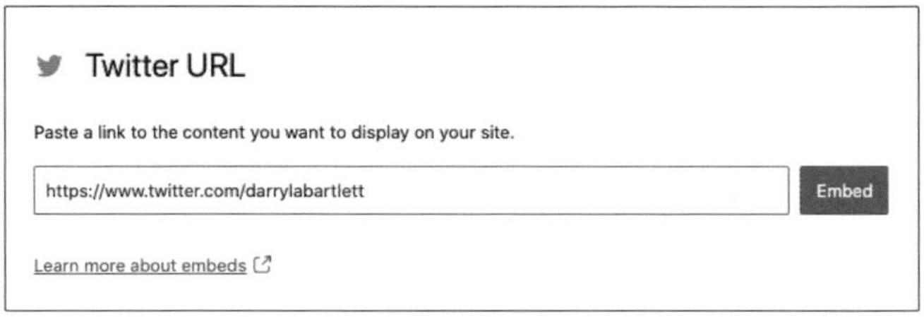

5. Your Twitter block should now show a preview of your feed. Don't forget to click **Update** or **Publish** to save changes to your post or page

Live Chat

Live chat is one of the quickest methods of providing customer services. Customers can get answers to queries within minutes. This will create a much better impression and – potentially – more orders. Live chat is very simple to set up within WordPress with a plugin by 3CX.

1. Go to **Plugins** > **Add New**
2. Search for "3CX Free Live Chat"
3. Install and activate the plugin
4. Click **3CX Live Chat** from the dashboard
5. You will then be presented with the form shown below:

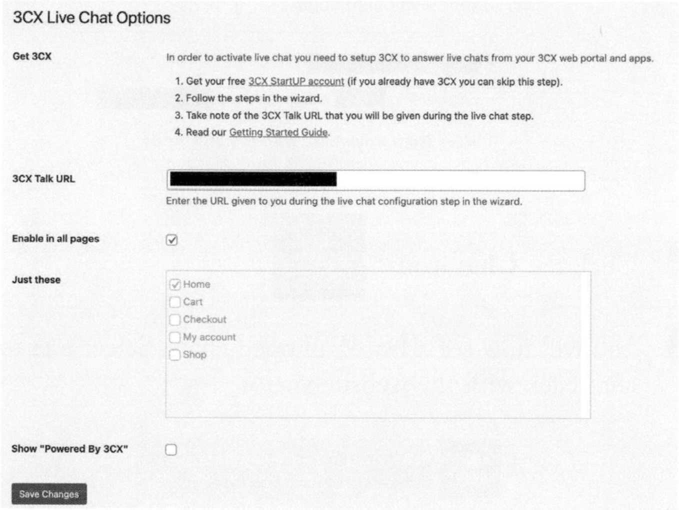

3CX Talk URL: You will be required to sign up for a free 3CX account (**https://www.3cx.com/startup/**) to get your Talk URL. Once you have received this, paste it into this field.

Enable in all pages: Check this box if you want live chat to appear on all your website pages.

Just these: You can also select various pages you want the live chat to appear on.

...cont'd

If you visit your website, you will notice that the user can already start a live chat, by clicking the message bubble in the bottom right.

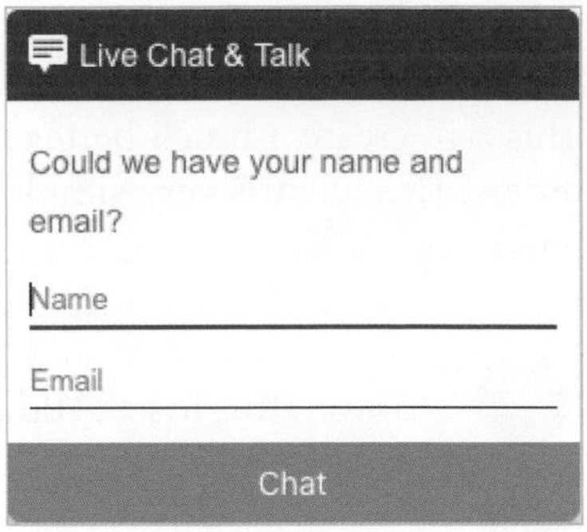

They can then fill out the form and click **Chat**.

Answering live chats

1. Go to the web client login address that you were sent inside your welcome email by 3CX. This email will also include your email and password, which you will need to log in

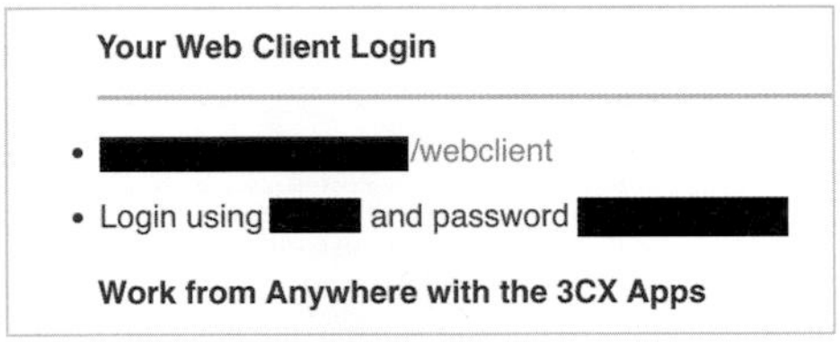

2. Click the **Chat** icon

3. You will now see a list of all open chats. Select one to chat back with the website visitor

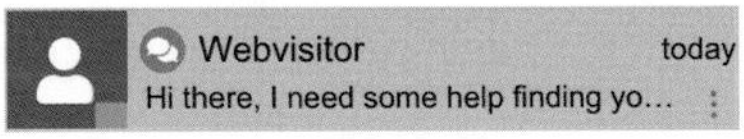

Select a chat

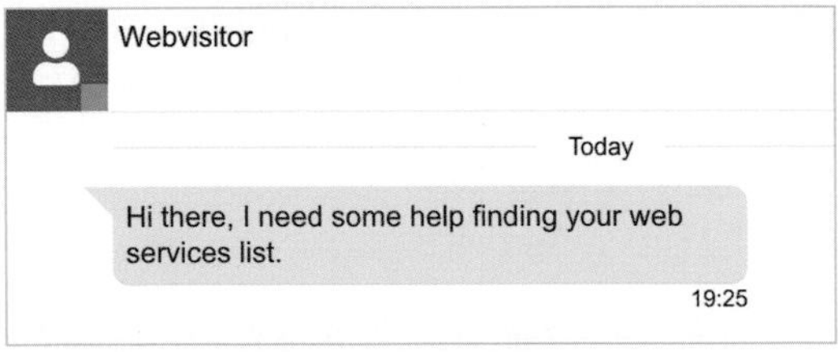

Open chat

Instagram Photos

Sharing photos these days is a massive trend. Instagram allows you to share your daily adventures through the medium of images and videos. If you are familiar with Instagram, you may want to share your uploads on your WordPress website. Once again, there are some great plugins that can help you with this. One of these is called **Smash Balloon Social Photo Feed**. It allows you to add a shortcode to your posts and pages or even add them into widget areas. To install **Smash Balloon Social Photo Feed**:

1. Go to **Plugins** > **Add New**
2. Search for "Smash Balloon Social Photo Feed"

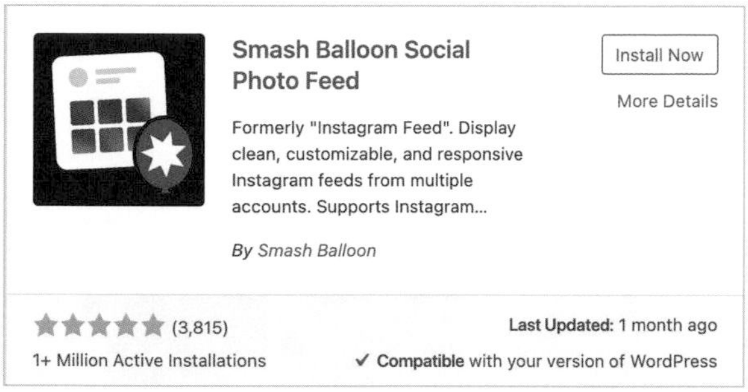

3. Install and activate the plugin, just the same as you have done with previous plugins. You will now notice that **Instagram Feed** has appeared in your dashboard, so click on it to get started
4. Select **+ Add New**
5. Select **User Timeline** as the feed type, and then click the **Add Source** button

6. Log in with your Instagram credentials – do this by clicking **Login with Instagram**

Hot tip

WordPress does come with its own Instagram block; however, it only allows you to use one post. **Smash Balloon Social Photo Feed** allows you to show off your whole feed.

...cont'd

Once your account is connected, select your account and click **Next**.

Beware

Remember that any future photos that you post to Instagram will automatically appear on your website or blog.

7. You can use the **Customize** tab to personalize your Instagram widget. From here, you are able to edit the height, padding, color scheme, etc. You can also choose how many posts you want to show on mobile and desktop

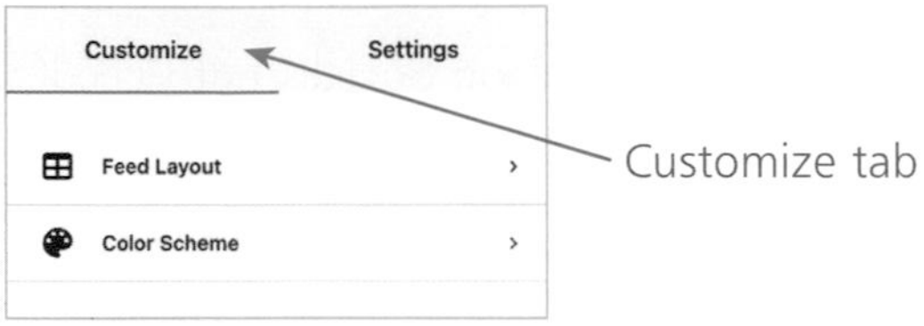

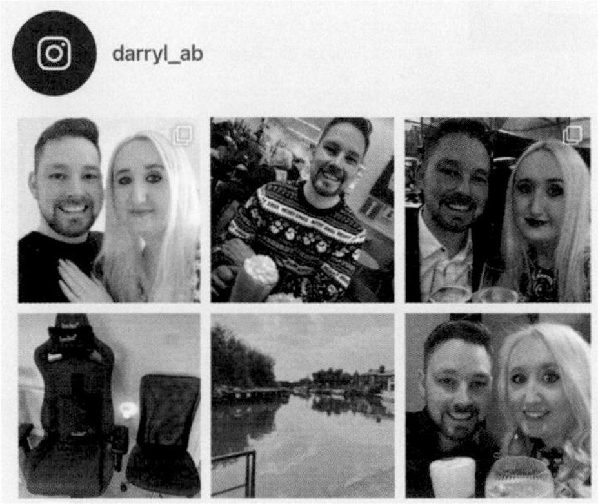

Feed preview

8. When you are happy, click the **Save** button on the top right-hand side

9. Finally, you will need to insert a shortcode block into your page or post and add in your Instagram shortcode: **[instagram-feed feed=1]**

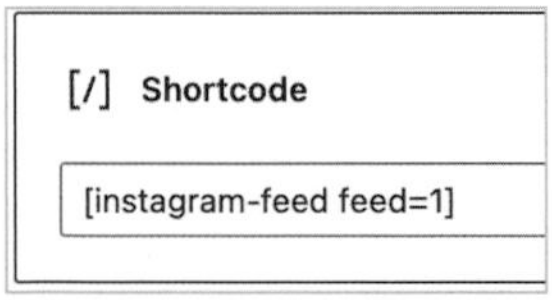

Hot tip

If you can't remember how to insert a shortcode block, then please refer to page 57.

9 User Interaction

This chapter explains various ways that users can interact with your website. It also covers setting up user membership and translation tools.

Comments

Comments are a good way for your users to reach out to you, and allow you to build two-way communication with your visitors. They also allow you to build up a community, and encourage visitors to return to your website or blog. It is more common to see comments on a blog rather than a website. However, the importance of making sure there is a blog on any website seems to be rising.

Hot tip

Allowing comments on your website or blog will encourage users to return to your site.

One thing to bear in mind with regard to comments is that as well as managing them, you should allow both positive and negative comments. Users will respect you more for this.

Managing comments

When users make comments through your website or blog, they will appear in the **Comments** section of WordPress. To access this, click **Comments** from the dashboard.

Comments

You will now be presented with a screen that will show all your website comments. Remember that some comments will be spam (see page 122).

Along the top there are six different sections: **All**, **Mine**, **Pending**, **Approved**, **Spam**, and **Trash**.

Comments
All (1) | Mine (0) | Pending (1) | Approved (0) | Spam (0) | Trash (9)
Bulk actions
Apply
All comment types
Filter
Author
Comment
David Smith
david.smith@wordpress
eagle.com
This has been very helpful in making a deci
Author
Comment
Bulk actions
Apply

When your comments come in, they are likely to go into your **Pending** section, and you will need to approve the comments before they go live.

You can change these various settings in **Settings** > **Discussion** (see pages 99-101).

Approving comments

To approve a comment, you will need to hover your mouse over the comment, and click the **Approve** link.

Approve | Reply | Quick Edit | Edit | Spam | Trash

Other options

You will also see a number of other options:

Reply: This allows you to reply to the comment. The reply will become public on the website.

Quick Edit: This allows you to make a quick edit to the comment using a small window.

Edit: This will take you to a full-sized page to edit the comment. This is useful if the comment is quite a long one.

Spam: This link will mark the comment as spam.

Trash: This will send the comment to the trash folder.

Editing user comments

There is a plugin called **Simple Comment Editing** that allows anonymous users to edit their own comments within a certain period of time. This also applies to users that don't have the privileges to edit comments in the dashboard. To install the **Simple Comment Editing** plugin:

1. Go to **Plugins** > **Add New**
2. Type in "Simple Comment Editing" and click **Search Plugins**
3. Install and activate the plugin

Once the plugin is activated, users can edit their comments for up to five minutes after posting.

Hot tip

It is not advised to edit user comments without the permission of the author. The email address of the comment author is shown along with the comment so that you can get in contact with them easily.

Akismet & Spam

When it comes to spam, there is a good plugin called Akismet that filters out spam for you. Akismet will come pre-installed with WordPress, but you will need to set it up before it works.

1. Go to **akismet.com** and register for an application programming interface (API) key

2. Go to **Plugins** and click **Settings** under **Akismet Anti-Spam** to enter your key

Enter your API key
Connect with API key

Once you have an Akismet account set up, your website will then be automatically be protected from spam, so if someone comments and the system recognizes it as spam, then it will automatically be placed in the Spam folder.

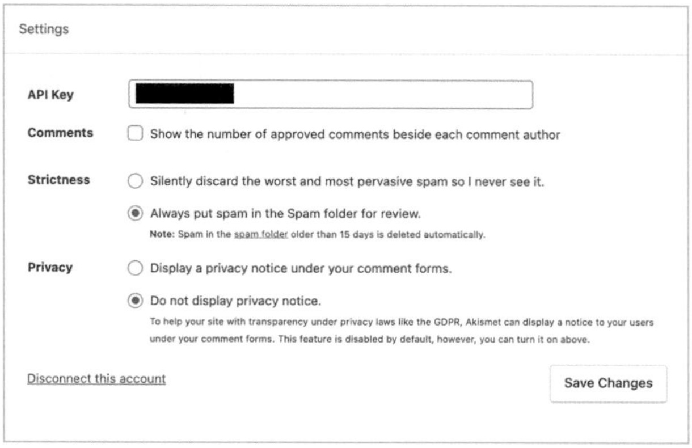
Settings
API Key
[redacted]
Comments
Show the number of approved comments beside each comment author
Strictness
Silently discard the worst and most pervasive spam so I never see it.
Always put spam in the Spam folder for review.
Note: Spam in the spam folder older than 15 days is deleted automatically.
Privacy
Display a privacy notice under your comment forms.
Do not display privacy notice.
To help your site with transparency under privacy laws like the GDPR, Akismet can display a notice to your users under your comment forms. This feature is disabled by default, however, you can turn it on above.
Disconnect this account
Save Changes

You can choose whether or not to discard spam without seeing it, or put it in the Spam folder for review.

There is also a **Check for Spam** button in the **Comments** section that you can press to check through all your current comments.

Comments
All (1) | Mine (0) | Pending (1) | Approved (0) | Spam (0) | Trash (9)
Bulk actions
Apply
All comment types
Filter
Check for Spam
Author
Comment
David Smith
david.smith@wordpresseagl e.com
This has been very helpful in making a decision.

Beware

If **JetPack** has been installed, you might find Akismet under **Jetpack** > **Akismet Anti-Spam**. (JetPack is a plugin that provides features like site stats, high-speed content delivery network (CDN) for images, related posts, downtime monitoring, brute-force attack protection, automated sharing to social networks, sidebar customization and SEO tools. Sometimes, it is pre-installed by web hosts.)

Hot tip

In this day and age, you definitely need a plugin to sort through your spam. Akismet is a great choice and will save you a lot of time.

Forums

Thanks to WordPress plugins, it is possible to create online discussion forums with WordPress. Let's take a look at how you can integrate forums onto your WordPress website using a plugin called **bbPress**.

1. From the dashboard go to **Plugins** > **Add New**
2. Search for a plugin called "bbPress", and install it

bbPress
Install Now
bbPress is forum software for WordPress.
More Details
By The bbPress Contributors
(320)
Last Updated: 8 months ago
200,000+ Active Installations
Untested with your version of WordPress

Don't forget

Try to create forums relevant to your website. Users will want to talk about issues relevant to your website content.

Setting up forums

Now that you have the plugin installed, you are ready to start creating forums for your website. You will notice down the left-hand side of the dashboard there are three options that have been added (**Forums**, **Topics**, **Replies**).

Forums
Topics
Replies

Forums: This is where you can add new forums and manage any existing ones.

Topics: This lists topics in every category. You can also add topics here or manage topic tags.

Replies: Here, you can manage replies to every post in each forum.

...cont'd

1. To create a new forum, click the **Forums** link

2. Click the **Add New** button

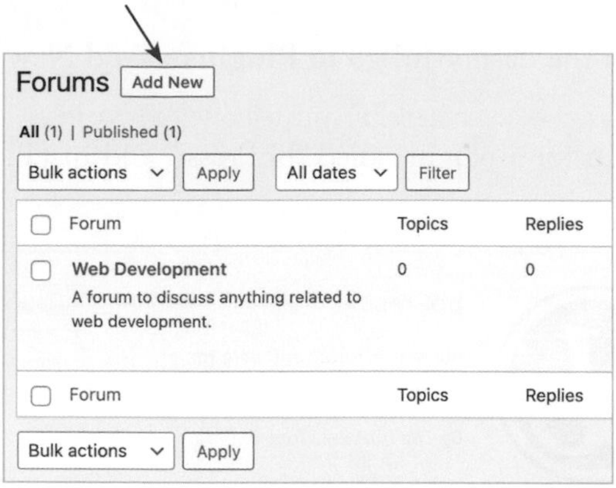
Forums
Add New
All (1) | Published (1)
Bulk actions
Apply
All dates
Filter
Forum
Topics
Replies
Web Development
A forum to discuss anything related to web development.
0
0
Forum
Topics
Replies
Bulk actions
Apply

3. This process is as simple as setting up a regular post or page. Enter a title for the forum and a description

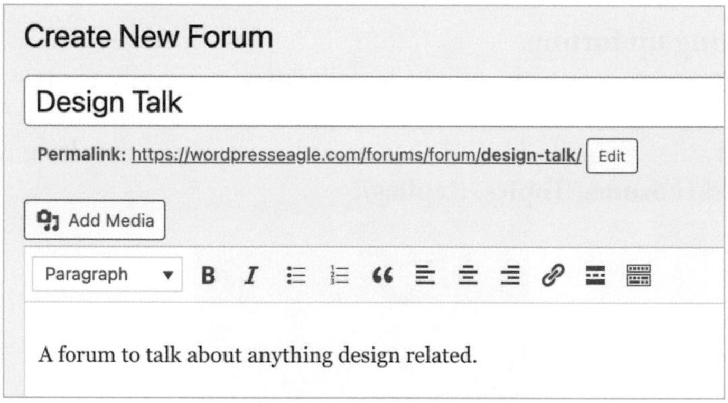
Create New Forum
Design Talk
Permalink: https://wordpresseagle.com/forums/forum/design-talk/
Edit
Add Media
Paragraph
A forum to talk about anything design related.

4. The last thing to do before you publish is to set the forum attributes

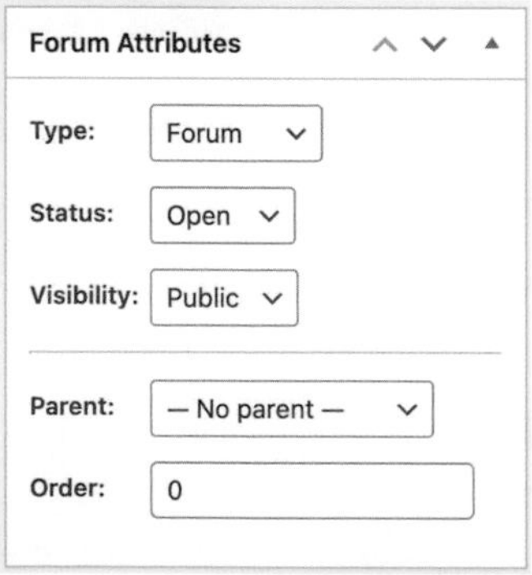
Forum Attributes
Type:
Forum
Status:
Open
Visibility:
Public
Parent:
— No parent —
Order:
0

Type: Set as Forum or Category.

Status: Here, you can set the forum as Open or Closed. If the forum is open, then people can post new topics. If the forum is closed then no new topics can be posted, although old topics will still be there to read.

Visibility: You can set whether you want the forum to be Public, Private or Hidden.

Parent: If your forum is a sub forum, then set the parent here.

Order: This is where you set the forum order. This determines the running order of forums down the page.

5. Click **Publish** to set up the forum

You will see when you go to the forums page (**http://www.yourdomain.com/forums/**) that your forum is now displayed.

Forum
Design Talk
A forum to talk about anything design related.

If you first click on your forum, you will see that the forum is empty. This is because no topics have been set up yet by you or any of your users. You can create topics from the live site itself or from the backend, which we will cover on pages 127-128.

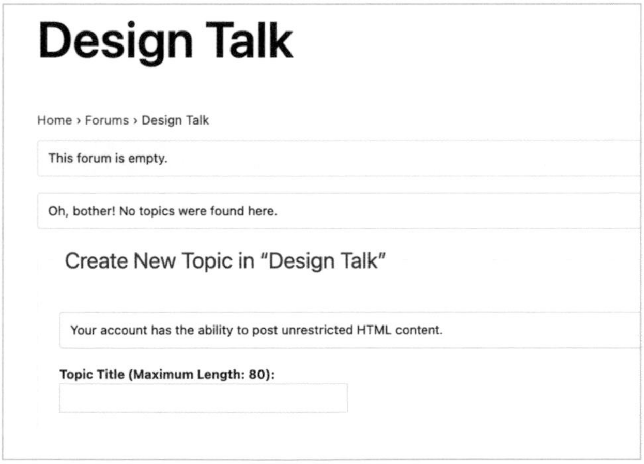
Design Talk
Home › Forums › Design Talk
This forum is empty.
Oh, bother! No topics were found here.
Create New Topic in "Design Talk"
Your account has the ability to post unrestricted HTML content.
Topic Title (Maximum Length: 80):

Beware

Try to keep advertising forums to more active members, or you could end up with visitors spamming your forums.

Editing existing forums

It's very simple to edit existing forums, so if you need to change the title, description, status, visibility, etc. then you can do it very easily.

1. Select **Forums** > **All Forums** from the dashboard. This will display all forums you have created

Bulk actions
Apply
All dates
Filter
Forum
Design Talk
A forum to talk about anything design related.

2. Click on a forum you wish to edit. This will bring up a page similar to when you created a forum. You can now make your changes. Don't forget to save your changes

Edit Forum
Add New
Design Talk
Permalink: https://wordpresseagle.com/forums/forum/design-talk/
Edit
Add Media
Paragraph
A forum to talk about anything design related.

One thing to bear in mind when having a forum on your website is that you will need to make sure users can register on your website.

Make sure you have checked the **Membership** box under the **Settings** > **General** page.

Membership
Anyone can register

Adding topics

You may wish to let your users set up topics on your forum, but you can also create them yourself. You can do this from the frontend as you will already be logged in. However, let's go through the process of adding a topic from the backend.

1. Click **Topics** from the dashboard. This will display all the current topics in your forum

2. To add a new topic, click **Add New**

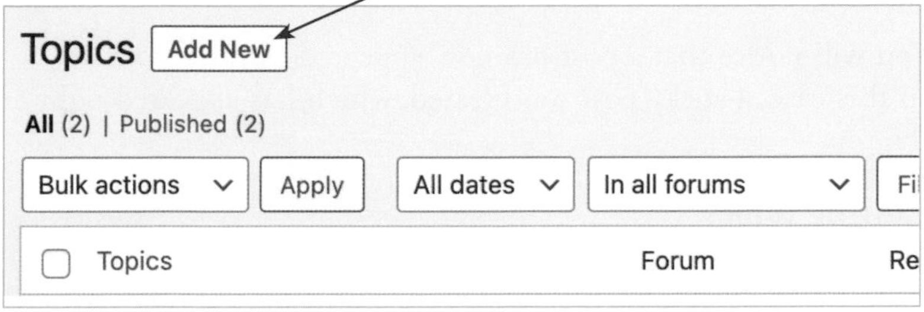
Topics
Add New
All (2) | Published (2)
Bulk actions
Apply
All dates
In all forums
Topics
Forum

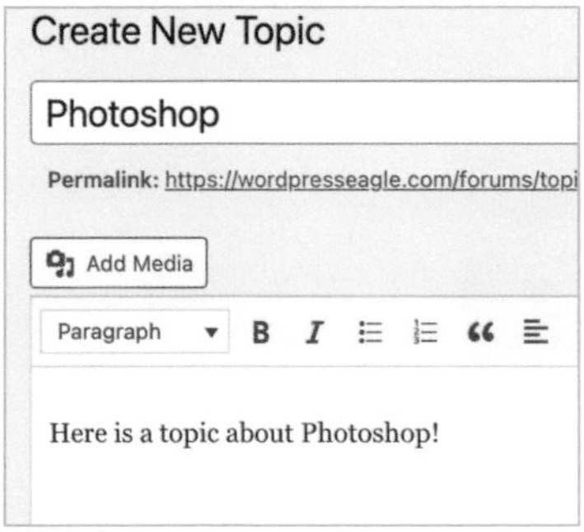
Create New Topic
Photoshop
Permalink: https://wordpresseagle.com/forums/topi
Add Media
Paragraph
Here is a topic about Photoshop!

3. Just like you did when you created a forum, you will need to create a topic name and a description

4. You will also need to set topic attributes

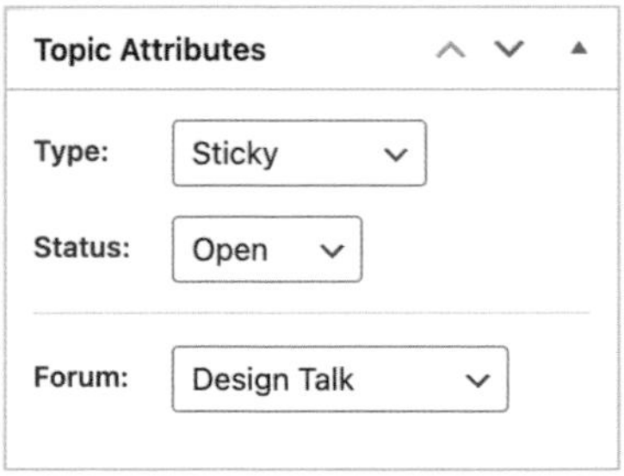
Topic Attributes
Type:
Sticky
Status:
Open
Forum:
Design Talk

Type: This could be a regular topic, or you could use **Sticky,** which appears at the top of that particular forum, or **Super sticky**, which stays at the top of all forums.
Status: You will need to set this to **Open**.
Forum: Select which forum you want the topic to appear in.

Hot tip

Try to add a couple of topics to your forum before it goes live. This way, it gives visitors something to talk about and will encourage them to post.

...cont'd

5. Click **Publish** to make your topic live

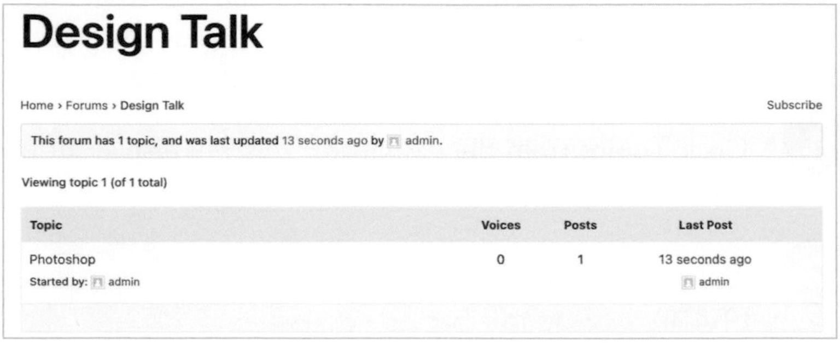
Design Talk
Home › Forums › Design Talk
Subscribe
This forum has 1 topic, and was last updated 13 seconds ago by admin.
Viewing topic 1 (of 1 total)
Topic
Voices
Posts
Last Post
Photoshop
Started by: admin
0
1
13 seconds ago
admin

You will notice that a post has now appeared in the forum. In this case, a sticky post was created, which has appeared right at the top.

Editing topics

When users add topics on your website, you can easily monitor them by going to **Topics** > **All Topics** and going through each one. You are still able to change the status of each individual topic that a user adds.

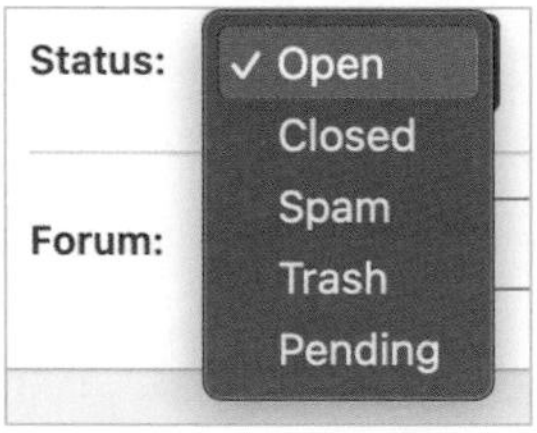
Status:
✓ Open
Closed
Spam
Trash
Pending
Forum:

Replies

The **Replies** section is a good way to monitor replies to topics on your forums. All your replies will appear in the **Replies** > **All Replies** section, which appears in the dashboard.

You can add replies yourself from here, although it is probably best to do this from an individual post on the live site. It also makes things less complex.

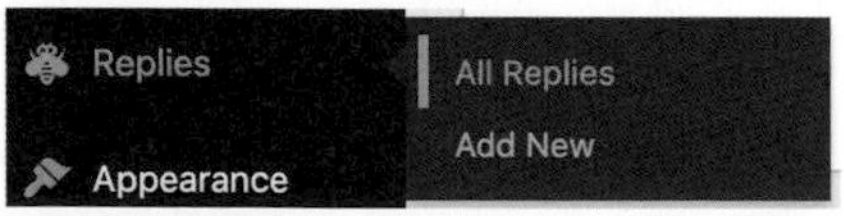
Replies
Appearance
All Replies
Add New

Contact Forms

Contact forms have to be the most vital element when it comes to communicating with your website visitors. Every website should have one, whether it's a blog or a business website. WordPress has some great plugins to set contact forms up on your website. We'll now illustrate one called **Contact Form 7**. Let's get started.

Don't forget

Make sure your contact page and contact form can be easily spotted by visitors.

1. Go to **Plugins** > **Add New** from the dashboard

2. Search for "Contact Form 7", then install and activate the plugin

3. Once installed, you should have a new **Contact** link on the left-hand side of your dashboard. Go ahead and click this

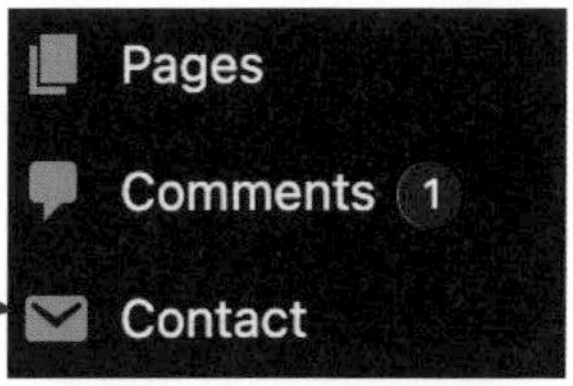

4. Click **Add New** from the top of the page

5. Choose a name for the contact form

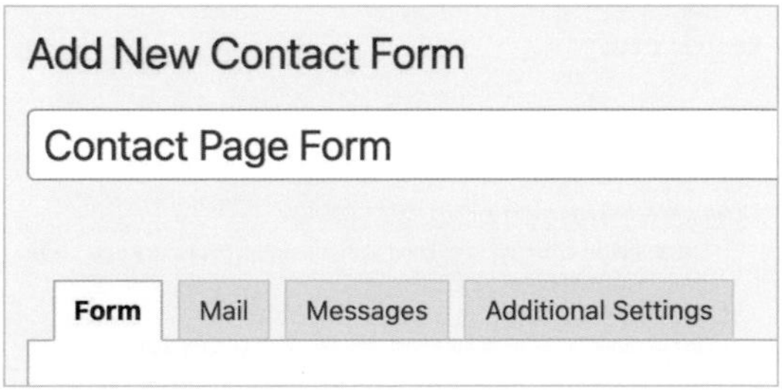

You will notice there are four tabs just under the title. Underneath the **Form** tab, you will notice a default form has already been set up for you.

...cont'd

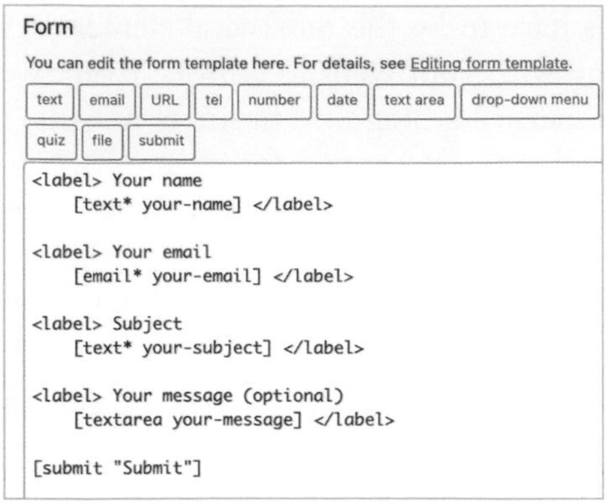
Form
You can edit the form template here. For details, see Editing form template.
text
email
URL
tel
number
date
text area
drop-down menu
quiz
file
submit
<label> Your name
[text* your-name] </label>
<label> Your email
[email* your-email] </label>
<label> Subject
[text* your-subject] </label>
<label> Your message (optional)
[textarea your-message] </label>
[submit "Submit"]

Hot tip

Try not to add too many fields to your form. Most people use name, email, phone and message.

6. Add your own field names between <p> </p> or leave the default ones in place if you are happy

7. **Mail**: The mail settings will be filled out already. Make sure the **To** field is filled out with the address you want mail sent to

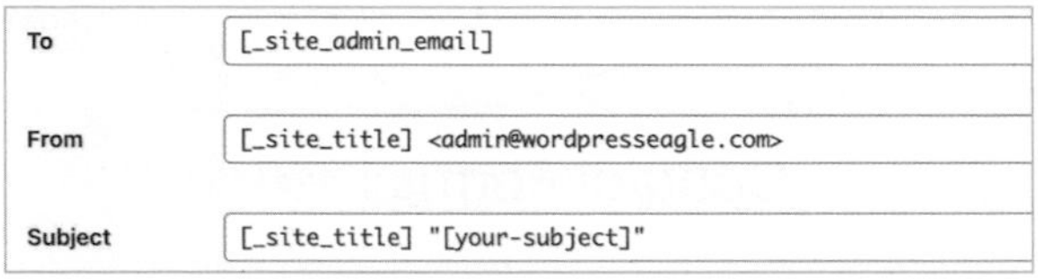
To
[_site_admin_email]
From
[_site_title] <admin@wordpresseagle.com>
Subject
[_site_title] "[your-subject]"

8. **Messages**: This section is used to set up some default messages, if a message contains errors or if messages fail to send, etc.

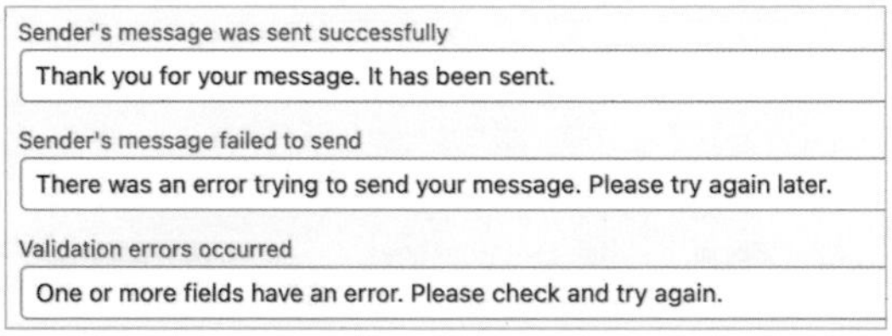
Sender's message was sent successfully
Thank you for your message. It has been sent.
Sender's message failed to send
There was an error trying to send your message. Please try again later.
Validation errors occurred
One or more fields have an error. Please check and try again.

Beware

Some emails may come through to your spam folder. This is very much dependent on your email provider.

9. To finish, you will need to click **Save**. You will be given a shortcode that you will need to use when adding a shortcode block to your page. It will look something like the one below

Copy this shortcode and paste it into your post, page, or text widget content:
[contact-form-7 id="15" title="Contact Form"]

Website Translation

There may come a time where you want to expand your reach. Translating your website is a great way of reaching new readers or customers. There are various plugins that can help you make your website multilingual. One of the best ones is called **GTranslate**. It has three versions – **Free**, **Pro**, and **Enterprise**. Upon installation of the plugin, your website will automatically be translated, making it simple and easy not just for you but also for your readers.

Installing GTranslate

1. Visit **www.gtranslate.io** and download the plugin

2. Go to **Plugins** > **Add New** from the WordPress dashboard

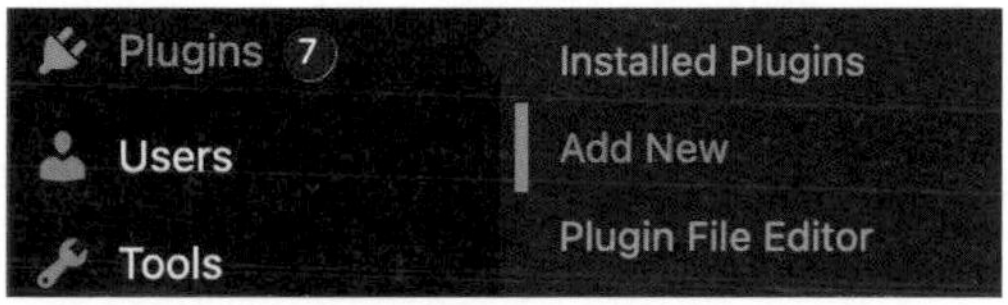

3. Select **Upload Plugin** at the top

4. As you have done before, select **Choose File** and select the zip file that you downloaded from the GTranslate website

...cont'd

5. Click **Install Now**. Remember to activate the plugin so you can get it working straight away

Configuring GTranslate

1. Go to **Settings** > **GTranslate** from the WordPress dashboard

Permalinks
Privacy
GTranslate

2. You will now be presented with a number of options with regard to how you want the translation to function

Widget look:
Nice dropdown with flags
Translate from:
English

You will also see a preview of your GTranslate widget:

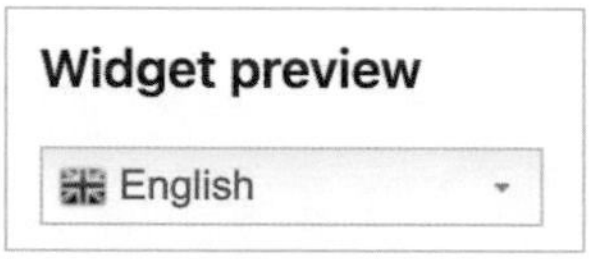
Widget preview
English

You can choose from a number of different looks, flag languages, languages to translate from, etc. You will also find your widget code here.

3. When you are happy, click **Save Changes** at the bottom of the page

Save Changes

Inserting GTranslate using widgets

There are a number of ways you can insert GTranslate into your website or blog. The best way is by inserting it as a widget. When you installed the GTranslate plugin, it automatically created a widget, ready for you to insert into a particular area on your web page.

1. Head over to **Appearance** > **Widgets** from the WordPress dashboard

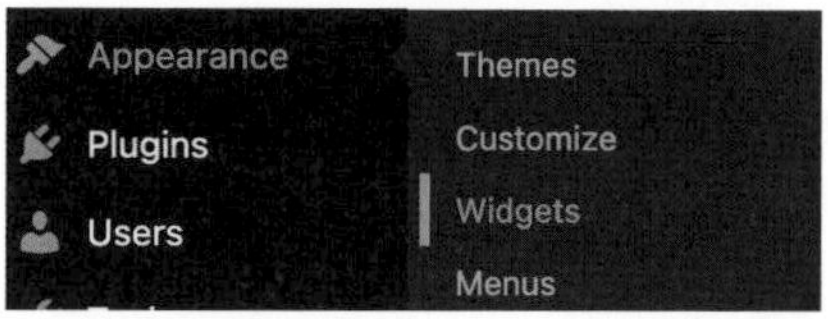

2. Search for the **GTranslate** widget and then drag it into your preferred sidebar

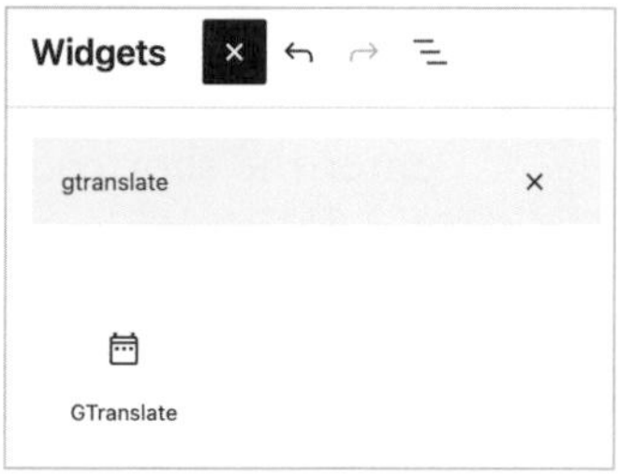

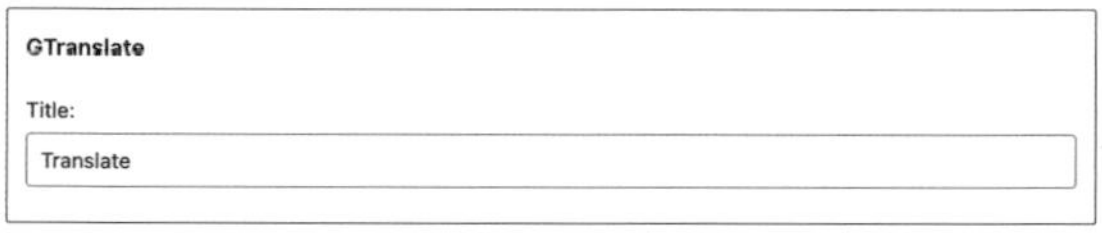

3. Remember to set a title, and then click **Save**

Your widget should now appear on your live website, and the translation should work when you change language. You can make adjustments to the settings at any time.

If you need help with widget setup, then refer back to pages 39-41.

...cont'd

You can also add GTranslate to your PHP template files and to individual pages.

Inserting GTranslate inside pages or posts

1. Head over to one of your pages or posts by selecting **Pages** or **Posts** from your dashboard and picking a page or post where you want to insert the GTranslate widget

2. Now, insert a shortcode block using the + button and enter the shortcode [gtranslate]. Click **Update** when you are finished

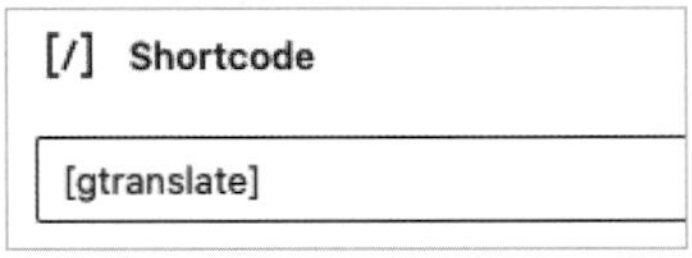

Inserting GTranslate into your PHP files

1. Go to **Appearance** > **Theme File Editor** from your WordPress dashboard

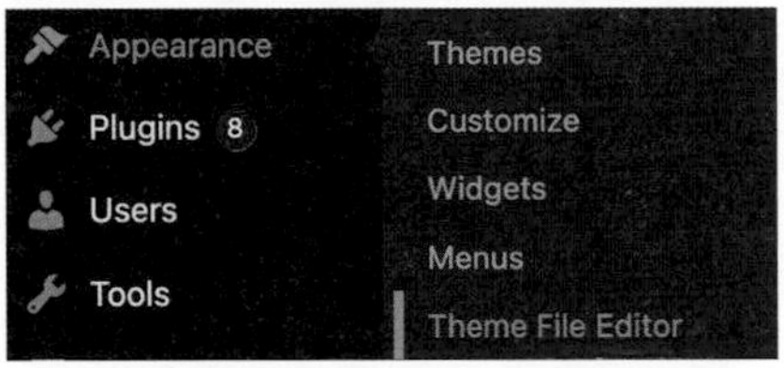

2. Select a template file (for example, header.php) and insert this piece of PHP code:
<?php echo do_shortcode('[gtranslate]'); ?>

```
<?php echo do_shortcode('[gtranslate]'); ?>
```

Beware

Not all themes will allow you access to the Editor area, so you may need to access the PHP file through FTP. You will be introduced to accessing your files through FTP on pages 163-165.

Membership Levels

You may want to set up membership levels for your users. For example, you may have an educational website where users can download content, or a premium area for paid users. There is a fantastic plugin for WordPress called **Paid Memberships Pro** that can help you with this.

Installing Paid Memberships Pro

1. From your dashboard select **Plugins** > **Add New**
2. Search for "Paid Memberships Pro" and click **Install Now**

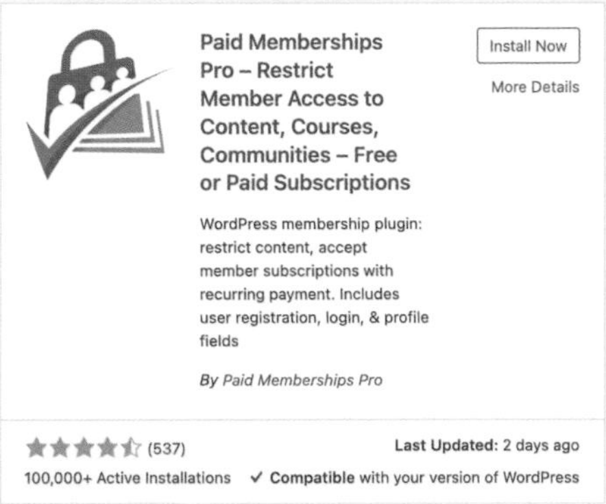

3. Activate your plugin after installation

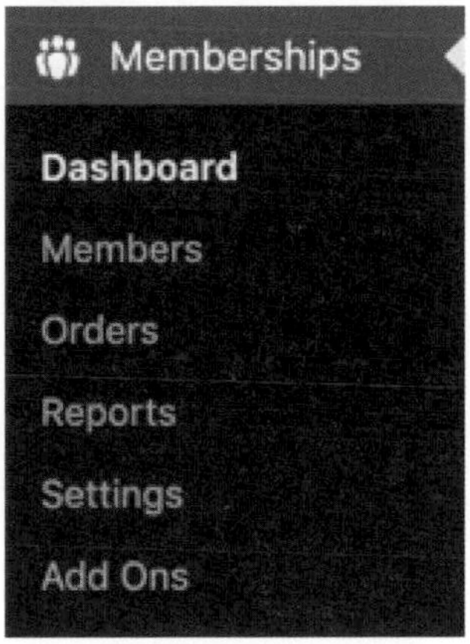

4. You should see on the dashboard that there is now an option called **Memberships**, as shown to the left. There are quite a few options here. Begin by selecting **Dashboard**

You will now be directed to the main section of the plugin, where you can run through the initial setup and view membership stats, sales and revenue, recent orders, etc. Let's begin by adding a membership level.

Adding a new membership level

1. Select **Create a Membership Level** from under **Initial Setup**

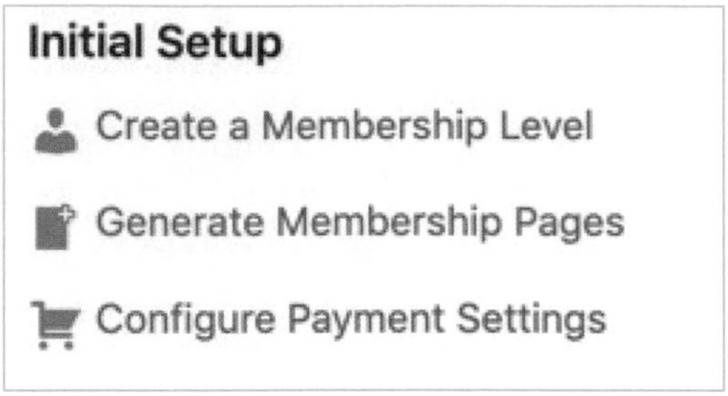
Initial Setup
Create a Membership Level
Generate Membership Pages
Configure Payment Settings

2. Set up your membership level using the following options:

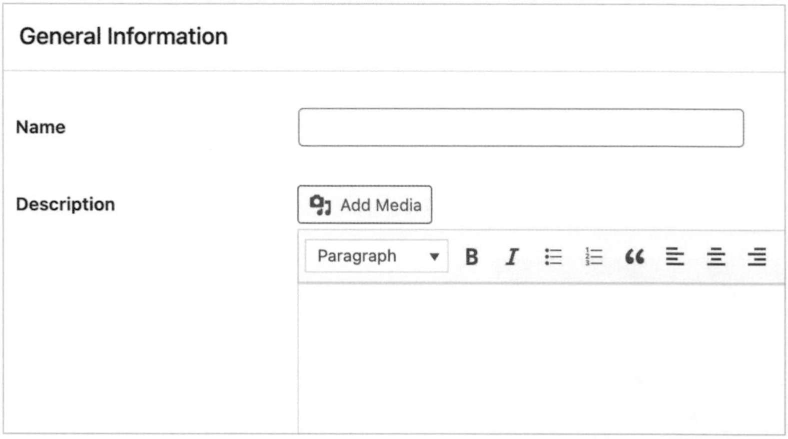
General Information
Name
Description
Add Media
Paragraph

Name: Enter a name for your membership level – for example, Basic Membership.

Description: Enter a description – this needs to be something that the user will understand.

Confirmation Message: This is a message that will display to the user upon signup.

Initial Payment: This amount is what the user will pay at signup.

Recurring Subscription: Choose whether or not the subscription is recurring.

Hot tip

Keep the descriptions simple and easy for the visitor to understand. They will want to know exactly what they are signing up for.

Disable New Signups: At first, you don't need to check this box. You would only check it if you wanted to disable new signups to this particular membership.

Membership Expiration: Check this box to disable access when membership expires.

Content Settings/Categories: Here, you can select which categories your membership covers. For example, you may have a **Design** membership that only **Design** members can access.

3. Finish your settings by clicking **Save Level**, which will complete the setup

Setting up pages for members only

When you created your membership, you were able to set up post categories for particular memberships, but you also need to be able to set up pages to be visible only to particular memberships. Thankfully, this is a very easy step, and only takes a short time to set up.

1. Open up a page you have already created
2. On the right-hand side, you will see a box that will allow you to select the appropriate membership

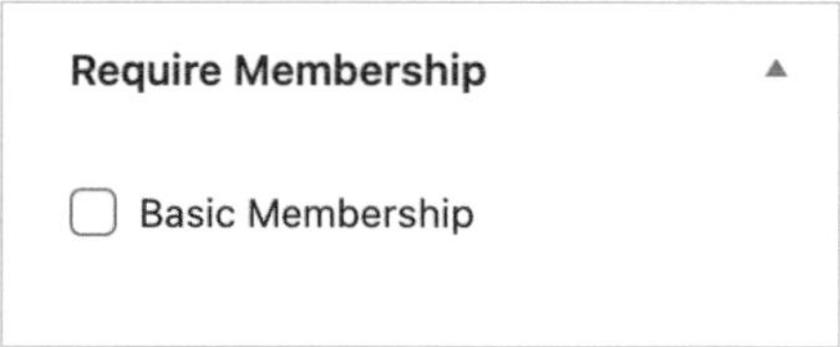
Require Membership
Basic Membership

3. Check the box for that particular membership. In the example above, you would check the **Basic Membership** box, as you only want members who have basic membership to access the page
4. Update or publish the page. This will make sure that only those particular members can access that page

Hot tip

Create test accounts so that you can make sure that users can view your content with the correct membership.

...cont'd

Page settings

You now need to create and assign various WordPress pages for your **Paid Memberships Pro** pages. These are things like account pages where the user can edit their details; checkout pages for paid membership; a page where the user can cancel their account; plus many more. The plugin can automatically create these pages for you, and automatically assign them.

1. Go to **Memberships** > **Settings** from the dashboard

2. Go to **Pages** from the submenu

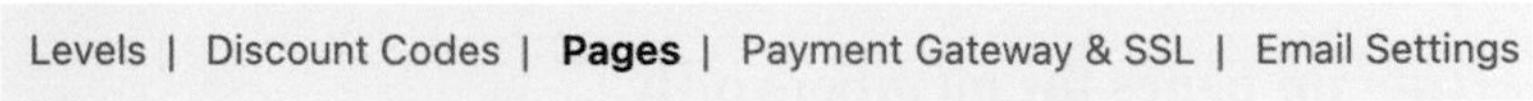

3. Click on the **Generate Pages For Me** button. This will automatically set up the necessary pages

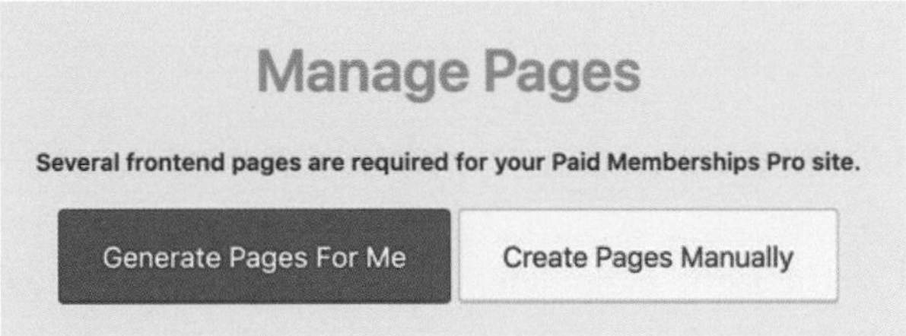

If you go to your live website, there should be an option called **Membership Account** in the main menu. This is a page that was automatically generated by **Paid Memberships Pro**. This is where the user can sign up for any of the memberships you created.

If the **Membership Account** page is not in your menu, be sure to add it yourself. See pages 37-38 for how to add pages to the menu.

...cont'd

On the **Membership Account** page, the user can then select which membership level they wish to sign up for.

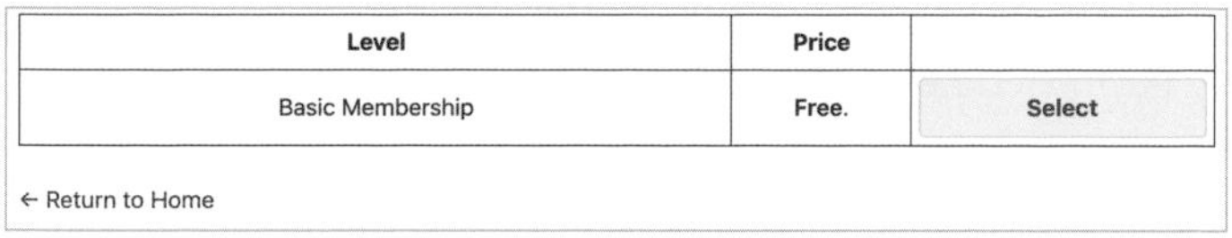
Level
Price
Basic Membership
Free.
Select
← Return to Home

The user can then fill out the fields to sign up. If they already have an account they can also choose to sign in.

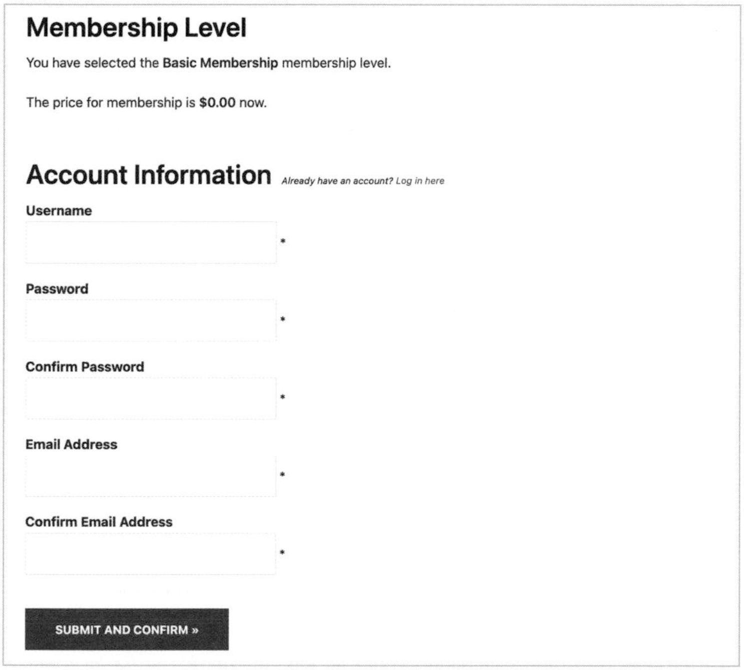
Membership Level
You have selected the Basic Membership membership level.
The price for membership is $0.00 now.
Account Information
Already have an account? Log in here
Username
Password
Confirm Password
Email Address
Confirm Email Address
SUBMIT AND CONFIRM »

The user can then view their account by selecting that same **Membership Account** link in their menu. This will allow them to change their current membership, change their password and view invoices if they have paid for membership.

My Account
James Smith
Username: JamesSmith
Email: [redacted]
Edit Profile | Change Password | Log Out

Don't forget

When the user signs up for a membership, they will automatically get a welcome email.

Payment settings

If you wish to receive payments for membership, then you will need to configure the payment settings.

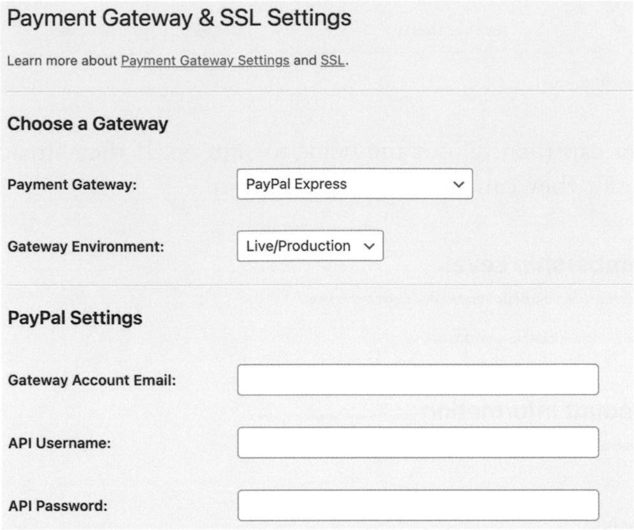
Payment Gateway & SSL Settings
Learn more about Payment Gateway Settings and SSL.
Choose a Gateway
Payment Gateway:
PayPal Express
Gateway Environment:
Live/Production
PayPal Settings
Gateway Account Email:
API Username:
API Password:

Beware

You will need to set **Gateway Environment** to **Live/Production**, or all transactions will be test payments.

To set up your payment options:

1. Go to **Memberships** > **Settings** and select **Payment Gateway & SSL** from the submenu

The setup options will depend on which payment methods you decide to accept. PayPal is one of the best choices for online payments. You will need to set up your API details (**API Username**, **API Password**, **API Signature**) by going to the PayPal developer website: **https://developer.paypal.com**

Email settings

1. Go to **Memberships** > **Settings** and select **Email** from the submenu

This section is self-explanatory. It will set up various email settings – for example, you may want to receive a new email when a user cancels their account or when a user changes their membership level.

10 Tips & Tricks

This chapter will take you through some of the techniques to enhance your WordPress websites even further.

Google Analytics

Google Analytics is a great way of gaining detailed statistics about your website visitors. This could be extremely useful, especially if you want to find out how many daily visitors you are getting, or to monitor where the visitors to your site are coming from.

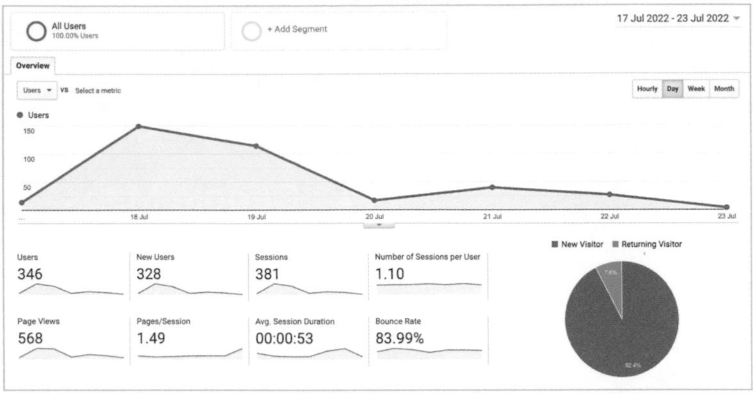

What Google Analytics can tell me

- How many visitors your website has had (hourly, daily, weekly, and monthly).
- Where your visitors are coming from.
- Web browsers that your visitors are using.
- Keywords used by your visitors in search engines to get to your website.

Signing up for Google Analytics

First of all, you need to sign up to Google Analytics.

1. Go to **www.google.com/analytics/** and follow the on-screen instructions to set up your website
2. Click **Admin** in the bottom left

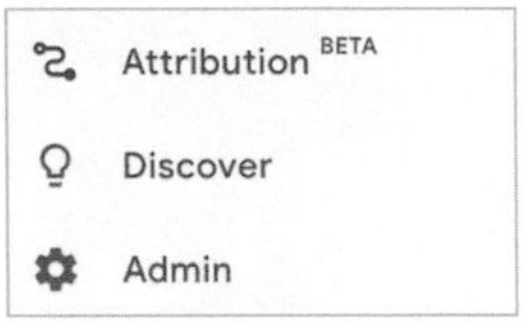

3. Click **Tracking Code** underneath **Tracking Info**

Don't forget

You will need a Google account to set up **Google Analytics**. You can get one here: **https://accounts.google.com/signup/v2/webcreateaccount**

You will be given a code that you can enter into pages on your website:

```
<!-- Global site tag (gtag.js) - Google Analytics -->
<script async src="https://www.googletagmanager.com
<script>
  window.dataLayer = window.dataLayer || [];
  function gtag(){dataLayer.push(arguments);}
  gtag('js', new Date());

  gtag('config', '[redacted]');
</script>
```

To get **Google Analytics** onto your WordPress website so that you can start gaining valuable statistics:

1. Copy your code from the screen above

2. From your dashboard go to **Appearance** > **Theme File Editor**

3. Select **Header.php** from the right-hand side. The code window will now display **header.php** on the left-hand side

4. Place the **Google Analytics** code that you just copied and place it before the closing **</head>** tag

```
    <?php wp_head(); ?>

    <!-- Global site tag (gtag.js) - Google Anal
    <script async src="https://www.googletagmana
    <script>
    window.dataLayer = window.dataLayer || [];
    function gtag(){dataLayer.push(arguments);}
    gtag('js', new Date());

    gtag('config', '[redacted]');
    </script>

</head>

<body <?php body_class(); ?>>
```

Before closing **</head>** tag

5. Click **Save Changes**. Analytics will now start tracking activity. It will take 24 hours before your **Google Analytics** dashboard will display any activity

Hot tip

Google Analytics is a key tool for businesses, as it can show you where your customers are coming from and even tell you which marketing strategies are working out the best.

Google Maps

Having a website map is useful if you want to show customers where your business is located. **WP Go Maps** is a free plugin that gives you many options for your map.

1. Go to **Plugins** > **Add New**
2. Type in "WP Go Maps" and click **Search Plugins**

3. Click **Install Now** under **WP Go Maps**. Don't forget to activate it once it's been installed

You should see an option called **Maps** on the left-hand side of the dashboard.

4. Click **Maps** > **Maps**

There should be one map already created called **New Map.** This is where your list of maps will appear.

5. Click the **Edit** button on the same line as **My first map**

ID	Title	Width	Height	Type	Action
1	My first map	100%	400px	Roadmap	Edit

Hot tip

WP Go Maps can use **Google Maps** or **Open Layer** as the map engine; however, this section uses **Google Maps**.

Don't forget

The plugin will prompt you for a Google Maps JavaScript API key. You can get this by following the instructions here: **https://developers.google.com/maps/documentation/javascript/get-api-key**

From here, you will be presented with some map options:

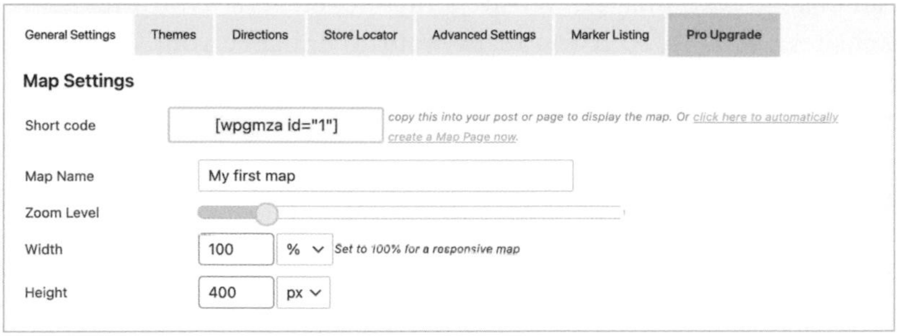
General Settings
Themes
Directions
Store Locator
Advanced Settings
Marker Listing
Pro Upgrade
Map Settings
Short code
[wpgmza id="1"]
copy this into your post or page to display the map. Or click here to automatically create a Map Page now.
Map Name
My first map
Zoom Level
Width
100
%
Set to 100% for a responsive map
Height
400
px

Short code: You can copy and paste this onto one of your posts or pages to display the map.

Map Name: Choose a name for the map.

Width/Height: Here, you can set your map width and height.

Map Alignment: Left, Center, or Right.

Map type: Here, you can select whether or not the map displays the road, a satellite image, or hybrid or terrain views.

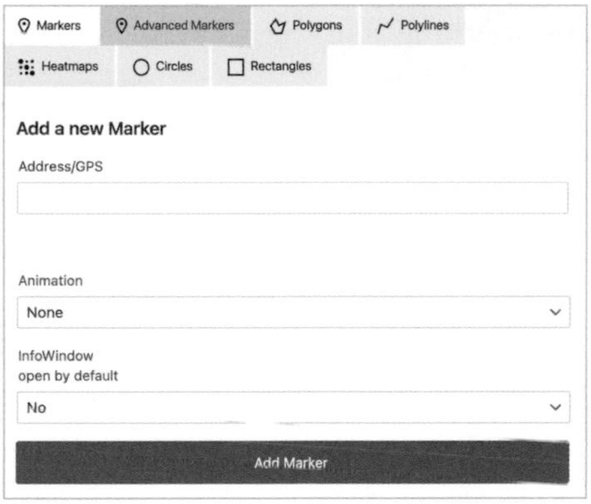
Markers
Advanced Markers
Polygons
Polylines
Heatmaps
Circles
Rectangles
Add a new Marker
Address/GPS
Animation
None
InfoWindow
open by default
No
Add Marker

6. Enter the address where you want your marker to be placed. Then, click **Add Marker**. The preview should update

7. You can now add the map to your post or page using the WP Go Maps block

WP Go Maps

Hot tip

You might be prompted to select a map engine. Make sure you select **Google Maps**.

Don't forget

Remember to save your map after making changes.

Hot tip

You can also use the shortcode to add your map to a post or page.

Using CSS

Using CSS is a great way to alter the way your website looks. You can change text, images, website structure, etc. All WordPress websites use CSS, so if you really want to enhance your website, then this is a great tool. Let's have a look at ways that CSS can help you.

Hot tip

CSS is a style language that defines the layout of web pages. It covers things like fonts, colors, margins, backgrounds, widths, etc.

1. First, download or open the Google Chrome web browser (**www.google.com/chrome**)

2. Go to your WordPress website and right-click on one of your elements – in this case, a post title. Then, click on **Inspect element** from the drop-down list

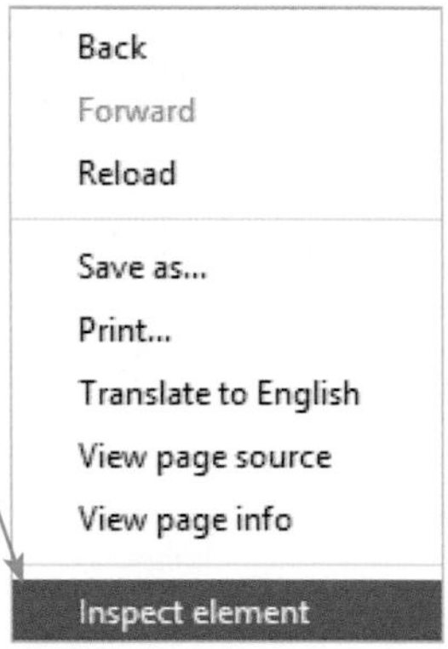

An Element Inspector will appear at the bottom or side of the page, which looks something like the one shown below:

Beware

Do not mess with CSS unless you know what you're doing. Learn more with **CSS in easy steps**!

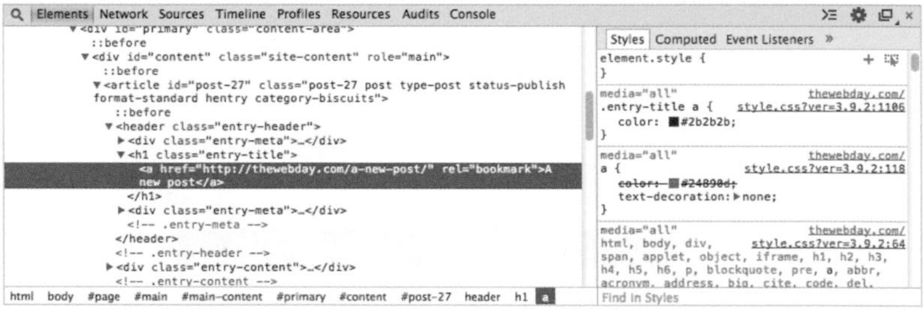

Hot tip

Using the **Inspect Element** tool is a great way of understanding CSS. It's also a good way to tweak the code to see how it will work before adding it to a stylesheet.

The box on the right-hand side or at the bottom displays attributes for that particular element. In this case, it's the title for one of the posts. This element is called **.entry-title a**

```
media="all"                   thewebday.com/
.entry-title a {   style.css?ver=3.9.2:1106
   color: ■#2b2b2b;
}
```

You can change the code here to get a preview of what the website would look like if you were to change the CSS code.

Change the text color to red and change the font size to 38px by clicking in the Element Inspector and adding the following lines:

color: red;
font-size: 38px;

```
media="all"                thewebday.com/
.entry-title a {     style.css?ver=3.9.2:1106
   color: ■red;
   font-size: 38px;
}
```

You will now notice that the live website provides a preview of how it looks. So, the text now looks like this:

HELLO WORLD!

This is only a preview and doesn't change the live site. To do this, you need to go into the editor and change the code from there.

1. Go to **Appearance** > **Theme File Editor**

2. Select **Stylesheet (style.css)** from the right-hand side

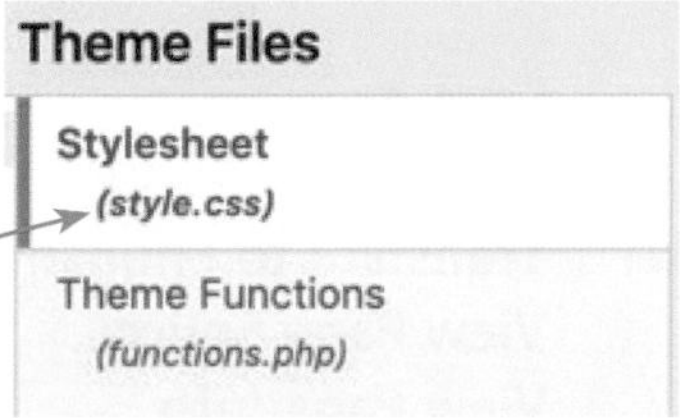
Theme Files
Stylesheet
(style.css)
Theme Functions
(functions.php)

```
.entry-title {
    font-size: 33px;
    font-weight: 300;
    line-height: 1.0909090909;
    margin-bottom: 12px;
    margin: 0 0 12px 0;
    text-transform: uppercase;
}

.entry-title a {
    color: #2b2b2b;
}

.entry-title a:hover {
    color: #41a62a;
}
```

The code for the stylesheet will now appear on the left-hand side. You need to find the element name. In this case, it would be **.entry-title a**

Don't forget

Your elements will all have different names. It all depends on what the theme developer has named them.

Don't forget

Developing your skills in CSS is a fantastic way to enhance your website. It is key if you are looking to start out as a developer.

...cont'd

3. Now, type in the changes you want to make. When you have finished, click **Update File** and the changes will appear live on your website

```
    line-height: 1.0909090909;
    margin-bottom: 12px;
    margin: 0 0 12px 0;
    text-transform: uppercase;
}

.entry-title a {
    color: red;
    font-size: 38px;
}

.entry-title a:hover {
```

Element code

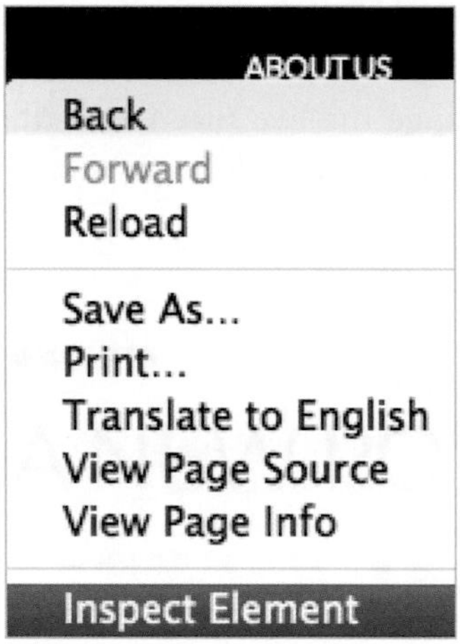
ABOUT US
Back
Forward
Reload
Save As...
Print...
Translate to English
View Page Source
View Page Info
Inspect Element

Let's try one more example.

1. Right click-on the header menu on the website and click **Inspect Element**

Once again, a menu will appear at the bottom of the page, along with the selected element on the right-hand side.

```
.header-main {      style.css?ver=3.9.2:3352

}
```

2. To make the menu color green, you would add the code **background-color: green;** to the element, as shown below:

.header-main {
background-color: green;
}

The website preview in the browser has changed – it is now green. Next, go back to **Appearance** > **Editor** and change the code for that element in the stylesheet (style.css) file.

There is a lot more to CSS than this. You can change all kinds of elements, but this is just to help you to understand the process behind the design.

Some basic samples of CSS code

Below are some samples of CSS and their meanings. You can try them out on your own elements.

text-transform: uppercase;
This code will transform the text into uppercase. For example, if your text was "hello", then it would be changed to "HELLO".

border-bottom: thick dotted black;
This code will add a black dotted border at the bottom of the element. You can use border-top, border-left, etc. too.

float: left;
Using the float element will specify if the box floats to the left or the right. In this instance, it's to the left. You can also choose "none", which means the box will not float.

padding-right: 50px;
Padding will clear the area around that particular element. In this instance, it will add a 50px area to the right of the element. You can also use padding-left, padding-top, etc.

background-image: url("biscuit.png");
You can add background images using the code above. The image is usually repeated by default until the element is covered.

font-family: "Times New Roman", Georgia, Serif;
This will specify the font for a particular element. If the first font is not available, it will use the next one in the list.

Hot tip

Why not check out **CSS in easy steps** to learn more about CSS?

Newsletter Forms

If you'd like to send out a newsletter by email to your readers or customers, then adding a newsletter signup form to your website is a really good idea. Any new readers that visit your website can then easily sign up. Sending out newsletters is a good way of keeping visitors coming back to your website. **Mailchimp** is a great way to create and distribute newsletters, and you don't need to have any technical knowledge.

Hot tip

Mailchimp is a very simple tool to use to create email campaigns. It does not require any coding knowledge and integrates nicely into WordPress.

To create a signup form on your website, so that every time someone subscribes it will add them to one of your **Mailchimp** lists:

1. Create a **Mailchimp** account if you don't already have one. You can sign up at **www.mailchimp.com**

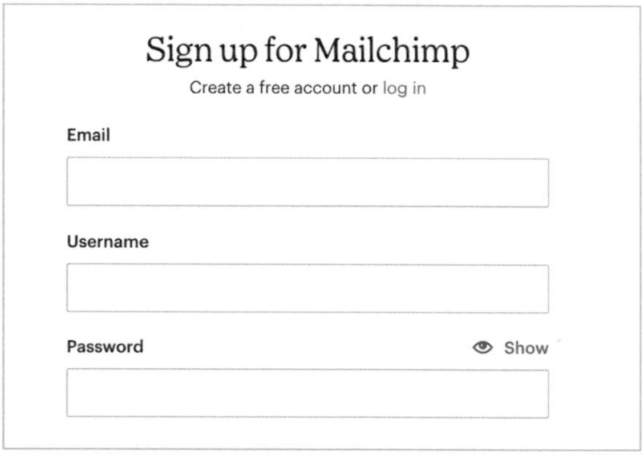

2. Go to **Plugins** > **Install New** and search for **Easy Forms for Mailchimp**

3. Install and activate the plugin

...cont'd

Configuring Easy Forms for Mailchimp

You will notice a new link on the left-hand side of the dashboard called **Easy Forms**.

1 Click **Easy Forms** > **Settings**

Easy Forms
Opt-in Forms
Mailing Lists
Settings
Support
Add-Ons

2 You will be presented with this form

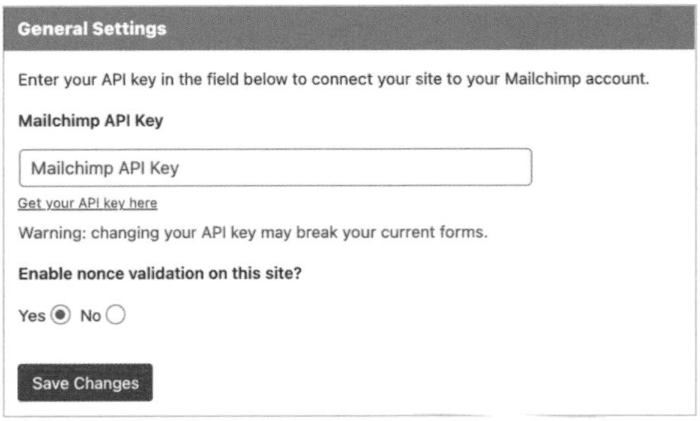
General Settings
Enter your API key in the field below to connect your site to your Mailchimp account.
Mailchimp API Key
Mailchimp API Key
Get your API key here
Warning: changing your API key may break your current forms.
Enable nonce validation on this site?
Yes
No
Save Changes

Mailchimp API Key: You can get hold of this from your Mailchimp account.

3 Log in to Mailchimp. Click your name on the bottom left-hand side and select **Account & billing**

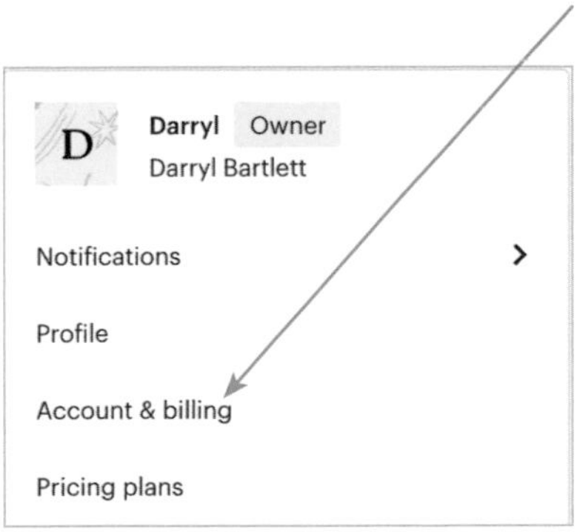
D
Darryl
Owner
Darryl Bartlett
Notifications
Profile
Account & billing
Pricing plans

...cont'd

4. Click **Extras** along the top bar and then select **API keys**

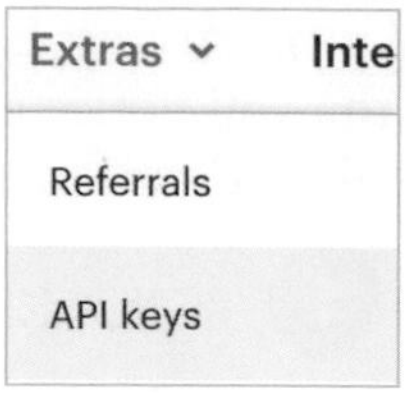

5. Click **Create A Key** under **Your API Keys**

6. Finally, copy your API key from the field

7. Head back to your **Mailchimp** settings in the dashboard. Paste your code into the **Mailchimp API Key** box

8. Click **Save Changes**

Audience settings

You are now almost ready to start creating forms for your website; however, you may want to change some audience settings first. When you signed up, a default audience will have been set up for you so that users can be added.

1. Log in to Mailchimp and select **Audience** from the left-hand navigation

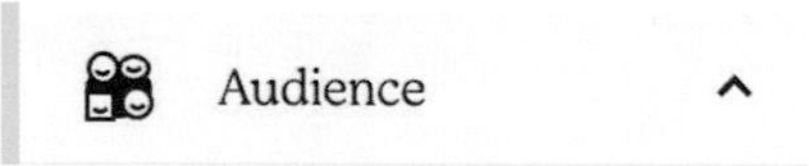

2. Select **All contacts** from the drop-down menu

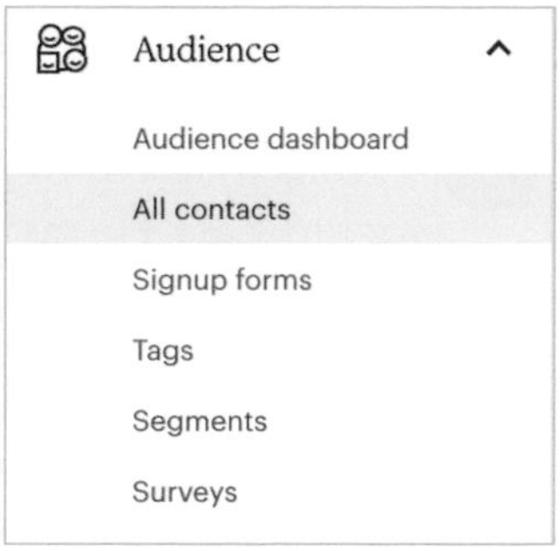

3. Click **Settings** > **Audience name and defaults**

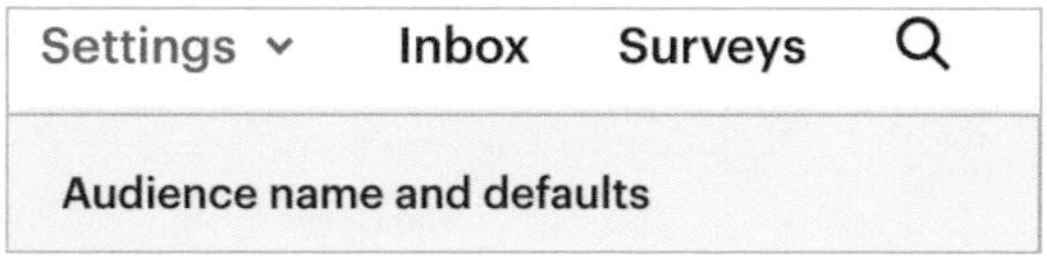

4. Update the following fields:

Audience name: This can be anything you like. Your subscribers will see this when they sign up.

Default From name: When users receive your newsletter, this is the name they will see. Use something like your company name.

Default From email address: This is the email that your subscribers will reply to.

5. Click **Save Audience And Campaign Defaults**

6. Go back to **Settings** and select **Required email footer content** from the list

7. Update the following fields:

Remind people how they signed up: You will need to write a short sentence here to remind recipients how they got on your list. In this case, it will be because they subscribed through the website.

Contact information: This is likely to already be filled out. It will contain your company details and will appear at the bottom of emails.

In your newsletter campaigns, remember to only use email addresses from customers who have signed up via the website, or who have given you permission.

...cont'd

Adding Mailchimp forms

Don't forget

Remember to save the changes.

1. From your WordPress dashboard, go to **Easy Forms** > **Opt-in Forms**

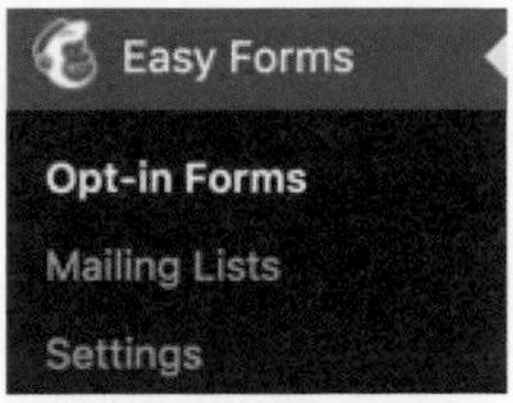
Easy Forms
Opt-in Forms
Mailing Lists
Settings

2. Fill out the **Create a New Signup Form** widget on the right-hand side:

   Form Name: Choose a name for your form.
   Form Description: Type a relevant description.
   Associated List: Your audience name should automatically be picked up.

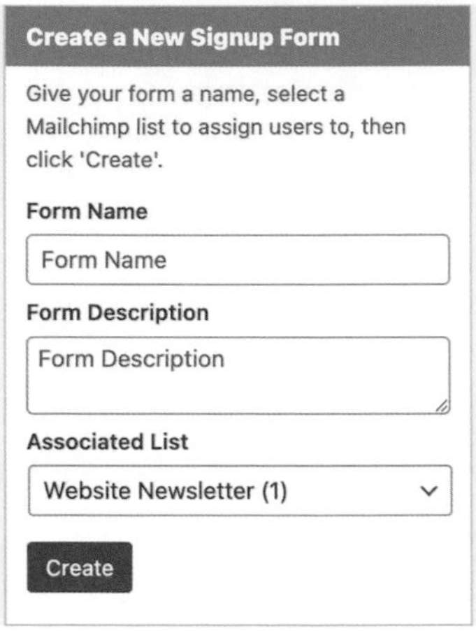
Create a New Signup Form
Give your form a name, select a Mailchimp list to assign users to, then click 'Create'.
Form Name
Form Name
Form Description
Form Description
Associated List
Website Newsletter (1)
Create

3. Click **Create** to set up your form

Create

4. Inside the **Form Fields** and **Interest Groups** settings you will see a list of several form fields

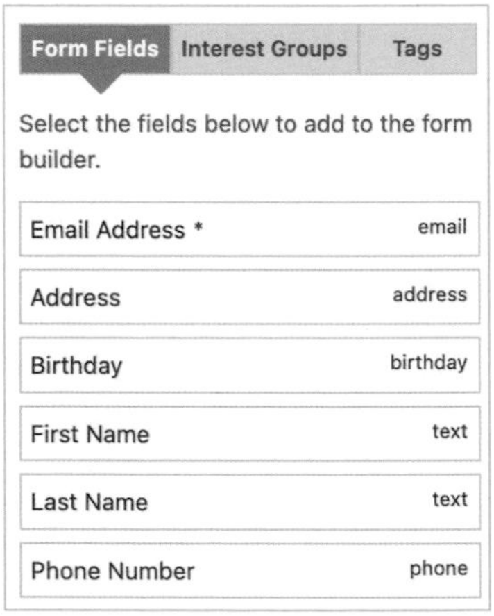
Form Fields
Interest Groups
Tags
Select the fields below to add to the form builder.
Email Address *
email
Address
address
Birthday
birthday
First Name
text
Last Name
text
Phone Number
phone

5. Select Email Address, First Name and Last Name, and click the **Add to Form Builder** button

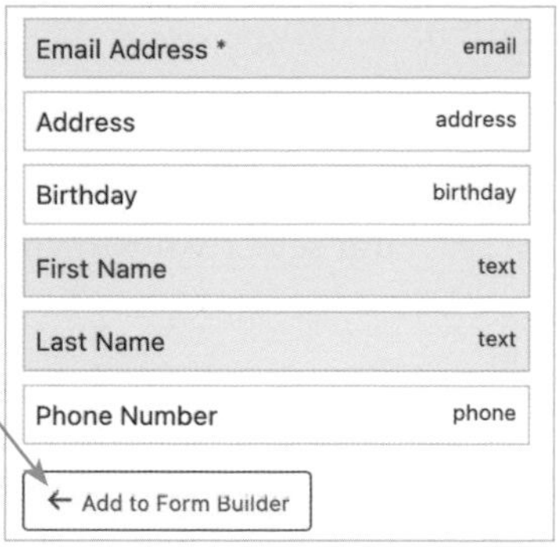
Email Address * email
Address address
Birthday birthday
First Name text
Last Name text
Phone Number phone
Add to Form Builder

6. The three fields will now display under the **Form Builder** section. Click **Update Form** to bring your form up-to-date

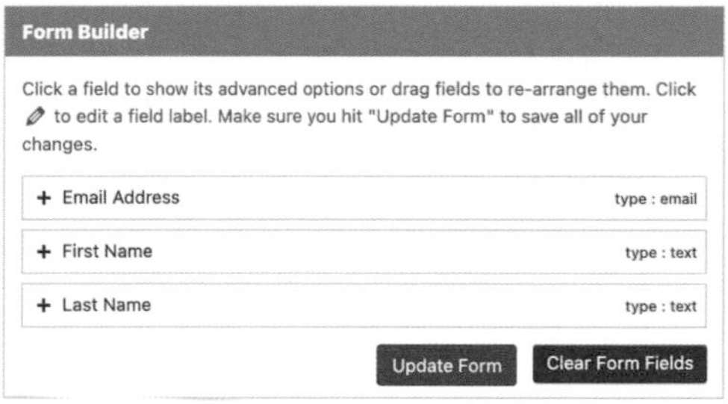
Form Builder
Click a field to show its advanced options or drag fields to re-arrange them. Click to edit a field label. Make sure you hit "Update Form" to save all of your changes.
Email Address type : email
First Name type : text
Last Name type : text
Update Form
Clear Form Fields

7. Copy the shortcode that has been generated by the plugin

Shortcode
[yikes-mailchimp form="1"]

8. Finally, open up the post/page where you want the form to go. Add in a shortcode block and paste in the shortcode from Step 7. Click **Update** to save the changes

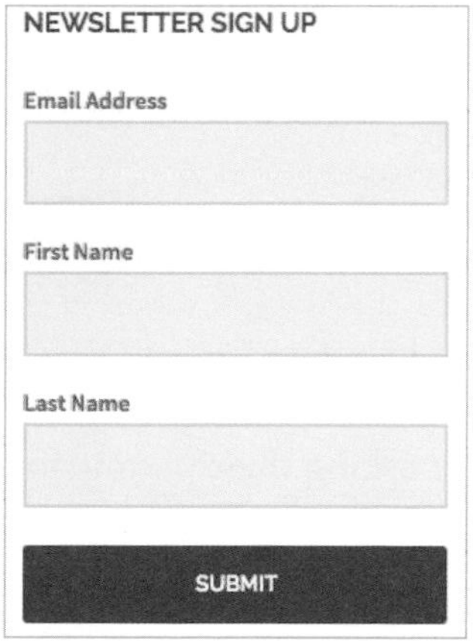
NEWSLETTER SIGN UP
Email Address
First Name
Last Name
SUBMIT

Now, every time a user signs up, their email address will be added to your list, ready for when you create an email campaign with **Mailchimp**.

Hot tip

You can also insert your Mailchimp forms in widget areas by going to **Appearance** > **Widgets** and dragging the **Easy Forms for Mailchimp** widget into your chosen widget area.

Don't forget

If you need help inserting a shortcode on a page or post, please refer back to page 57.

Opt-in settings

1. Go to **Easy Forms** > **Opt-in Forms** from the dashboard and select your form

	ID	Form Name	Form Description	List	Impressions	Submissions	Conversion Rate
☐	1	**Newsletter Sign Up**	Sign up to our newsletter for the latest deals.	Website Newsletter	0	0	%0
☐	ID	Form Name	Form Description	List	Impressions	Submissions	Conversion Rate

2. Click **+ Opt-in Settings**

Single or Double Opt-in

You can choose whether or not you want a single or double opt-in. A single opt-in is when the user signs up via the form, and it doesn't require them to verify their subscription by email. A double opt-in will send out an email to the user asking them to verify their email address.

Update Existing Subscriber (Yes/No)

If you choose to select **Yes** to this option, then an existing subscriber's information will be automatically updated rather than displaying a **User already subscribed** message.

Send Update Email (Yes/No)

If you select **Yes**, then it will automatically send an email to the user asking their permission to update their profile information. If you choose **No**, then their profile will be updated without any further interaction.

Don't forget

Don't force users to sign up. Try to explain the benefits of signing up for your newsletter. Sometimes, adding an incentive can help.

Sitemaps

A sitemap lists all the pages of your website. It can tell search engines about the organization of your site content, and when new or existing pages are updated and available for crawling (see tip). There is a good plugin called **XML Sitemaps** that generates an XML sitemap.

1. Go to **Plugins** > **Add New**
2. Type in "XML Sitemaps" and click **Search Plugins**

XML Sitemaps
Install Now
This plugin will improve SEO by helping search enginess better index your site using sitemaps.
More Details
By Auctollo
(2,134)
Last Updated: 1 month ago
1+ Million Active Installations
✓ Compatible with your version of WordPress

3. Install and activate the plugin
4. A **sitemap.xml** file will automatically be created. However, you can customize the settings by going to **Settings** > **XML-Sitemap**

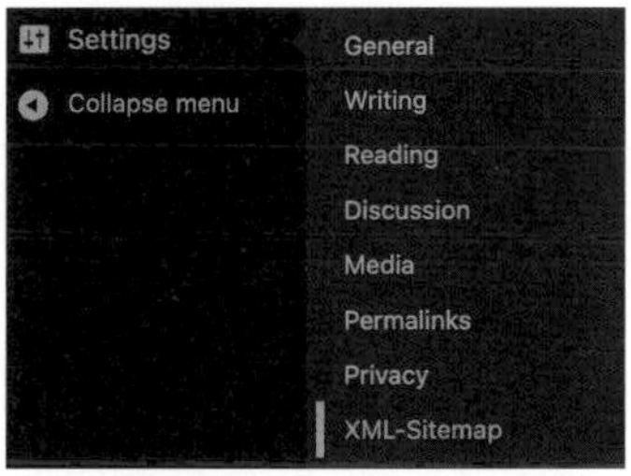
Settings
Collapse menu
General
Writing
Reading
Discussion
Media
Permalinks
Privacy
XML-Sitemap

5. Your sitemap will now be live. There are some optional settings that you might wish to change

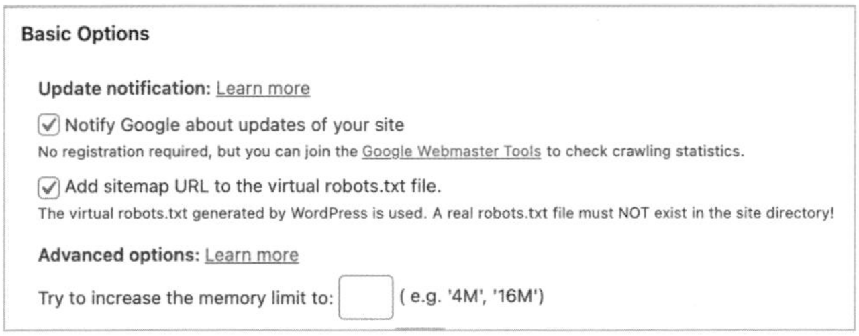
Basic Options
Update notification: Learn more
Notify Google about updates of your site
No registration required, but you can join the Google Webmaster Tools to check crawling statistics.
Add sitemap URL to the virtual robots.txt file.
The virtual robots.txt generated by WordPress is used. A real robots.txt file must NOT exist in the site directory!
Advanced options: Learn more
Try to increase the memory limit to: (e.g. '4M', '16M')

Don't forget

A crawler is a program that most search engines use to find what's new on the internet. It basically crawls the web and collects documents to build a searchable index for the different search engines. The program starts at a website and follows every hyperlink on each page.

...cont'd

Don't forget

Pinging is used to notify various online search engines that a blog/website has been updated. Typically, a search engine will follow links and index the new post quicker as a result.

Update notification

Notify Google about updates of your website: Google will be notified every time content is updated or added.

Notify Bing about updates of your site: Bing (formerly MSN Live Search) will be notified every time content is updated or added.

Add sitemap URL to the virtual robots.txt file: This will allow search engines that don't support ping to find your sitemap.

Advanced options

Most of these options you don't need to worry about. Make sure that **Include sitemap in HTML format** is checked, as an HTML sitemap allows site visitors to easily navigate a website.
It is basically a text version of your site navigation.

Additional pages

Here, you specify pages that should be included in your sitemap, but may not belong to your blog or website. For example, if your domain is *www.biscuit.com* and your blog is located on *www.biscuit.com/blog* then you might want to include your homepage, **www.biscuit.com**

Post priority

In this section, you can specify how the priority of each post will be calculated. Posts with high-priority values are likely to get indexed faster and crawled more often. You can set them to have the same priority, use the number of comments, or use the comment average.

Sitemap content

Here, you can select what you want to include in your sitemap. The homepage, posts and pages will be automatically selected. You can, however, add things like categories, author pages and archives.

Excluded items

You can choose to exclude particular posts, pages and categories from your sitemap. Just select the categories, or type the posts or pages you want to exclude.

Change frequencies & priorities

You can give an indication to search engines of how often content changes on your website, and you are also able to give search engines an indication of the priorities of your page types.

Google Fonts

In the early days of the web, the internet was filled with boring standard fonts, mainly because developers were limited to using fonts commonly found on most computers. These days, developers have a lot of choice thanks to web fonts. **Google Fonts** is just one way you can change the fonts on your website without the user having to have the font already stored on their computer.

Getting started with Google Fonts

Before you get **Google Fonts** set up on your WordPress website, we are going to have a look at how you can discover great fonts on the **Google Fonts** website. Let's begin by going to **https://fonts.google.com**

Search fonts
Sentence
Type something
40px
Categories
Language
Font properties
Show only variable fonts
1429 of 1429 families
About these results
Sort by: Trending

You will notice a number of filters along the top of the page that will help you find the type of font you are looking for.

Different font previews will appear down the center of the page:

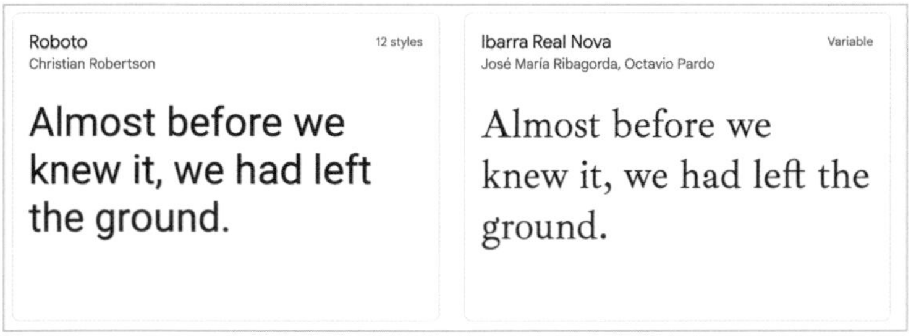
Roboto
12 styles
Christian Robertson
Almost before we knew it, we had left the ground.
Ibarra Real Nova
Variable
José María Ribagorda, Octavio Pardo
Almost before we knew it, we had left the ground.

You can see how a line of text will look in a particular font by typing some text in the sentence text box in the filters.

Custom
Hello WordPress

Using WP Google Fonts

There is a great plugin you can use called **WP Google Fonts** that is especially helpful for beginners, if you don't want to get involved with adding code.

Don't forget

You don't have to download the fonts to use them on your website.

...cont'd

1. Go to **Plugins** > **Add New**
2. Search for **WP Google Fonts** in the search bar, install and then activate

F
WP Google Fonts
Install Now
More Details
The WP Google Fonts plugin allows you to easily add fonts from the Google Font Directory to your Wordpress theme.
By Noah Kagan
(38)
80,000+ Active Installations
Last Updated: 9 months ago
Untested with your version of WordPress

3. Click **Google Fonts** from the dashboard

Hot tip

Check out the previews of your font on the **Google Fonts** website so that you know how your font will look.

A font selection page will appear that allows you to choose six different fonts for your website. You can add one font to each of the six drop-down boxes.

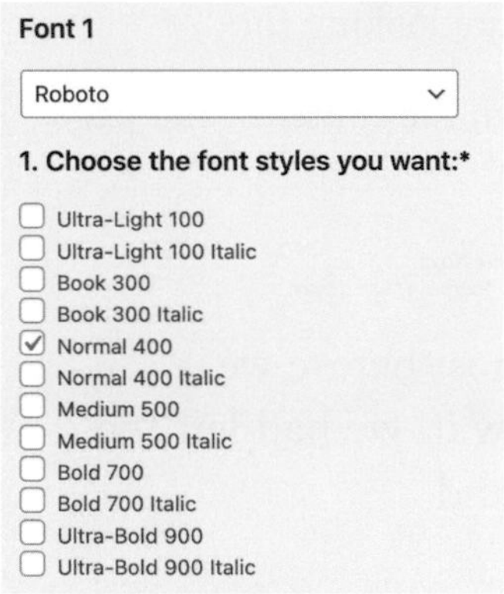
Font 1
Roboto
1. Choose the font styles you want:*
Ultra-Light 100
Ultra-Light 100 Italic
Book 300
Book 300 Italic
Normal 400
Normal 400 Italic
Medium 500
Medium 500 Italic
Bold 700
Bold 700 Italic
Ultra-Bold 900
Ultra-Bold 900 Italic

Font selection

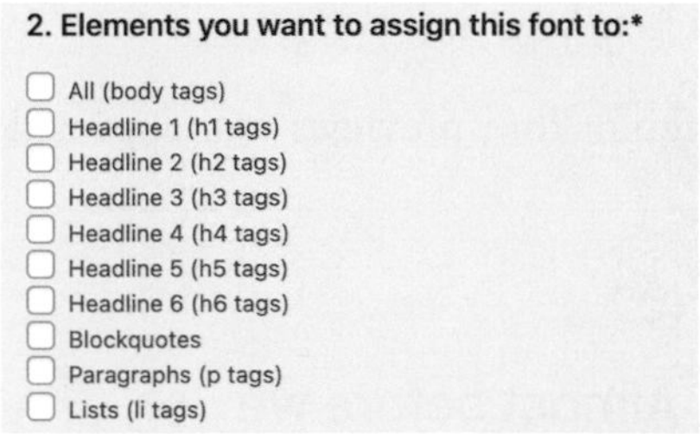
2. Elements you want to assign this font to:*
All (body tags)
Headline 1 (h1 tags)
Headline 2 (h2 tags)
Headline 3 (h3 tags)
Headline 4 (h4 tags)
Headline 5 (h5 tags)
Headline 6 (h6 tags)
Blockquotes
Paragraphs (p tags)
Lists (li tags)

Font options

1. Choose the font styles you want: Some fonts will have their own different styles – for example, **Regular** or **Bold**.
2. Elements you want to assign this font to: Here, you select the elements you want to assign the font to. You might want to assign it to header 1, or the main paragraph text.
3. Custom CSS (optional): You can add your own custom CSS.
4. Choose character sets you want: Make sure you select any character sets you want.
5. Save All Fonts: Saves the changes to all font selections.

Save All Fonts

Don't forget

Save your changes so that your elements will update straight away with the new font choices.

11 Advanced WordPress

This final chapter covers more advanced topics, including setting up FTP; website backups; creating a theme; responsive design; and security.

WordPress & PHP

PHP is the server-side web development language behind WordPress. You don't need to know PHP to use WordPress. However, it is a good way to add extra functionality or enhance your website even further. It also comes in handy if you want to develop your own themes or plugins. We will show you how to create your own theme on pages 166-174.

WordPress theme files

A WordPress theme consists of several files. These are the basic ones that are the key fundamentals behind the main website:

- **footer.php**: This file controls the footer (at the very bottom of the page). Footers are great for adding copyright notices, etc.
- **header.php**: This file controls the header. Most of your pages will share the same header.
- **index.php**: This file usually sets up the homepage unless there is a **home.php** file. This file can also be used to generate other pages. For example, if WordPress cannot find the file specific to that page, then it will use the **index.php** file.
- **sidebar.php**: This file controls all the sidebar content.
- **style.css**: This controls the styling for your website – for example, your layout, look, elements and colors, etc.
- **single.php**: This file will set up all single-page posts on your blog or website.
- **page.php**: This file will control all your pages.
- **archive.php**: This file will control the layout of the archive pages. For example, you may have a page in a **June 2010** category.

You will find all these files in your WordPress editor by going to **Appearance** > **Theme File Editor** from the dashboard.

Setting up FTP

File Transfer Protocol (FTP) allows you to move files from your computer to your hosting account in a quick and simple manner. Most web developers will use FTP as they can transfer lots of files, and it allows them to manage their website just by using an FTP client. An FTP client, such as FileZilla, is a piece of downloadable software that allows you to easily move files from your computer to a web host or another computer. To get FTP set up, you will need to do two things:

Hot tip

FTP is a much quicker way to move files from your computer to your hosting account.

Setting up an FTP account with HostGator

The first thing we need to do is set up an FTP account. The process is very similar with most hosting companies, and a lot of web hosts will provide documentation on their website. If you are using HostGator, then follow these steps to set up your FTP account:

1. Log in to your HostGator portal, just like you did in Chapter 1 (see page 12)

2. Click **Launch cPanel**

3. Click **FTP Accounts** under the **FILES** section

4. Complete the form (see screenshot on page 164):

   Log In: Choose a login name. This will eventually be login@yourdomain.com.

   Password: Enter a password for the account.

   Password (Again): Re-enter the password.

   Directory: Make sure this ends with **public_html**, as shown in the screenshot on page 164.

   Quota: Set a quota for the FTP account.

...cont'd

Log In
[redacted]
@wordpresseagle.com
Password
[redacted]
Password (Again)
[redacted]
Strength
Very Strong (97/100)
Password Generator
Directory
/home3/wordpgle/
public_html
Quota
2000
MB
Unlimited

5. Now, all you need to do is click **Create FTP Account** and you're ready to go

Create FTP Account

Downloading and configuring the FileZilla FTP client

You will need an FTP client to access your files. FileZilla is a great choice.

1. Download it at **https://filezilla-project.org**

2. Open up the application

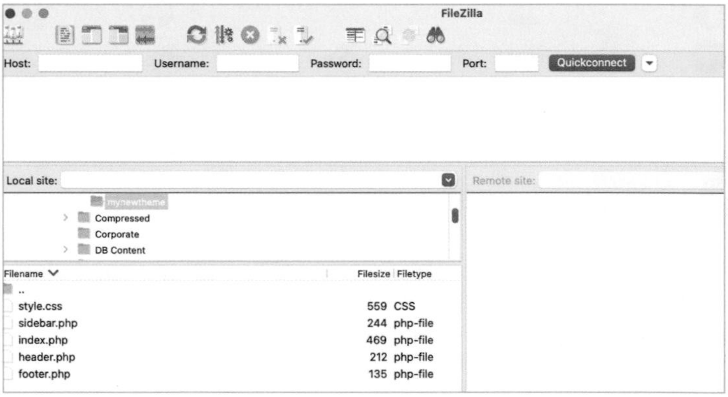
FileZilla
Host:
Username:
Password:
Port:
Quickconnect
Local site:
Remote site:
Compressed
Corporate
DB Content
Filename
Filesize
Filetype
style.css 559 CSS
sidebar.php 244 php-file
index.php 469 php-file
header.php 212 php-file
footer.php 135 php-file

At the top of the application, there is a bar with a number of fields you need to fill out.

3. Enter your host (**ftp.yourdomain.com**), username (the one you set up under FTP accounts), and your password. Now, click **Quickconnect**

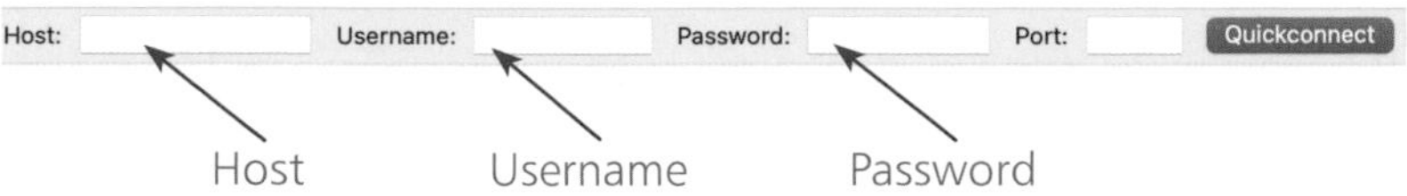
Host:
Username:
Password:
Port:
Quickconnect
Host
Username
Password

If the status reads **Directory listing of "/" successful** then you are connected.

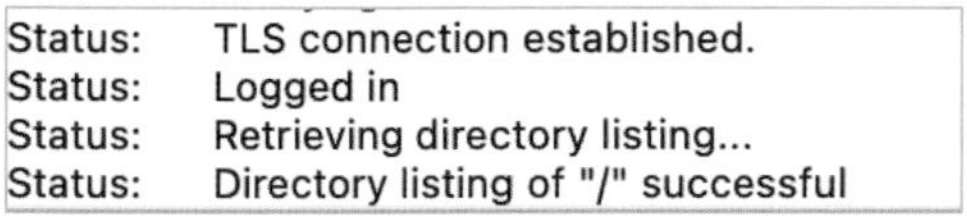
Status: TLS connection established.
Status: Logged in
Status: Retrieving directory listing...
Status: Directory listing of "/" successful

The window on the right will display all your hosting files. The window on the left will display all the files on your computer. If you wish to upload a file from your computer, all you need to do is drag the file from the left-hand window (computer files) to the right-hand window (host files).

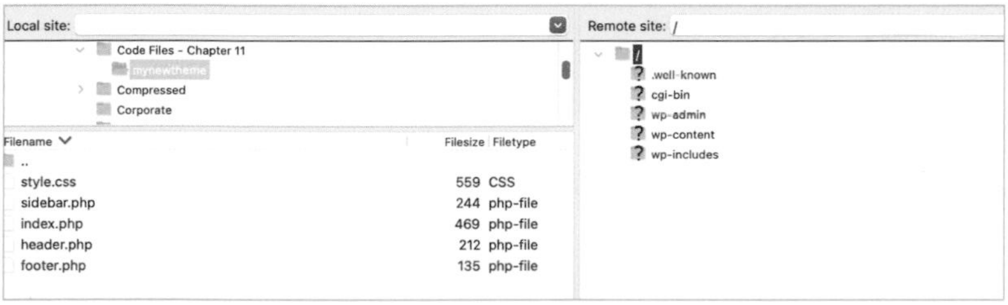
Local site:
Code Files - Chapter 11
mynewtheme
Compressed
Corporate
Filename
Filesize
Filetype
style.css 559 CSS
sidebar.php 244 php-file
index.php 469 php-file
header.php 212 php-file
footer.php 135 php-file
Remote site: /
.well-known
cgi-bin
wp-admin
wp-content
wp-includes

Left-hand window (computer files) Right-hand window (host files)

If you are looking to edit PHP files, or the stylesheet for the theme you currently have activated, then in the right-hand FileZilla window navigate to **wp-content** > **themes** > **themename**. You can find your theme name in the dashboard by going to **Appearance** > **Themes**.

You should now see your theme files (**header.php, footer.php**, and **style.css**, etc.) You can double-click them to open right there. However, it is advised to drag a copy to your computer to edit.

Hot tip

You might need to set a port number. Usually, this is 21.

Don't forget

Make sure you keep a backup of your files.

Beware

Depending on your broadband connection, it can take some time to transfer files.

Creating a Theme

Earlier in the book, you were shown how to add and upload themes. Now, we will show you how to create a basic one. This should help you gain a better knowledge of HTML and PHP, and will help create better websites.

Remember the PHP files that we talked about on page 162 that make up a WordPress theme? We will show you how to create five of them to make up our theme:

- **index.php**
- **header.php**
- **footer.php**
- **sidebar.php**
- **style.css**

Hot tip

Take a look at **Web Design in easy steps** for key principles of good web design.

Text editor

You'll need a text editor to create these files: something like Notepad, or you can use a professional code editor like Visual Studio.

Don't forget

Remember to use a text editor that you are comfortable with. It may take some time to familiarize yourself with the layout.

Index file (index.php)

We are going to begin by creating the main template file.

1. Open up your text editor and enter the following code:

```
<?php get_header(); ?>
<div id="main">
<div id="content">
<?php if (have_posts()) : while (have_posts()) : the_post(); ?>
<h1><?php the_title(); ?></h1>
<h4>Posted on <?php the_time(‘F jS, Y’) ?></h4>
<p><?php the_content(__(‘(more...)’)); ?></p>
<hr> <?php endwhile; else: ?>
<p><?php _e(‘Sorry, there are no posts available at this time.’);
?></p><?php endif; ?>
</div>
<?php get_sidebar(); ?>
</div>
<div id="delimiter">
</div>
<?php get_footer(); ?>
```

```
index.php ●
index.php
<?php get_header(); ?>
<div id="main">
<div id="content">
<?php if (have_posts()) : while (have_posts()) : the_post(); ?>
<h1><?php the_title(); ?></h1>
<h4>Posted on <?php the_time('F jS, Y') ?></h4>
<p><?php the_content(__('(more...)')); ?></p>
<hr> <?php endwhile; else: ?>
<p><?php _e('Sorry, there are no posts available at this time.');
?></p><?php endif; ?>
</div>
<?php get_sidebar(); ?>
</div>
<div id="delimiter">
</div>
<?php get_footer(); ?>
```

1. Make sure you save your file as **index.php**

Index file explained

<?php get_header(); ?>
This will grab the header and include it in this page. As mentioned before, the header is used in all pages on a website.

```
<?php if (have_posts()) : while (have_posts()) : the_post(); ?>
<h1><?php the_title(); ?></h1>
<h4>Posted on <?php the_time('F jS, Y') ?></h4>
<p><?php the_content(__('(more...)')); ?></p>
<hr> <?php endwhile; else: ?>
<p><?php _e('Sorry, there are no posts available at this time.');
?></p><?php endif; ?>
```

This will bring in the posts on your website. As you can see, it brings in the title, time posted and the content of the post. If there are no posts on the website, then it will leave a message saying **Sorry, there are no posts available at this time**. If you set your homepage to display a static page, then that content will appear there instead.

<?php get_sidebar(); ?>
Bring in the sidebar code and get this inserted into your page.

<?php get_footer(); ?>
Finally, bring in the footer. This is the last thing you will bring in to your page.

Hot tip

PHP in easy steps will teach you how to write PHP server-side scripts.

...cont'd

Header file

1. Create a new file in your text editor and enter the following:

```
<html>
<head>
<title>My Page Title</title>
<link rel="stylesheet" href="<?php bloginfo('stylesheet_url'); ?>">
</head>
<body>
<div id="wrapper">
<div id="header">
<h1>Some Title for the Top</h1>
</div>
```

2. Save the file as **header.php**

The **header.php** file will be used throughout all of your WordPress web pages.

Header file explained

<title>My Page Title</title>
This will assign a title to the website at the top of the browser.

<link rel="stylesheet" href="<?php bloginfo('stylesheet_url'); ?>">

This tells WordPress to load the **style.css** file.

<div id="wrapper">
<div id="header">

Notice how you have created some div tags here. We will later go on to style these in our **style.css** file.

A **<div>** tag is used to specify a section within an HTML document.

A **<div id>** tag is used to identify a single element that only appears once, a bit like a header. A <div class> tag is used to identify elements that are used more than once – for example, a widget or an image area.

<h1>Some Title for the Top</h1>
We have added a title in your header saying "Some Title for the Top", but you can come up with something creative. This is styled using <h1>, which is Header 1.

Footer file

1. Create a new file in your text editor and enter the following:

```
<div id="footer">
<h1>This is our footer</h1>
<a href="https://www.ineasysteps.com">In Easy Steps</a>
</div>
</div>
</body>
</html>
```

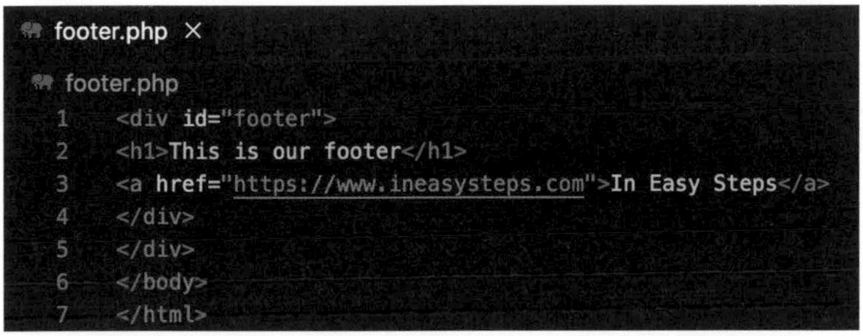

2. Save the file as **footer.php**

Hot tip

The footer is a good place for things like copyright notices.

Footer file explained

<div id="footer">
Here, we create a **<div>** tag that we can use in the stylesheet (**style.css**) later on.

<h1>This is our footer</h1>
We are going to add a title to our footer; we do not usually do this when it comes to developing websites.

...cont'd

In this scenario, we have specified the title to point out the footer.

<a href="https//www.ineasysteps.com">In Easy Steps</a>

This will add a link in the footer. The first part specifies the actual link of the website, and the last part is how the actual link will appear on the page.

Sidebar file

1. Create a new file in your text editor and enter the following:

```
<div id="sidebar">
<h2 ><?php _e('Categories'); ?></h2>
<ul >
<?php wp_list_cats('sort_column=name&optioncount=1&hierarchi
cal=0'); ?>
</ul>
<h2 ><?php _e('Archives'); ?></h2>
<ul >
<?php wp_get_archives('type=monthly'); ?>
</ul>
</div>
```

2. Save the file as **sidebar.php**

Sidebar file explained

Here, we are looking to create links to our categories and archives, so let's break this down.

<div id="sidebar">
First, we are setting up a **<div>** tag, so we can set this up in the stylesheet.

<h2 ><?php _e('Categories'); ?></h2>
This will show the word **Categories** in <h2> styling.

Don't forget

It is important to add the **.php** extension at the end of your files when saving.

Hot tip

In this example, the sidebar will appear on the right-hand side. It is a great place to display a list of posts, or maybe even a list of your content categories.

<?php wp_list_cats('sort_column=name&optioncount=1&hierarchical=0'); ?>
This will set up our list of categories down the side of the page.

<h2 ><?php _e('Archives'); ?></h2>
This will set up another title saying **Archives**. This is styled using the <h2> attributes.

<?php wp_get_archives('type=monthly'); ?>
This will display our archives by month.

Stylesheet file

Now we have the foundations set in place, we are going to begin styling our elements.

1. Enter the following into a new file:

```
body { text-align: center; }
#wrapper { display: block; border: 1px #a2a2a2 solid; width: 90%;
margin: 0px auto; }
#header { border: 2px #a2a2a2 solid; background-color: red; }
#content { width: 75%; border: 2px #a2a2a2 solid; float: left; }
#sidebar { width: 23%; border: 2px #a2a2a2 solid; float: right; }
#delimiter { clear: both; }
#footer { border: 2px #a2a2a2 solid; }
.title { font-size: 11pt; font-family: verdana; font-weight: bold; }
h1 { font-size: 40px; }
h2 { font-size: 22px; }
p { font-size: 14px; }
#footer h1 { font-size: 35px; }
```

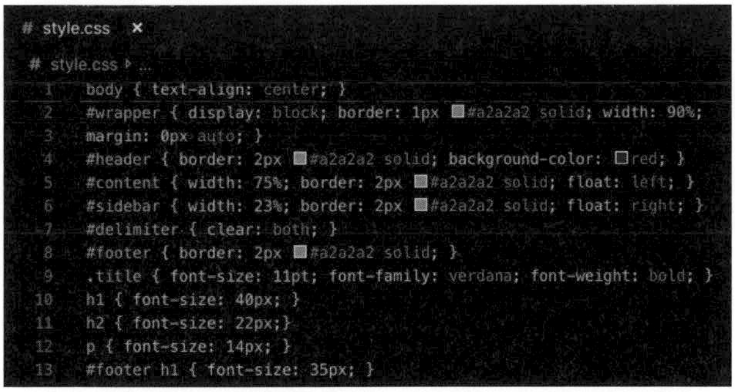

2. Save the file as **style.css**

Hot tip

A stylesheet is a key element in styling the elements on your website.

...cont'd

Stylesheet file explained

body { text-align: center; }
Here, we are aligning all body content to the center.

#wrapper { display: block; border: 1px #a2a2a2 solid; width: 90%; margin: 0px auto; }
Here, we are setting the details for our wrapper – this is where all our main content will go. We are setting this to a width of 90% and setting the border and margin attributes for it.

#header { border: 2px #a2a2a2 solid; background-color: red; }
Here, we set the thickness and color of the border of the header. We are also setting the background of the header to red.

#sidebar { width: 23%; border: 2px #a2a2a2 solid; float: right; }
We are setting our sidebar to 23%, giving it a border and making sure the content floats to the right.

#footer { border: 2px #a2a2a2 solid; }
Here, we set the thickness and color of the border for the footer.

.title { font-size: 11pt; font-family: verdana; font-weight: bold; }
h1 { font-size: 40px; }
h2 { font-size: 22px; }
p { font-size: 14px; }
#footer h1 { font-size: 35px; }
Here, we are setting the font sizes for our headers and paragraphs. On page 170, we set up the heading **Categories** under <h2>. In this stylesheet, we have set up h2 with a font size of 22px.

This is how our website will look once it goes live:

Uploading files

Once you have finished writing and saving your files, you can upload them to your webspace.

1. Open up **FileZilla**
2. Enter your FTP details, as you created on page 163

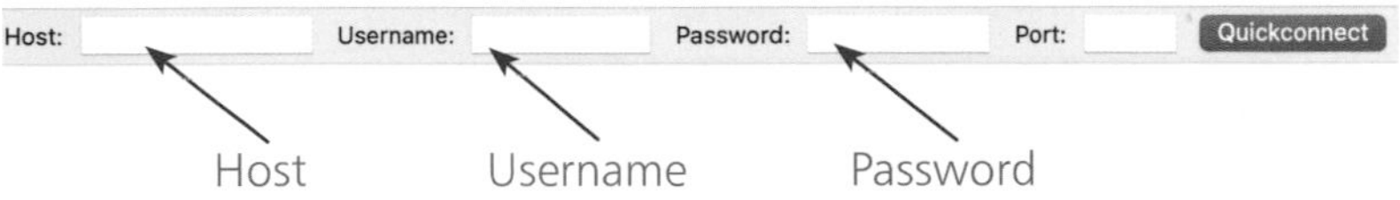
Host:
Username:
Password:
Port:
Quickconnect
Host
Username
Password

3. Once you are logged in, find your theme files on your computer in the window on the left-hand side

Filename	Filesize	Filetype
..		
style.css	559	CSS
sidebar.php	244	php-file
index.php	469	php-file
header.php	212	php-file
footer.php	135	php-file

4. In the right-hand panel, navigate to **wp-content** > **themes**. In this folder, create your own folder, and name it. In this example, we have called it **my-first-theme**. Create a directory by right-clicking in the window and selecting **Create directory**

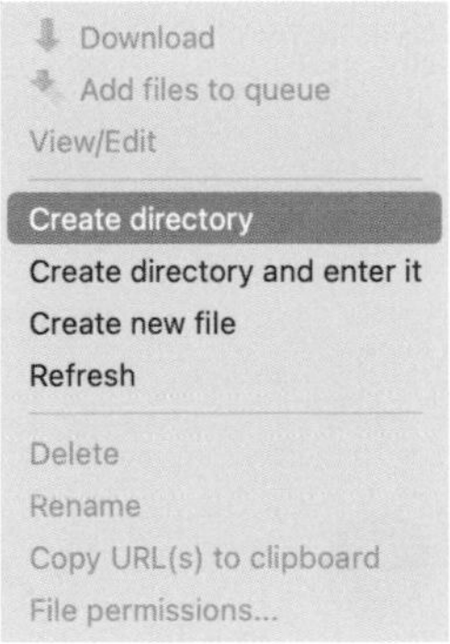
Download
Add files to queue
View/Edit
Create directory
Create directory and enter it
Create new file
Refresh
Delete
Rename
Copy URL(s) to clipboard
File permissions...

Create directory
Please enter the name of the directory which should be created:
/wp-content/themes/my-first-theme
Cancel
OK

Don't forget

For now, make sure all your files are in the same directory to avoid errors.

...cont'd

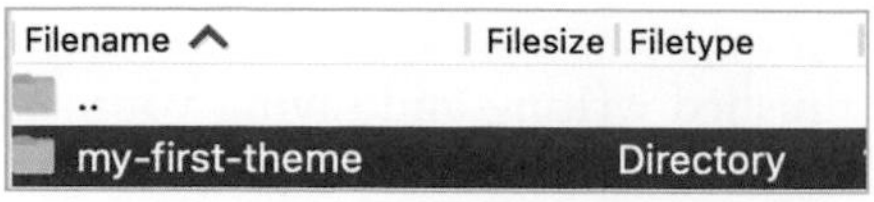
Filename
Filesize
Filetype
..
my-first-theme
Directory

5. Once you have created the directory, double-click it to open it. Now, drag across the files from the left-hand window to the right to upload your files

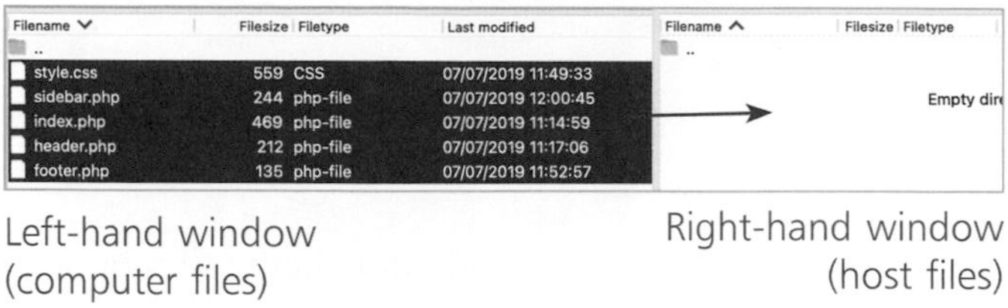
Left-hand window
(computer files)
Right-hand window
(host files)

6. You now need to activate your new theme in WordPress. Log in to the dashboard and go to **Appearance** > **Themes**. You will notice your theme appears there

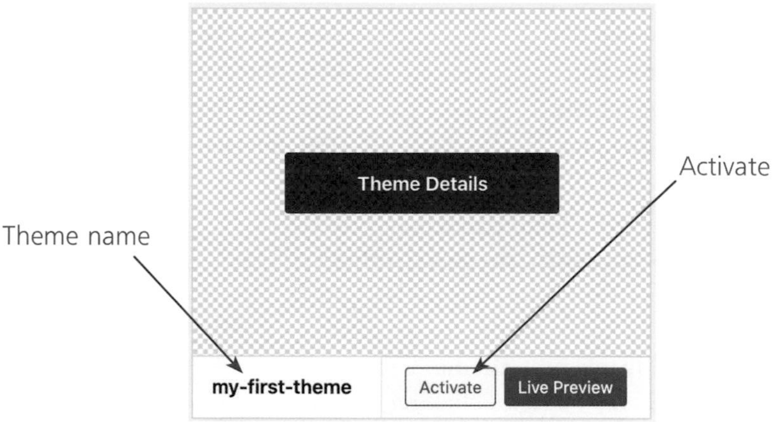
Theme Details
Theme name
Activate
my-first-theme
Activate
Live Preview

7. Now, click **Activate** and your theme should now be available on your live website

You can change back to another theme at any time by going back to **Appearance** > **Themes** from your dashboard.

Don't forget

When activating a custom theme, there may come a time where the top WordPress bar might go missing. You can, however, access the WordPress dashboard by going to **www.yourdomain.com/wp-admin/**

WordPress Backup

You should keep a backup of your whole WordPress website in case of a disaster or if you move web hosts. Earlier on in the book, we explained how to export posts and pages (see page 104). However, this is not the best method for backing up, because a WordPress website has multiple areas – things like stylesheets, plugins, etc. You need to make sure the whole thing is backed up so that once your website is restored, it will be in the same state it was when you backed up.

File backup

First of all, you need to back up all your files. You can do this using the FTP program FileZilla, introduced on pages 163-165.

1. Open up **FileZilla**
2. Enter your FTP details

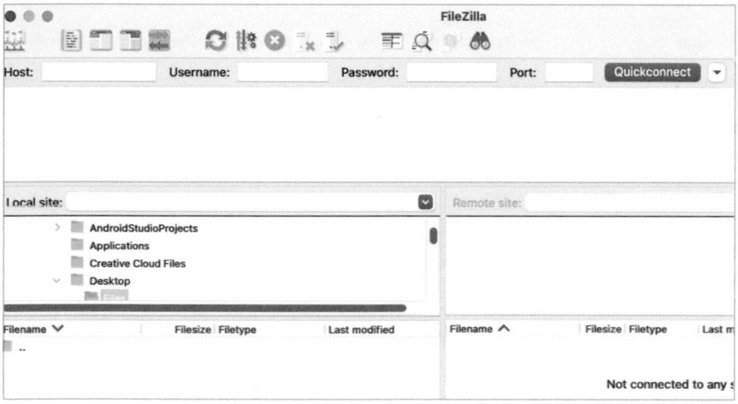

3. Make sure you create a directory on your computer where you want to store the backup

As well as keeping a backup on your computer, it may be a good idea to store your files on a backup disk or in the cloud.

...cont'd

4 Now, double-click that directory in the left-hand window panel, ready to transfer the files across

Local site:
Desktop
Files
Backup
Filename
Filesize
Filetype
Last modified
..

5 As you are logged in and in the correct directory, you can now select all the files in the right-hand panel. To make things easier, select one of the folders in the right-hand panel and then press **Ctrl + A (Cmd + A on Mac)** on your keyboard so that all the files are selected

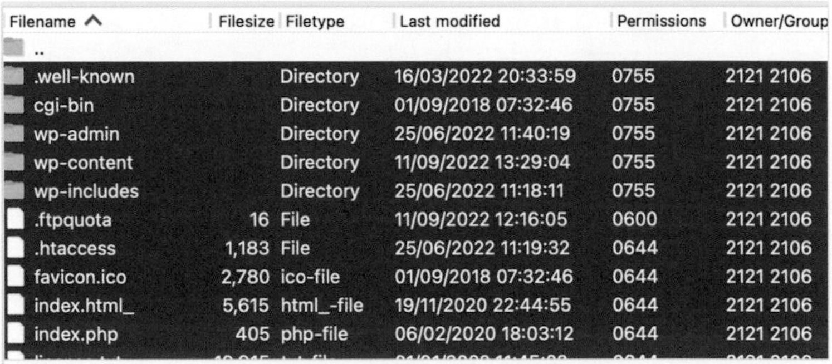
Filename | Filesize | Filetype | Last modified | Permissions | Owner/Group
..
.well-known Directory 16/03/2022 20:33:59 0755 2121 2106
cgi-bin Directory 01/09/2018 07:32:46 0755 2121 2106
wp-admin Directory 25/06/2022 11:40:19 0755 2121 2106
wp-content Directory 11/09/2022 13:29:04 0755 2121 2106
wp-includes Directory 25/06/2022 11:18:11 0755 2121 2106
.ftpquota 16 File 11/09/2022 12:16:05 0600 2121 2106
.htaccess 1,183 File 25/06/2022 11:19:32 0644 2121 2106
favicon.ico 2,780 ico-file 01/09/2018 07:32:46 0644 2121 2106
index.html_ 5,615 html_-file 19/11/2020 22:44:55 0644 2121 2106
index.php 405 php-file 06/02/2020 18:03:12 0644 2121 2106

6 Now, all you need to do is drag across the files from the right-hand window to the left-hand window, as shown in the screenshot below. This copies the files to the location on your Desktop

Filename
Filesize
Filetype
Last modified
..
Drag Here
Filename
Filesize
Filetype
..
.well-known Directory
cgi-bin Directory
wp-admin Directory
wp-content Directory
wp-includes Directory
.ftpquota 16 File

Now you have copied all the files, you need to make a backup of the database. You can use **phpMyAdmin,** which is located in your hosting Control Panel. We covered installing WordPress from the Control Panel in Chapter 1. Go back to this Control Panel to back up your website database.

Beware

Make sure you have copied across every file, to avoid errors when restoring a backup.

Database backup

1. Go to **Launch cPanel** (like on page 163)

2. You will need to scroll down until you find **phpMyAdmin**

3. Select **Databases** along the top

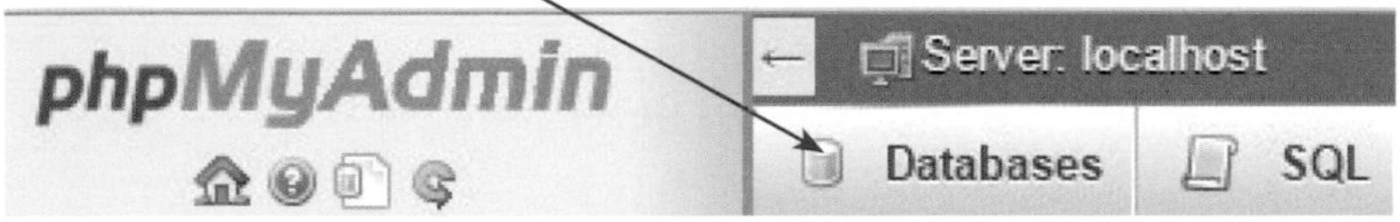

4. You will be presented with a list of databases, as shown on page 178. It is likely that you only have one database at this time; this is the WordPress database

...cont'd

You will need to click on the database (it will appear as a link under **Databases**).

5 You will be presented with a list of tables relating to WordPress. A lot of them will start with "**wp_**" – for example, "**wp_users**". Ignore these and select **Export** along the top

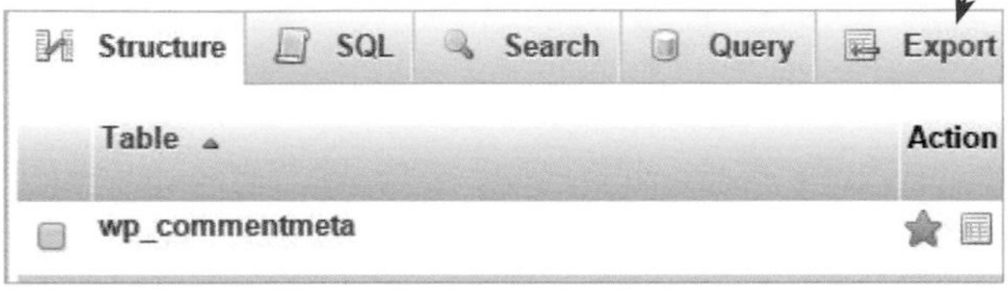

6 Select an export method and format. Select **Quick - display only the minimal options** under **Export Method**, and for the format, select **SQL**

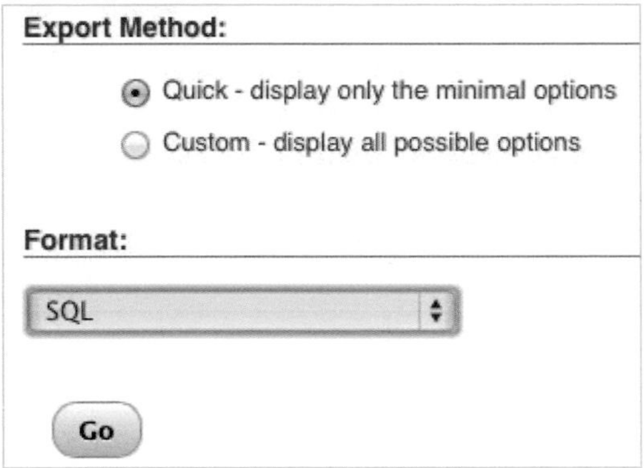

7 Finally, press the **Go** button. This will download the database locally to your computer

Make sure the database file is saved, along with your website files. You now have a complete backup of your website.

Responsive Design

There are more and more people using mobile phones and tablets to access the internet these days. This makes it extremely important to make sure websites are responsive so that they appear and function properly across all devices.

Hot tip

These days, your website needs to cater for all kinds of devices, from smartphones to tablets. This means web developers need to look at customizing their sites for different resolutions.

Using a responsive theme

You could use a responsive theme, which would save a lot of time. ThemeForest do a good selection of responsive themes (**www.themeforest.net**), or you could search for "Responsive" when adding a new theme from the WordPress dashboard (see pagcs 31-33). However, even if you have selected a great responsive theme, there might be times where you might want to move elements around – a bit like introducing CSS (see pages 146-149).

Testing on different devices

You might very well own a selection of devices to test your website on, but this can be an expensive option. There are a number of browser tools you can use to test out your website's appearance across numerous devices.

One of the best ones to use is the **Web Developer** extension by Chris Pederick. It is available for both Chrome and Firefox, and makes it easy to view your website using various resolutions.

Adding the Web Developer extension

In this case we will use Firefox, but you can add it to Chrome if you wish.

1. Open up Firefox
2. Navigate to **https://addons.mozilla.org/en-GB/firefox/addon/web-developer/**
3. Select **Web Developer** by chrispederick and click **Add to Firefox**

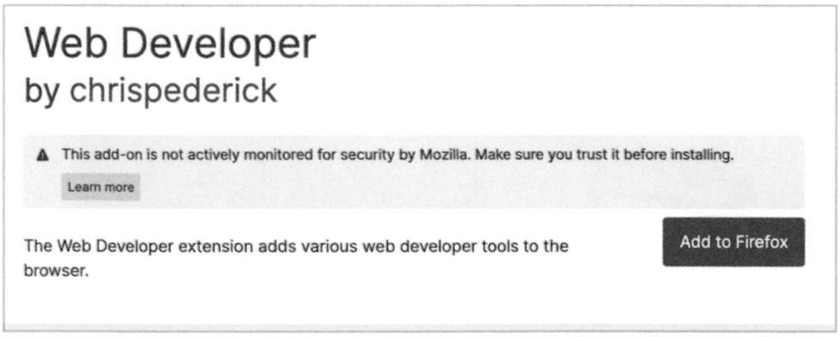
Web Developer
by chrispederick
This add-on is not actively monitored for security by Mozilla. Make sure you trust it before installing.
Learn more
The Web Developer extension adds various web developer tools to the browser.
Add to Firefox

...cont'd

4. If you select the **Web Developer** icon on the far right of the Firefox browser, you will notice that you now have some extra tools to work with

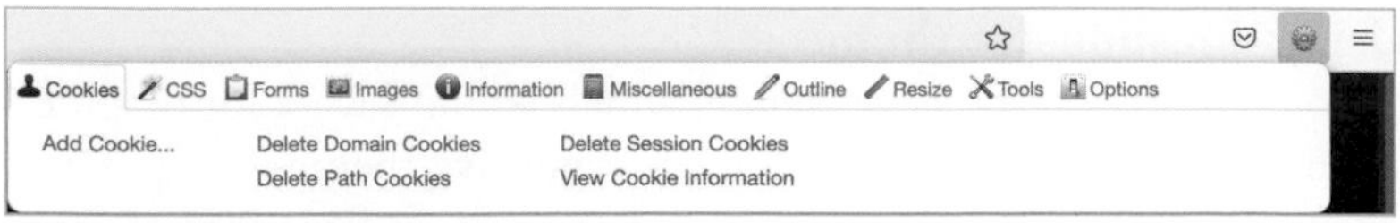

Working with the Web Developer extension

Now you have the extension installed, you are ready to view how your website looks across various resolutions.

1. Navigate to your WordPress website using the address bar

2. Select **View Responsive Layouts** from the **Resize** tab in the Web Developer extension tool

You should see that Firefox will bring up a number of viewpoints, displaying how your website will look using different devices.

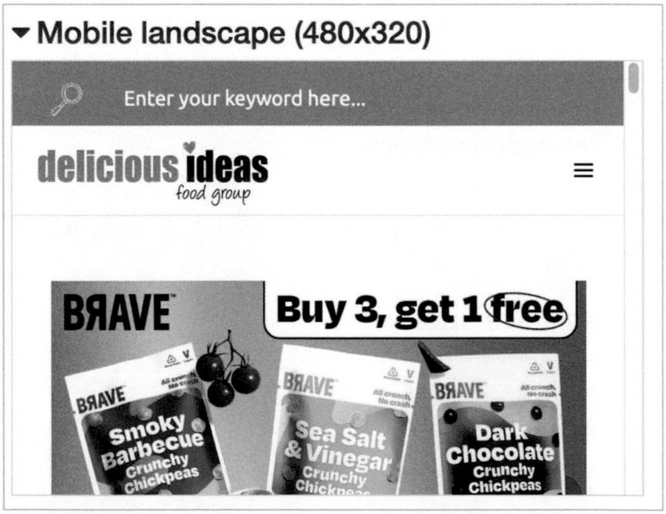

If you chose a responsive WordPress template when starting out development of your website, then most layouts should already look pretty good.

Don't forget

There is nothing like testing your website on an actual device. If you have a mobile or tablet, be sure to test it out on the real thing.

Making changes to a responsive template

You are now going to make changes to your mobile responsive layout.

We will be using the Element Inspector (see page 146) alongside the Firefox Web Developer extension.

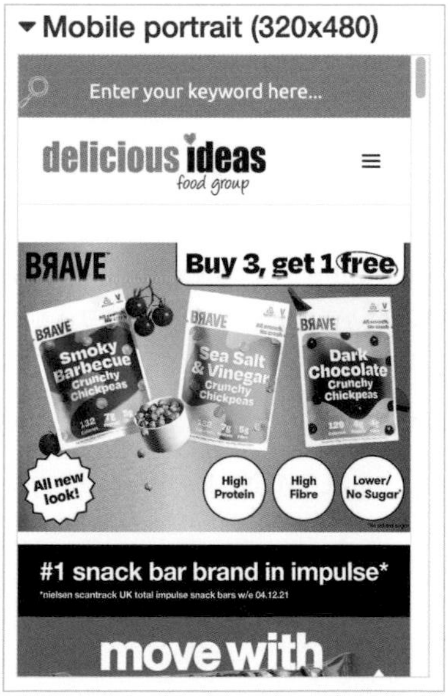

Use the viewpoint at the top labeled **Mobile portrait (320x480)** to make changes to your mobile portrait mode.

If you have a smartphone, then you could view how your website displays on your device.

...cont'd

1. Right-click on one of the elements inside the mobile portrait viewpoint and click **Inspect**

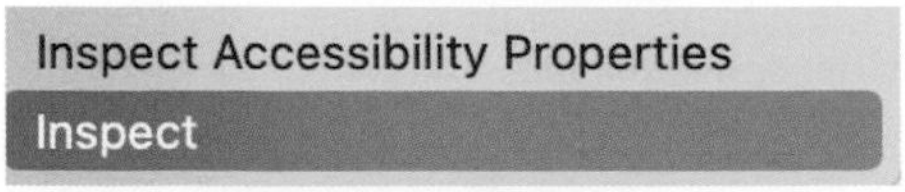
Inspect Accessibility Properties
Inspect

2. You will notice the Inspector appears at the bottom of the page, just like it did on page 146 when we introduced you to CSS. In this example we have right-clicked on the search window in our Inspector, which is **mkdf-search-slide-window-top**. Yours will be something different, depending on the element you selected

Enter your keyword here...

Element Selected

<div class="mkdf-wrapper">
<div class="mkdf-wrapper-inner"> overflow
<div class="mkdf-top-bar"> … </div>
<form class="mkdf-search-slide-window-top" action="https://delicious-ideas.com/" method="get">
<div class="mkdf-grid">
<div class="mkdf-search-form-inner">

3. You should now notice that on the right-hand side, there is a specific piece of CSS for that element, and if you see a **min-width** or **max-width** query, then it has a particular piece of CSS set for that screen size

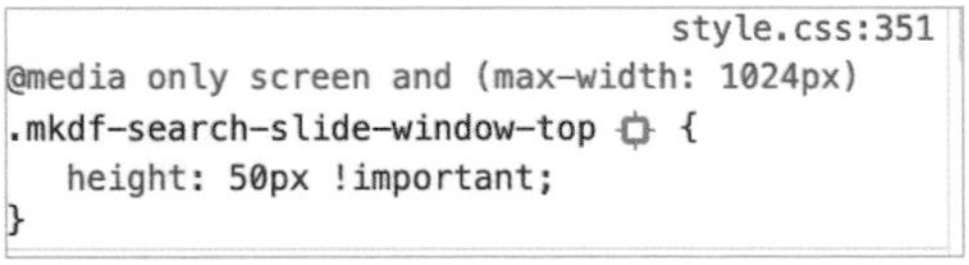
style.css:351
@media only screen and (max-width: 1024px)
.mkdf-search-slide-window-top {
height: 50px !important;
}

You should see something that looks like the following piece of code if you have managed to select an element adjusted for a particular screen size:

```
@media only screen and (max-width: 1024px) {

        ELEMENT NAME {

        }

}
```

Don't forget

The Inspector may look different for each browser. It also may change dependent on whether or not you if you have dark mode enabled for your OS.

Don't forget

If you are using a responsive template from a third-party website, remember that not all elements will have been modified for a particular screen size. The **max-width** and **min-width** queries could also be a lot higher.

This will set the element details for any screen size with a maximum width of up to 1024 pixels. As shown on pages 146-149, you can test how you want your element to look. This will only change the element for that particular screen size.

It is important to make sure in the Inspector that you can see the **max-width** or **min-width** only code. If that does not appear, then you will be changing the code for all screen sizes. It will always look similar to the following:

```
                                     style.css:351
@media only screen and (max-width: 1024px)
```

It also displays the line of code in the stylesheet where the element detail is listed. In this example, it is line 351 of the **style.css** file.

4. You now need to open up your **style.css** file. You can do this by downloading it through FTP, or by going to **Appearance** > **Theme File Editor** and selecting your **style.css** file

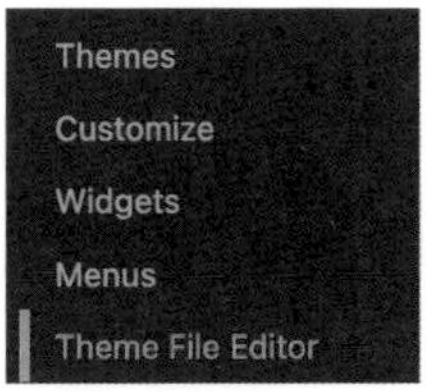
Themes
Customize
Widgets
Menus
Theme File Editor

5. Find the element you need to change, but make sure it is under the correct screen size. You can do this by sticking to the line number that was displayed in your Inspector. In the example above, it was line number 351

```
349 @media only screen and (max-width: 1024px){
350
351     .mkdf-search-slide-window-top {
352         height: 50px !important;
353     }
354 }
```

Hot tip

Using a code editor is a much better way to find pieces of code that have already been generated. Try to find an editor that displays the line number next to each line.

6. After you have saved your changes, make sure you clear your browser cache. Sometimes during development you will need to do this, as your website might not update right away. You can do this in Firefox by selecting **History** > **Clear All History** from the main toolbar

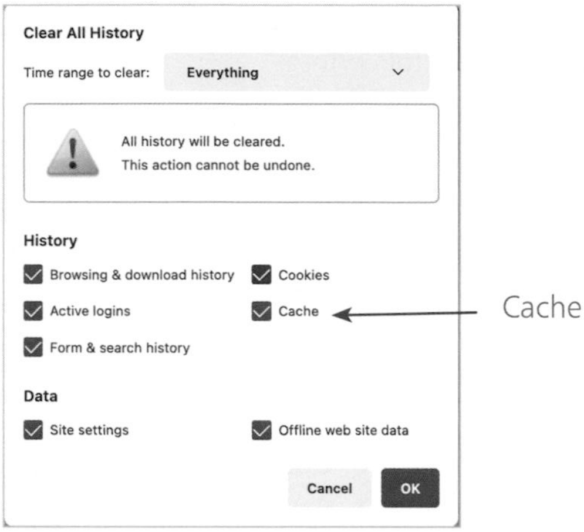
Clear All History
Time range to clear:
Everything
All history will be cleared.
This action cannot be undone.
History
Browsing & download history
Cookies
Active logins
Cache
Form & search history
Data
Site settings
Offline web site data
Cancel
OK
Cache

7. Now, you will need to boot up your website again in Firefox using the responsive mode layout that was introduced on page 179. You can also boot up your WordPress website on your mobile/tablet device

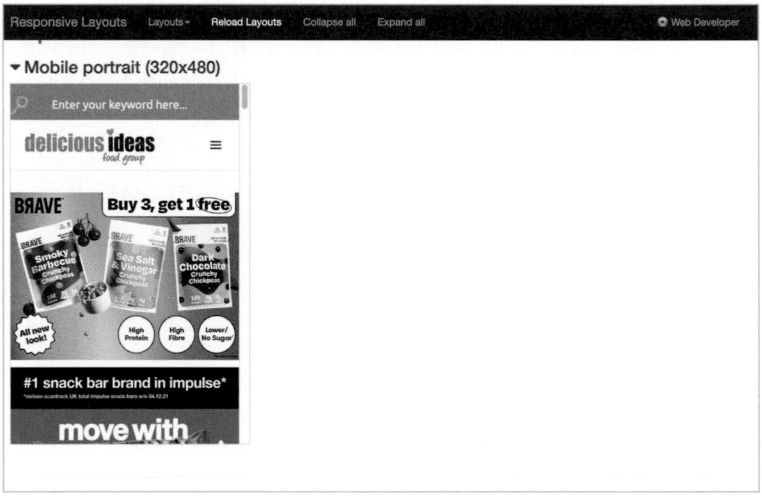
Responsive Layouts
Layouts
Reload Layouts
Collapse all
Expand all
Web Developer
Mobile portrait (320x480)
Enter your keyword here...
delicious ideas
food group
BRAVE
Buy 3, get 1 free
#1 snack bar brand in impulse*
move with

Adding responsive layouts to a stylesheet

If you are building your WordPress template from scratch, or you are using a non-responsive template, then there is a good chance you will not have responsive layouts set up in your stylesheet. You will need to go into your **style.css** file to set these up manually.

The first thing you need to do is familiarize yourself with the layouts that you will need. A good way to do this is to use the widths provided in the Firefox responsive layouts.

Mobile portrait (320x480)

The above example is 320x480. This means the width is 320 pixels and the height is 480 pixels. Each individual layout will be different. For example, mobile landscape will be 480x320.

Open up your **style.css** file and go right to the bottom. The stylesheet is read from top to bottom, so the resolutions will need to go from highest to lowest. Therefore, the mobile resolutions will be the last ones to go on the sheet.

@media only screen and (max-width: 767px) {

Enter element styles here

}

@media only screen and (max-width: 480px) {

Enter element styles here

}

It is best to set up each media screen first and then preview your changes using the Firefox responsive layouts so that you can get a good idea of your changes.

Hide Login

We are going to finish off this book by looking at a very important topic – security. On WordPress websites, you can log in by adding **wp-admin** or **wp-login** at the end of your URL. This makes your website susceptible to attacks. We are going to look at a plugin that allows you to change the URL of your login page.

1. Go to **Plugins** > **Add New**

2. Search for **WPS Hide Login**

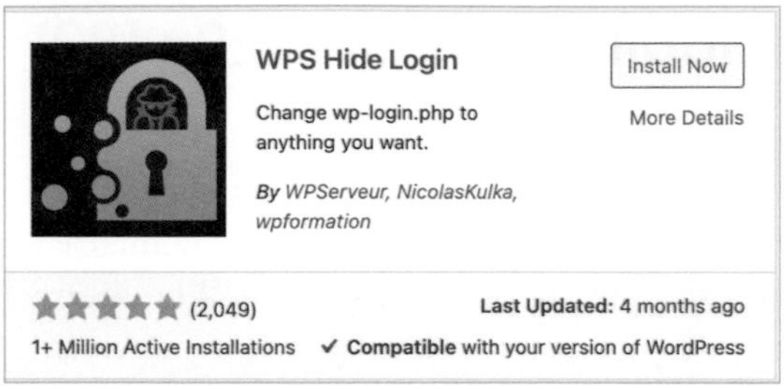
WPS Hide Login
Install Now
Change wp-login.php to anything you want.
More Details
By WPServeur, NicolasKulka, wpformation
(2,049)
Last Updated: 4 months ago
1+ Million Active Installations
✓ Compatible with your version of WordPress

3. Install and activate the plugin

Changing your login URL

Now you have the plugin installed, you can change your login URL.

1. Go to **Settings** > **WPS Hide Login**

2. Update your login and redirection URLs

Login url
https://wordpresseagle.com/
myloginurl
/
Protect your website by changing the login URL and preventing access to the wp-login.php page and the wp-admin directory to non-connected people.
Redirection url
https://wordpresseagle.com/
404
/
Redirect URL when someone tries to access the wp-login.php page and the wp-admin directory while not logged in.

Login url: This is the URL you want to use for your login page. Make sure you are using something unique.

Redirection url: This is the URL you want visitors to be redirected to if they try to access **wp-admin** or **wp-login**.

Numbers & Symbols

A

B

C

D

E

F

G

H

I

J

L

M

N

O

P

R

S

T

U

V

W

X

Y

Notes